CHARLES HORTON COOLEY

HUMAN NATURE AND THE SOCIAL ORDER

Introduction by Philip Rieff

Foreword by George Herbert Mead

Transaction Publishers
New Brunswick (U.S.A.) and London (U.K.)

Social Science Classics

The American Presidency, Laski

Critiques of Research in the Social Sciences, Blumer

Cultural Sciences, Znaniecki

Earth-Hunger and Other Essays, Summer

The Engineers and the Price System, Veblen

An Essay on the History of Civil Society, Ferguson

General Economic History, Weber

The Growth of the Mind, Koffka

Guild Socialism Restated, Cole

Human Nature and the Social Order, Cooley

Human Nature in Politics, Wallas

Jews and Modern Capitalism, Sombart

Myth of the Nation and Vision of Revolution, Talmon

News and the Human Interest Story, Hughes

Outlines of Sociology, Gumplowicz

A Preface to Morals, Lippmann

Progressive Democracy, Croly

The Psychology of Marxian Socialism, de Man

The Psychology of Socialism, Le Bon

Recollections, de Tocqueville

The Rise & Fall of Elites, Pareto

Social and Cultural Dynamics, Sorokin

Social Organization, Cooley

The Social Role of the Man of Knowledge, Znaniecki

Society in America, Martineau

The Sociological Eye, Hughes

The Theory of Business Enterprise, Veblen

Toward a General Theory of Action, Parsons and Shils

The Theory of Economic Development, Schumpeter

The Transformation of Democracy, Pareto

Young Germany, Laqueur

HUMAN NATURE AND THE
SOCIAL ORDER

Fifth printing 2005

Transaction edition 1983. Original edition copyright 1902 by Charles
Scribner's Sons, © 1922 revised edition by Charles Horton Cooley, © 1930
by Elsie Cooley, © 1964 by Schocken Books, Inc.

Library of Congress Catalog Number: 82-11002
ISBN: 0-87855-918-3
Printed in the United States of America

Library of Congress Cataloging-in-Publication Data

Cooley, Charles Horton, 1864-1929.
    Human nature and the social order.

(Social science classics series)
    Reprint. Previously published: New York: Schocken Books, 1964.
(Schocken paperbacks)
    Includes index.
    1. Social psychology. 2. Sociology. 3. Individualism. I. Title.
    II. Series

HM251.C8   1984 302.5   82-11002
ISBN 0-87855-918-3

CONTENTS

Introduction by Philip Rieff   ix

Foreword by George Herbert Mead   xxi

INTRODUCTION

HEREDITY AND INSTINCT

PAGE

The Evolutionary Point of View—Two Channels of Life—
What We Get from Heredity and What from Society—
Our Mode of Life does not Alter the Heredity of our
Children—Selection in Heredity—Eugenics—Heredity
and Progress—Interaction of Heredity and Social En-
vironment—Are they Antagonistic?—The Teachability
of Human Heredity—Long Infancy—Teachable He-
redity Implies a Diverse and Changing Life—What is
Instinct?—Instinctive Emotion in Man—Examples of
Instinctive Emotional Disposition—Human Conduct
Not to be Explained by the Direct Working of Instinct
—Reason as Organization of Plastic Instinct—Human
History—What is Human Nature?—Does Human Na-
ture Change?   3

CHAPTER I

SOCIETY AND THE INDIVIDUAL

An Organic Relation—They are Aspects of the Same Thing
—The Fallacy of Setting Them in Opposition—Various
Forms of this Fallacy—Familiar Questions and How they
may be Answered   35

CHAPTER II

SUGGESTION AND CHOICE

The Meaning of these Terms and their Relation to Each
Other—Individual and Social Aspects of Will or Choice—
Suggestion and Choice in Children—The Scope of Suggestion Commonly Underestimated—Practical Limitations upon Deliberate Choice—Illustrations of the
Action of the *Milieu*—Class Atmospheres—Our Unconsciousness of our Epoch—The Greater or Less Activity of Choice Reflects the State of Society—Suggestibility   51

CONTENTS

CHAPTER III

SOCIABILITY AND PERSONAL IDEAS

PAGE

Aim of this Chapter—The Sociability of Children—
Imaginary Conversation and its Significance—The Na-
ture of the Impulse to Communicate—There is no Sepa-
ration between Real and Imaginary Persons—Nor be-
tween Thought and Intercourse—The Study and Inter-
pretation of Expression by Children—The Symbol or
Sensuous Nucleus of Personal Ideas—Personal Atmos-
phere—Personal Physiognomy in Art and Literature—
In the Idea of Social Groups—Sentiment in Personal
Ideas—The Personal Idea is the Immediate Social Reality
—Society must be Studied in the Imagination—The
Possible Reality of Incorporeal Persons—The Material
Notion of Personality Contrasted with the Notion Based
on a Study of Personal Ideas—Self and Other in Personal
Ideas—Personal Opposition—Further Illustration and
Defense of the View of Persons and of Society Here Set
Forth   81

CHAPTER IV

SYMPATHY OR UNDERSTANDING AS AN ASPECT OF SOCIETY

The Meaning of Sympathy as here Used—Its Relation to
Thought, Sentiment, and Social Experience—The Range
of Sympathy is a Measure of Personality, *e.g.*, of
Power, of Moral Rank, and of Sanity—A Man's Sympathies Reflect the State of the Social Order—Specialization and Breadth—Sympathy Reflects Social Process
in the Mingling of Likeness with Difference—Also in
that it is a Process of Selection Guided by Feeling—The
Meaning of Love in Social Discussion—Love in Relation
to Self—The Study of Sympathy Reveals the Vital Unity
of Human Life   136

CHAPTER V

THE SOCIAL SELF—1. THE MEANING OF "I"

The "Empirical Self"—"I" as a State of Feeling—Its
Relation to the Body—As a Sense of Power or Causation—As a Sense of Speciality or Differentiation in

CONTENTS

PAGE

a Social Life — When the Body is "I"; Inanimate
Objects—The Reflected or Looking-glass "I"—"I" is
Rooted in the Past and Varies with Social Conditions- -
Its Relation to Habit—To Disinterested Love—How
Children Learn the Meaning of "I"—The Speculative
or Metaphysical "I" in Children—The Looking-glass
"I" in Children—The Same in Adolescence—"I" in Re-
lation to Sex—Simplicity and Affectation—Social Self-
feeling is Universal—The Group Self or "We" .   .   .   168

CHAPTER VI

THE SOCIAL SELF—2. VARIOUS PHASES OF "I"

Egotism and Selfishness—The Use of "I" in Literature and
Conversation—Intense Self-feeling Necessary to Produc-
tivity—Other Phases of the Social Self—Pride *versus*
Vanity—Self-respect, Honor, Self-reverence—Humility
—Maladies of the Social Self—Withdrawal—Self-trans-
formation—Phases of the Self Caused by Incongruity
between the Person and his Surroundings—The Self in
Social Problems   211

CHAPTER VII

HOSTILITY

Simple or Animal Anger—Social Anger—The Function of
Hostility—The Doctrine of Non-resistance—Control and
Transformation of Hostility by Reason—Hostility as
Pleasure or Pain—The Importance of Accepted Social
Standards—Fear   264

CHAPTER VIII

EMULATION

Conformity—Non-Conformity—The Two Viewed as Complementary Phases of Life—Rivalry—Rivalry in Social
Service—Conditions under which Emulation in Service
may Prevail—Hero-worship   293

CHAPTER IX

LEADERSHIP OR PERSONAL ASCENDANCY

Leadership Defines and Organizes Vague Tendency—
Power as Based upon the Mental State of the One
Subject to It—The Mental Traits of a Leader: Sig-

CONTENTS

PAGE

nificance and Breadth—Why the Fame and Power of a Man often Transcend his Real Character—Ascendancy of Belief and Hope—Mystery—Good Faith and Imposture—Does the Leader really Lead? 317

CHAPTER X
THE SOCIAL ASPECT OF CONSCIENCE

The Right as the Rational—Significance of this View—The Right as the Onward—The Right as Habit—Right is not the Social as against the Individual—It is, in a Sense, the Social as against the Sensual—The Right as a Synthesis of Personal Influences—Personal Authority—Confession, Prayer, Publicity—Truth—Dependence of Right upon Imagination—Conscience Reflects a Social Group—Ideal Persons as Factors in Conscience—Some Ideas of Right are Universal 358

CHAPTER XI
PERSONAL DEGENERACY

Is a Phase of the Question of Right and Wrong—Relation to the Idea of Development—Justification and Meaning of the Phrase "Personal Degeneracy"—Hereditary and Social Factors in Personal Degeneracy—Degeneracy as a Mental Trait—Conscience in Degeneracy—Group Degeneracy—Crime, Insanity, and Responsibility—Practical Effect of the Organic View Upon Responsibility —Upon Punishment 402

CHAPTER XII
FREEDOM

The Meaning of Freedom—Freedom and Discipline—Freedom as a Phase of the Social Order—Freedom Involves Incidental Strain and Degeneracy 422

INDEX 435

INTRODUCTION

by PHILIP RIEFF

"The imaginations people have of one another," Cooley wrote, "are the solid facts of society." *Human Nature and the Social Order* is a classic examination, first published in 1902 and then again in a revised edition in 1922, of the flash point at which the human imagination ignites to produce the infinitely adjustable social temperature without which man has not yet learned to live. That flash point may produce the cold of the concentration camp or the warmth of the family. Cooley can account for both; his theory of human nature predicates no ontology but only the social order itself. In this brilliantly written work, Cooley, pushing the modern genius for social analysis against all ontological traditions of human nature, destroys, in a way that has persuaded generations of readers, the belief that human nature has some content and meaning superior to the social order of which it is the representative conception.

That there is a human nature,* mirroring in each man the social order in which men act out their lives, seemed to Cooley something more than an article of faith, a *fides quarens intellectum*. It is the very language of faith, supplying every culture with its self-revelation, and therefore with its self-understanding. The social

* "Shewing the two contrary states of the human soul," as Blake puts it.

ix

order requires some such faith. And yet this too may have become an article of faith, for those who, following Cooley, have been systematically autobiographical enough to recognize the changeable contents of their symbolic interactions.

What distinguishes Cooley, as sociologist, from all those philosophers, psychologists, theologians, artists, novelists, poets and holy men who have written on human nature before him, is that he does not propose a position but rather examines the dynamics which make this mode of self-understanding socially necessary. *Human Nature and the Social Order* contains no maneuverings for moral position. Cooley does not strive to gain that high symbolic ground from which the great forgers of human nature have organized the egos of others, as, in the act of seeing the nature of the human, they must organize their own.

Primarily by linking doctrines of human nature to social orders, Cooley asserts how widely diffused and varied both are, inducing terror and consolation among men about themselves, in ways that facilitate their particular habits of action for and against each other. Doctrines separating human nature from social order, for all their brilliant complexities, belong to those great dead cultures in which men knew chiefly what they believed. In doctrines of human nature(s)* they found a way of putting a face on their group identity, thus forging the missing link between self and society. That link broken, there is the privacy of madness or a more social disorder. Without an imagery of self, a common consciousness, a culture would be characterized mainly by doubts about its own existence, as ours is nowadays.

* In Western societies, these doctrines are dualist, characteristically.

INTRODUCTION

Culture survives. Every social order produces a doctrine of human nature, an imagery of individual development (as from original sin to ultimate salvation), implicit in that order. Thus warmth is achieved, great communities founded. Every doctrine is an internal fix, from which each man must depart and yet maintain, by virtue of his graduated membership in the life-plan of that order, his self-esteem. Departing, each man achieves his mandatory sense of guilt, a motor for the driving in of social demand thus rendered moral. Granted a working balance of self-esteem and guilt, each man, collecting himself from elements of the social order, according to its ethos, measures the manner and distance of his drift through existence. There are combinations and complexities of fix and drift that have to be treated historically, empirically—treated finally, in Cooley's view, by a sociology united, in its highest style, to "systematic autobiography."

The intellectual ancestry of Cooley includes all those for whom autobiography is the highest science—that science being the least likely to freeze into a permanent truth. Montaigne understood the pathos of modern autobiographies; they render individualities endurable by rendering them problematic. Pulling up anchor, making autobiography itself the object of his ironic address, Montaigne set himself adrift on the sea of modern self-consciousness. From this voyage no one has yet had the genius to return, except as to some port of call. "If my health smiles on me and the day is clear," Montaigne remarked, "I am a worthy person." Here we have described, in one self-reference, the plan of the autobiographical culture to which we ourselves belong. Montaigne's "health" Pascal called sickness—but the issue has been

xi

settled, in Montaigne's favor, by successors like Cooley, who made society the subject of autobiography.

To the professional students of society, living as they do under the duress of life plans that have cracked up, or, perhaps, of non-plans not yet compelling enough to serve an equivalent function, doctrines of human nature, in all varieties everywhere, may be known, but only at the expense of belief. They appear as the embarrassing expedients with which every social order, until our own, has given shape and color to the emptiness that might otherwise expand inside and shiver the ego. When doctrines of human nature hold, like centers, the panic and emptiness may even be therapeutically elicited and contained, sending vicarious shivers through the *I* in the middle of everyone's head. Better than any sociologist or psychologist, Forster described in *Howard's End* the function of high culture. Leonard Bast goes to a concert, listens to Beethoven's *Ninth*, and, in its resonance, catches the silence around which every culture gulls every man into producing an appropriate insulation of experience. Of course that experience which is encouraged in the culture must also be mastered; otherwise, it is not insulating. In some cultures, the insulation of experience mastered may be more producible in the arts; in others, warfare or a theology may supply the functional equivalent. Thus, in Buddhist doctrine, the panic and emptiness can itself be experienced and rendered an integral part of the religious tasks set for mastery from earliest childhood.

Mastery is usually taught from earliest childhood, in a magnificent variety of modes, beginning always with the parental and sibling pedagogy. In the period after Cooley's, in the history of American social science, the study of children became a field of the first importance, not only because of Freud but also because of insights into the development of social communication supplied by Cooley, Mead, and William James. Those insights, adumbrated in this book, remain important for understanding how the naked ego is clothed and thus protected from the ontological emptiness.

Of course, the social order does swiftly clothe the actors born into it in the self-understandings they are, thereafter, reluctant to shed even for the rare privilege of a glimpse of themselves in their nothingness. The clothing, it may be argued, tentatively and in an exploratory way, has been tailored to make every man assume the role of emperor. But in a nation of emperors, who is to play the child? On the other hand, by this time in the history of Western culture, the child, or naivete about the sanctity of our social sentiments, may be superfluous. The emperors do not believe. They do not disbelieve. In the world of the nude, who is nude?

In the subtle business of detecting how emperors are clothed, none was more subtle, or more sympathetic to the enterprise, than Cooley. In this book he argues, beautifully and with full knowledge of the dangers inherent in the argument, the classical case that every society produces, out of its own structure, the myth within which it is thus empowered to live. It is required that "self-feeling" be thus fused, with enough social strength to keep the individual in that "middle-road" of civility and self-respect where Cooley found all truly civilized men, able to communicate and disagree—and yet maintain the social peace.

It is the "control of hostility by a sense of allegiance to rule," the social necessity of vetting all lasting animal angers that has led Cooley's successors in sociology to covet the possibility of a place in the new symbol industry. With both hostility and allegiance growingly inaccurate general terms from which to begin a description of the popular mind, alarmed students of our own social order call for the mass manufacture of emperor's clothes, advertising them all as rather useful and nice. They will give warmth, they look good, if not looked at too closely. But men like to look closely. Boredom supports animal curiosity; fashions of doctrinal denials come quickly on the heels of doctrinal affirmation until naivete is exhausted and all understand that it is a necessary game, a dressing-up of the ego. There is nothing, really, to believe—except the utility of belief itself. We are all Anglicans now, going to church because it is the civil thing to do on Sunday morning. Some old philosophers may continue to argue seriously on the nature of man, but that is because they are poorly educated in the new learning and ignore, in plain self-defense, their logical successors, the interior decorators.

Among our present cadres of interior decorators, the psychiatrists are probably the most widely remarked. The best of them know that our ego models have a long history of contradiction. Therefore, they build a model of nature that is contradictory. The natural is an idealization of the social. It is, perhaps, conflicting ego ideals that lead to contrary states of the soul.

Read a reputable book on modern interior decoration, titled *Understandable Psychiatry* (I choose it mainly because of the title—the point can be reproduced from a thousand texts) by Hinsie, published in 1948. This book demonstrates, to my satisfaction at least, what a hard time dying the idea of human nature has had. In fact, it is still alive and excessively popular nowadays, putting on the fashion of the time. Psychiatrists, in the late forties, being unembarrassed by the slightest training in philosophy or theology, not to mention sociology, went so far as to distinguish "first nature" from "second nature." First nature turns out to be "the undiluted and unmodified instincts," primitive "drives" emanating from the bodily tissues. This first nature distributes itself in the body, and is also taken up, so to say, into the mind. "Second nature" refers, of course, to the "super-ego." It is a term that is equivalent to "inner conscience," derived, of course, from parental management. First nature is somehow organic; second nature social. Here is perpetuated the myth that man has two natures, one supervising the other. In this way does psychiatry make itself understandable in the Western tradition. Just as the Jesuits forwarded education precisely to the point where it served their object of restoring the authority of the Church, and no farther, so the contemporary psychiatrist forwards a doctrine of two natures so far as it buttresses his therapeutic authority. The idea of human nature has always been thus associated with polemical and institutional uses. The rhetorical problem of contemporary dynamic psychiatry is how to put "instinct," which is hypostasized as the raw limit of social order, on the loftiest pedestal and yet keep it in subjection, like a beautiful and dangerous woman.

Exploring the Jesuits on intellect, or the psychoanalysts on instinct, the social psychology of knowledge (by which I would understand the sociological discipline to which Cooley's work was propaedeutic) exemplifies in itself the polemical uses of the doctrine of human nature, those purposes served by its particular conceptualization within this present social order. Certainly, Cooley was entirely opposed to any variety of ontological argument, whether human nature is the predicate of society, or vice versa. Like the philosophers Mead and James, the sociologist Cooley was too hard-headed an American to be interested in the European shadow play of the dialectic between essence and existence. To meddle thus with philosophical terms is no part of sociology. That ontology returns regularly to distract the social sciences is therefore only a measure of their faulty self-understanding.

I do not say that ontological argument ought to be summarily dismissed. Contemporary psychiatry conceives of anxiety, for example, not merely as something we *have* but also as something we *are*. Perhaps there is a healthy residue of philosophical tradition in the persistent tendency of modern psychology to treat every event or symptom (in appearance) as a correlative of a real personal subsistence (in reality). A particular symptom therefore becomes related to its hypostasis, although the relation is rarely more than assumed. Freud assumed an "organic" repression, although the relation between "organic" and "symbolic" repression is never worked out. Thus some shred of ontology makes its stand even in Freud, who was so impatient with what he called the "abstractness" of philosophy.

Human Nature and the Social Order is a sociological, as opposed to a philosophical, piece of work. It is, of course, subject to further sociological analysis. Cooley's book is itself a chapter in the doctrinal history of human nature. Referring to the chapter in this book on "The Social Conscience," Mead remarks that it is an "admirable ethical treatise" in the American style. "His sociology," Mead concludes, "was in a sense an account of the American community to which he [i.e., Cooley] belonged, and pre-supposed its normal healthful process." My point here has been that, in face of the evidence, Cooley's successors need no longer make this pre-supposition. Cooley represented a limited constituency, with a limited history. His small-town doctrine of human nature may appear as archaic now as that of the philosopher-aristocrats of Greek culture, in the context of Greek political theory and institutional practice. The intelligent and gentlemanly Cooleyan symbolic of human nature— White, Anglo-Saxon, Protestant and Liberal—may no longer serve to build up that controlling consensus which once constituted the specific genius of American culture. It is not yet clear what the new symbolic is, nor whether, in a technologically advanced and bureaucratically organized mass society, a controlling consensus, in the classical mode, is required for social order.

To say how a doctrine—or doctrinal element—functions is to exhibit the consensual purposes it serves in the social order. Thus, the main component elements of the doctrine of human nature among upper class and upper middle class Unitarians in the nineteenth century indicates that they meant by "reason" and "progress" (as the twin elements of human nature) to include the prerogatives of private property. "Reason" functioned differently for the leadership of the Paris Communards. In this sense, the question of truth, in sociological analysis, is limited to the truth of a specific consensus. No doctrine of human nature has yet indicated its independence from the social order in which it has appeared. These doctrines may be treated as salient ways in which societies organize their systems of moral demand.

All doctrines of human nature are subject to what Durkheim rightly called the "laws of collective ideation." In *Human Nature and the Social Order*, Cooley composed a psychology of cultural forms. His analysis of American culture, in the ideal form it took in his imagination, exhibits the modes of control and release by which our moral consensus was once achieved. Because "collective psychology is sociology,"* this work on the American collective psychology remains an exemplary display of sociological competence.

I have tried to indicate the way in which *Human Nature and the Social Order* is something more than an admirable ethical treatise. It is also a classic work on the process of social communication as the very stuff of which the self is made. To the study of this process both Cooley and Mead contributed insights that have become the trustworthy basis of contemporary social psychology.

Both Cooley and Mead went beyond the Wundtian concept of the gesture. A gesture is, as Mead would have it, that part of a social act which serves as a stimulus to other forms involved in the same social act. To both Cooley and Mead, the Darwinian notion of gesture proved mistaken. Gestures do not have as their primary function the "expression of emotion." They are, rather, parts of a complex system of social communication in which many different forms are involved. *We* observe animals and assume emotional attitudes which lie behind acts; they have that meaning *for us*. No consciousness is necessary for animals—animal communication does not necessarily involve consciousness. When, however, a man shakes his fist in another's face, we assume not only a hostile attitude but that *meaning* of hostility for him which it has for us—a fist is a significant symbol. We have a symbol which answers to a meaning in the experience of the first individual and which also calls out that meaning in the second individual.

Thus gesture may become language, or a significant

* Again, according to Durkheim.

INTRODUCTION

symbol. The gesture *as such* merely makes adjustment possible; the significant symbol makes meaning possible —and a truly social order. Sociology begins with this assumption of action meaningful to the actors. Only when we have significant symbols are mind and society, in the human sense, possible.

"Taking the attitude of the other" toward one's own conduct is, for Mead and Cooley, the essential characteristic of social conduct. Even the body is not a self, *as such;* it becomes a self only when it imagines itself in relation to others; without social experience, therefore, the self cannot develop. Social communication is thus fundamental to selfhood.

The theory of imitation, like the theory of gesture, proved an inadequate basis for modern social psychology. Meaning is something different from mocking. Intelligibility is something more than intelligence. A computer may exhibit intelligence without producing significant symbols. If a gesture calls out an appropriate response in others, it is possible to get complex cooperation, as in the case of ants or bees; but an imitation of another is not necessarily a significant symbol. In fact, imitation really depends on the individual influencing himself as others influence him, so that he undergoes the influence not only of the other but also of himself insofar as he uses the same vocal gesture. There is, therefore, no imitation *as such;* but if there is already present in the individual an action like the action of another, then there is a situation which makes so-called imitation possible. The critical importance of vocal gesture lies in its reciprocal character; it immensely facilitates role assumption. It is largely owing to language that we "see oursel's as ithers see us," for from infancy onward we address ourselves as others address us.

Extreme behaviorists like Watson held that all our thinking is explicit or implicit vocalization. In "silent thinking" we are simply starting to use certain words. Even so, the extreme behaviorists overlook the fact that these words, as stimuli, are essential elements in elaborate social processes, and carry with them the other components of those processes.

The meaning of "calling out in oneself the same response as in others" is illustrated by asking someone to do something. It becomes difficult to keep from doing it oneself; the prophet is stirred by his prophecy. The categorical imperative might be reinterpreted in this way, not as a sublime ethical doctrine but as routine psychological dynamics. And this was Cooley's polemical intention: so to reinterpret the categorical imperative that it became the inescapable meaning of social life.

COOLEY'S CONTRIBUTION TO AMERICAN SOCIAL THOUGHT[1]

by GEORGE HERBERT MEAD

"I have often thought that, in endowment, Goethe was almost the ideal sociologist, and that one who added to the more common traits his comprehension, his disinterestedness and his sense for organic unity and movement might accomplish almost anything." Cooley wrote this at almost the end of his third book, that on *Social Process*. It is indicative in a fundamental way of Cooley's conception of sociology and of the sort of mind which Cooley brought to his writings within this field. The men from whom he loves to quote are Thoreau, Emerson, Luther, Thomas à Kempis, and Charles Darwin. The style of his writing is that of Emerson, that is, the organization of his thought belonged rather to the felt unity of the structure that his thinking illuminated than to any closely knit concatenation of elements which analysis presented to thought. And Emersonian sentences stand out from his pages. For example, "The severely necessary can never be vulgar, while only nobleness can prevent the superfluous from being so."

It becomes then of peculiar importance to identify the living social reality which Cooley felt and upon which his thought throws light. It was, indeed, the society of which he was a part and which he could enter by way of his own human nature. No one could be less self-centered

[1] Reprinted from *American Journal of Sociology*. No. 5, Vol. XXXV, March, 1930 by permission of The University of Chicago Press.

than Cooley, but it was by way of the discovery of what went on in his own living with other people that he discovered the community with which the sociologist is concerned. His approach was that of objective introspection. The community that he discovered, so to speak from the inside, was a democracy, and inevitably an American democracy. I call it a discovery, for what anyone finds for himself and by his own way of search must be a discovery. Finding it in living, it was a process. Its organization was a manner of living. Its institutions were the habits of individuals. In a sense Cooley says the same thing in his three books, that is, he illuminates the same reality in different ways.

Society, then, [says Cooley] in its immediate aspect, is a relation among personal ideas. In order to have a society it is evidently necessary that persons should get together somewhere; and they get together only as personal ideas in the mind. Where else? What other possible *locus* can be assigned for the real contacts of persons, or in what other form can they come in contact except as impressions or ideas formed in this common *locus?* Society exists in my mind as the contact and reciprocal influence of certain ideas named "I," Thomas, Henry, Susan, Bridget, and so on. It exists in your mind as a similar group, and so in every mind.[1]

I do not see how any one can hold that we know persons directly except as imaginative ideas in the mind.[2]

I conclude, therefore, that the imaginations which people have of one another are the *solid facts* of society, and that to observe and interpret these must be a chief aim of sociology.[3]

In saying this I hope I do not seem to question the independent reality of persons or to confuse it with personal ideas.

[1] *Human Nature and the Social Order* (New York: Charles Scribner's Sons, 1902), p. 119.
[2] *Ibid.*, p. 120.
[3] *Ibid.*, p. 121.

FOREWORD

The man is one thing and the various ideas entertained about him are another; but the latter, the personal idea, is the immediate social reality, the thing in which men exist for one another, and work directly upon one another's lives.[4]

We may view social consciousness either in a particular mind or as a co-operative activity of many minds. The social ideas that I have are closely connected with those that other people have, and act and react upon them to form a whole. This gives us public consciousness, or to use a more familiar term, public opinion, in the broad sense of a group state of mind which is more or less distinctly aware of itself. By this last phrase I mean such a mutual understanding of one another's points of view on the part of the individuals or groups concerned as naturally results from discussion. . . .

In a congenial family life, for example, there may be a public consciousness which brings all the important thoughts and feelings of members into such a living and co-operative whole. In the mind of each member, also, this same thing exists as a social consciousness embracing a vivid sense of the personal traits and modes of thought and feeling of the other members. And finally quite inseparable from all this, is one's consciousness of himself, which is directly a reflection of the ideas about himself he attributes to the others, and is directly or indirectly altogether a product of social life. . . .

There are, then, at least three aspects of consciousness which we may usefully distinguish; self-consciousness, or what I think of myself; social consciousness (in its individual aspect), or what I think of other people; and public consciousness or a collective view of the foregoing as organized in a communicative group. And all three are phases of a single whole.[5]

From these passages I think we may form a definite conception of Cooley's doctrine of society. It is an affair of consciousness, and a consciousness that is necessarily

[4] *Ibid.*, p. 123.
[5] *Social Organization* (New York: Charles Scribner's Sons, 1909), p. 10.

social. One's consciousness of himself is directly a re-flection of the ideas about himself which he attributes to the others. Others exist in his imagination of them, and only there do they affect him, and only in the imaginations which others have of him does he affect them. These ideas differ from each other as they exist in the conscious experience of different people, but they also have cores of identical content, which in public consciousness act uniformly. This identity Cooley insists upon. It is as real as the differences. But its *locus* is found in the experience of the individuals. Furthermore its organization is that of the functional relations of the different members of the society, and its unity is that of organization, not that of a common stuff. As stuff it is psychical and as such the experience of different individuals. The advantage of this approach has been very considerable in the development of Cooley's social doctrine. The "other" lies in the same field as that of the "self." It can be recognized as quite as immediate as the self. The stream of consciousness is the carrier of both—the self and its society—and each can be seen to be dependent upon the other for its evolution in experience. The semimetaphysical problems of the individual and society, of egotism and altruism, of freedom and determinism, either disappear or remain in the form of different phases in the organization of a consciousness that is fundamentally social.

The self is no longer a Cartesian presupposition of consciousness. In conduct it is a precipitate about a fundamental impulse or instinct of appropriation and power, while the primary content appears as a feeling or sentiment, the self-feeling which defies further analysis. Here Cooley follows James very closely. Its development is wholly dependent upon another or others who

are necessarily as immediate as the self. Being a re-
sultant in experience, those objects, through relationship to which it emerges, cannot be dependent upon it for
their existence in experience. The other cannot appear
first as an experience of my own self, if my own self
appears through the reaction of the individual to others.
"A self-idea of this sort seems to have three principal
elements: the imagination of our appearance to the
other person; the imagination of his judgment of that
appearance, and some sort of self-feeling, such as pride
or mortification."[6] But the imagination cannot exist in
experience as the imagination of a self, but must exist
as an imagination within which both self and the other
have their origin and development. Cooley thus leaves
the "person" or the "man" as metaphysically antecedent
to the self and the others. This problem is not, however,
Cooley's problem. He is undertaking to locate and define
the "solid facts of society," to observe and interpret
which must be the chief aim of sociology. Ignoring the
philosophical problem does give him elbowroom. On the
one hand, the organic nature of society Cooley recognizes and emphasizes, and he can present it as the physical outside, so to speak, of the social consciousness which
he regards as psychical, as the organization of personal
ideas, which can get together only in the mind, it should
be said in the *minds* of persons or men. If one were to
push the analogy, there should be a public consciousness
which is the psychical counterpart of the social organism.

But Cooley draws back from such a departure from
direct experience. Public consciousness is the expression
of communication, discussion, and resides in the common ideas of persons, and in their organization. On the

[6] *Human Nature and the Social Order,* p. 184.

other hand, Cooley can regard the relations of selves and others in this society in terms of mental processes. Ideas have definition and reality only in their relationship to other ideas. If selves and others are ideas in people's minds, then the relation of the individual to society is as little a problem as is the relation of any idea to the group of ideas that define it. Furthermore, the goods or values that attach to any idea can only be defined in terms of the values that belong to the whole ideal structure to which the idea belongs. The beauty that belongs to your presentation of an arm of a statue could not possibly be stated apart from that of the beauty of the whole figure. The values that are the expression of an economist's theory of production cannot be presented except in terms of consumption. In the same fashion, if an individual consists of the ideas in his mind which he imagines that others entertain of him, and if the others exist as members of society as the ideas which he entertains in his imagination, it is evident that they will have common goods in so far as they are organized in his imagination into some social whole, such as a family.

That which distinguishes Luther from the vulgarly ambitious and aggressive people we know is not the quality of his self-feeling, but the fact that it was identified in his imagination and endeavors with sentiments and purposes that we look upon as noble, progressive and right. No one could be more ambitious than he was, or more determined to secure the social aggrandizement of his self; but in his case the self for which he was ambitious and resentful consisted largely of certain convictions regarding justification by faith, the sacrilege of the sale of indulgences, and, more generally, of an enfranchising spirit and mode of thought fit to awaken and lead the aspirations of the time.[7]

[7] *Ibid.*, p. 212.

In the mind this identification of the values of the individual and of the society he imagines is complete. In defining the selfish man Cooley says, "There is some essential narrowness or vulgarity of imagination which prevents him from grasping what we feel to be the true social situation, and having the sentiments which should respond to it."[8]

If you fix your attention on the individual phase of things and see life as a theatre of personal action, then the corresponding ideas of private will, responsibility, praise and blame rise before you; if you regard its total aspect you see tendency, evolution, law, and impersonal grandeur. Each of these is a half truth needing to be completed by the other; the larger truth, including both, being that life is an organic whole, presenting itself with equal reality in individual and general aspects.[9]

The fact for Cooley is that these social ideas and their organization are not presentations of a reality lying outside but the "solid facts of society." The metaphysical question as to the freedom of will of the individual apart from the social situation that exists in his imagination has no sociological meaning. So the data of the scientist's problem as they lie in his mind cannot *compel* him to present the hypothesis which his imagination evolves. He is free over against the problem. Whether his mind, dependent upon a nervous system, is compelled to think as it does in forming his hypothesis by physical and chemical causes has no bearing upon the absence of compulsion in his statement of the problem.

Mind is an organic whole made up of co-operating individualities, in somewhat the same way that the music of an

[8] *Ibid.*, p. 214.
[9] *Social Organization*, p. 20.

orchestra is made up of divergent but related sounds. . . .
When we study the social mind we merely fix our attention on
larger aspects and relations rather than on the narrower ones
of ordinary psychology.[10]

By communication is here meant the mechanism through
which human relations exist and develop—all the symbols of
mind, together with the means of conveying them through
space and preserving them in time. . . . All these taken together, in the intricacy of their actual combination, make up
an organic whole corresponding to the organic whole of human thought; and everything in the way of mental growth has
an external existence therein. The more closely we consider
this mechanism the more intimate will appear its relation to
the inner life of mankind, and nothing will more help us to
understand the latter than such consideration. . . . Without
communication the mind does not develop a true human nature, but remains in an abnormal and nondescript state neither
human nor properly brutal.[11]

In these passages is presented Cooley's conception of
the relation of social mind to the organic structure and
process of society. It is a structure and process which is
particularly found in the vehicles of communication, that
is, everything that interrelates the conduct of members of
society, and which become therefore symbols in their
minds. The structure and process are external, but they
are the structure and process of a living reality, whose
interrelationships make possible the social mind in the
individuals. Just as the conscious processes of the mind
of "ordinary psychology" correspond to the living processes of the physiological individual, so the social processes of the mind answer to the living processes of society. However, there is an essential difference between
the two. Our physical and biological observation presents

10 *Ibid.*, p. 7.
11 *Ibid.*, pp. 61–62.

us with the objects that make up society and its mechanisms, which can be stated and defined without recourse to a living social process. It is in fact necessary to endue these physiological and physical objects with the meanings which, for Cooley, reside in the mind before life can be breathed into the social organism. I will recur to this later, but it is of first importance to recognize the value for social psychology which flows from Cooley's finding of the solid facts of sociology in the mind.

It can be most sharply stated in Cooley's recognition that the self is not an immediate character of the mind but arises through the imagination of the ideas which others entertain of the individual, which has as its counterpart the organization of our ideas of others into their selves. It is out of this bi-polar process that social individuals appear. We do not discover others as individuals like ourselves. The mind is not first individual and then social. The mind itself in the individual arises through communication. This places Cooley's doctrine in advance of Baldwin's and Tarde's and even of James's. Tarde looked for a psychological mechanism which determined the individual through the attitudes and manners of the community, and found this in imitation. As a mechanism, imitation proves hopelessly inadequate. It becomes simply a covering term for the likeness of the characters of the individual and of the group. Baldwin sought to work out, in a so-called circular reaction that reinstated the favored impulse, a possible psychological mechanism, but without success. While James recognized early the influence of the social environment upon the individual in the formation of the personality, his psychological contribution to the social character of the self was rather in showing the spread of the self over its social environment than in the structure of the self through social interactions. The superiority of Cooley's position lies in his freedom to find in consciousness a social process going on, within which the self and the others arise. By placing both phases of this social process in the same consciousness, by regarding the self as the ideas entertained by others of the self, and the other as the ideas entertained of him by the self, the action of the others upon the self and of the self upon the others becomes simply the interaction of ideas upon each other within mind. In this process the oppositions as well as the accords can be recognized and both can be placed upon the same plane.

It is then to a process of social growth and integration, exhibited both in the individual consciousness and in society, that Cooley directs attention. The forming influence of the group takes place through the ideas which are aroused in mind, and these ideas are not primarily ideas that belong to a self. This study of the social growth of the self and the others Cooley carried out in the observation of his own children, and it was the same process which he could trace in the relation of the individual and society. It was the same social process that was going on, looked at now from the inside and now from the outside. Rivalries and conformity operating on the same level could be stated in terms of the interaction of ideas and in terms of social forces. It was Cooley's firm belief that the process was the same—the growth or decay of the social organism. He was peculiarly successful in analyzing the phase of social degeneration. He could show that unhealthful social conditions reflected themselves in degenerate selves, and he could indicate the responsibility of the environment for the degeneration, at the same time recognizing the responsibility that belonged to the self. He could study traits of character as they appeared in the personality and as they appeared in the social forces which these personalities embodied. He could exhibit the social habits within consciousness and in the institutions of the community. He could present the culture of the community as it informed and refined the mind of the individual and as it existed in the literature, art, and history of the nations. In general, just as Cooley, following a psycho-physical psychology, recognized the same life-process exhibiting itself in the sensitivity and motor process of the organism and in the consciousness of the organism, so he could relate the social consciousness of the same individual to the social organism to which it belonged. The social process was the same. It was viewed simply from two different standpoints, from without and from within. Such a view would have been impossible if all experience is lodged in a pre-existent self that must reach other selves through conscious or subconscious inference, and if the influence which selves exercise upon each other must take place through mechanisms which operate through the physiological and psychological apparatus of "ordinary psychology." These presupposed an individual that is in its experience pre-existent, and attains acquaintance with other objects through its inner experience. Tarde and Baldwin were after all operating with such psychological mechanisms. A self that can reach other selves only through the interpretation of states of consciousness that are primarily states of itself, can never be primarily a social self, no matter how social the group may be within which as a living organism it has its being. The question then arises whether the consciousness that belongs to Cooley's "person" or "man" within which the self and the other arise can serve as the inside of the social process of which the life of society is the outside. I am not raising a metaphysical question. The question is whether the "solid facts of society" can be found in such a consciousness. I think that Cooley was Emersonian in finding the individual self in an overself, but he does not depend upon such a doctrine for his sociology. He comes back to what he calls "ordinary psychology" for his interpretation of what goes on in the mind.

I have already indicated a serious difficulty that arises if we carry over the method of psychophysical parallelism into social psychology, accepting Cooley's interpretation of psychophysical parallelism. His interpretation is that consciousness is an inside experience of the life of the external organism. In "ordinary psychology" this sets up a parallelism between sensations, percepts, emotions, volitions, and so forth, and physiological processes; and Cooley seems to be committed to this "ordinary psychology." This implies that we can give a scientific account of the physiological process without introducing the parallel states of consciousness. But for Cooley selves and others lie inside of the consciousness of "ordinary psychology," and yet they also are the "solid facts" of sociology, that is, they are the field of the external social organism. Now, I have no interest in pressing a point of logical or terminological conflict. Cooley has in a sense met such a criticism by his assurance that his parallelism connotes an outside and an inside view of the same reality, not a parallelism between states or processes in two different realms of metaphysical being. The only pertinent question is whether he succeeds in presenting adequately the "solid facts of society" by means of his apparatus of social psychology.

In the first place it follows from Cooley's lodging of the self and the others in consciousness, while he accepts the parallelism of ordinary psychology, that he cannot and does not wish to identify the self with the physical organism. Now, while Cooley slips out of this segregation of the animal organism from social and so moral experience by merging the life-process and the social process in a universal onward evolution in which he had a profound faith, the actual effect was to take the mental organization of society as it lay in his own liberal and wholesome view as the standard by which primitive impulses must be tested. What impresses one in reading his chapter on "The Social Aspects of Conscience," in *Human Nature and the Social Order,* is that it is an admirable ethical treatise rather than a scientific analysis of the situation within which lie moral judgments and the whole apparatus of impulses. The healthful social order is mental, not in the sense that there have appeared there the intellectual processes of reflection, but in the sense of a developing culture which carries all the values of society which are the standards and tests of social theory and conduct. Such a culture has a *locus* in minds. It is not true that Cooley conceived of the best culture of his time as the final culture of mankind. He recognized that it is in a constant process of evolution, but it was true that Cooley was prescribing for society in so far as it was sick in terms of processes and standards that were for the time being established in minds, which could be distinguished from what was merely physical, animal, and brutal. He did not feel it to be his primary task to state the whole of human behavior in scientific terms which would be equally applicable to primitive impulses and to the so-called higher processes and cultural expressions. It followed that the beginnings of behavioristic and Freudian psychology did not attract him or suggest new avenues of approach.

In the second place, the problem of the application of scientific method to the study of society did not interest him. The importance of statistical methods he recognized, and those of community surveys, but the question as to the form in which social experience could be stated so as to be amenable to exact definition and formulation seemed to him unimportant. He rejected the economic interpretation of history, and presented his organic view of history in which all factors must be recognized as phases of a unitary life-process whose primary category was that of growth. In this sense evolution was for Cooley the conception that brought society within the realm of science, but evolution was for him a philosophy and a faith rather than a method. He made use of primitive society to illustrate his striking conception of primary groups and their face-to-face association and cooperation, but he made no attempt after the fashion of the French school to analyze primitive mind, nor did he undertake to understand human society through its development from its earlier forms. His method was that of an introspection which recognized the mind as the *locus* of the selves that act upon each other, but the methodological problem of the objectification of this mind he pushed aside as metaphysical. His method was therefore psychological. For him society was a psychical whole.[12]

The question that this method presents is this: Does Cooley's psychological account of the self lying in the mind serve as an adequate account of the social individual in the objective life of society? The crucial point, I think, is found in Cooley's assumption that the form which the self takes in the experience of the individual is that of the imaginative ideas which he finds in his mind that others have of him. And the others are the imaginative ideas which he entertains of them. Now we do make

[12] See *ibid.,* p. 31.

a distinction between selves—our own and those of
others—and our ideas of ourselves and of others, and we
assume that these selves and our ideas of them exist in
our experience. Our ideas of others and of our own selves
are frequently mistaken, while we assume that the real
selves were there in experience. We correct our errors
and reach the genuine personalities which were there all
the time. The stuff of these selves social psychologists
have found in impulses, fundamental wishes, and the
like, especially as these appear in crises in social experience. The question which Cooley's approach raises
is whether the form of a self belongs to this level of human experience, or whether this is reached only in the
imagination or idea of the other and of the self. Are
selves psychical, or do they belong to an objective phase
of experience which we set off against a psychical phase?
I think it can be shown that selves do belong to that objective experience, which, for example, we use to test all
scientific hypotheses, and which we distinguish from
our imaginations and our ideas, that is, from what we
term psychical. The evidence for this is found in the fact
that the human organism, in advance of the psychical experiences to which Cooley refers, assumes the attitude of
another which it addresses by vocal gesture, and in this
attitude addresses itself, thus giving rise to its own self
and to the other.[13] In the process of communication there
appears a social world of selves standing on the same
level of immediate reality as that of the physical world
that surrounds us. It is out of this social world that the
inner experiences arise which we term psychical, and
they serve largely in interpretation of this social world
as psychical sensations and percepts serve to interpret

[13] G. H. Mead, "The Genesis of Self and Social Control," *International Journal of Ethics*, Vol. XXXV, No. 3 (1925).

the physical objects of our environment. If this is true, social groups are not psychical but are immediately given, though inner experiences are essential for their interpretation. The *locus* of society is not in the mind, in the sense in which Cooley uses the term, and the approach to it is not by introspection, though what goes on in the inner forum of our experience is essential to meaningful communication.

Whether this account of the appearance of selves be correct or not, it is evident that the acceptance by the sociologist of a society of selves in advance of inner experiences opens the door to an analysis which is behavioristic. I refer to such analyses as those of W. I. Thomas, Park and Burgess, and Faris. In many respects Cooley's analyses are of this type, but they always presuppose a certain normal social order and process as given. It is the organization and process which his introspection revealed. One misses perhaps the neutral attitude of the scientist, and one feels that the door is closed to a more profound analysis. In other words, Cooley did not find selves and society arising in primitive processes of communication, so that he could grasp their reality in early human behavior. He felt that he grasped this reality when he found them within what was for him the normal social process. His sociology was in a sense an account of the American community to which he belonged, and pre-supposed its normal healthful process. This process was that of the primary group with its face-to-face organization and co-operation. Given the process, its healthful growth and its degenerations could be identified and described. Institutions and valuations were implicit within it. The gospel of Jesus and democracy were of the essence of it, and more fundamentally still it was the life of the spirit. Cooley never sought for the reality of this in the dim beginnings of human behavior.

If we can carry back the social behavior within which selves and others arise to a situation that antedates the appearance of the psychical as distinguished from an outer world, it will be to this primitive behavior that we can trace back the origins of the social patterns which are responsible not only for the structure of society but also for the criticism of that structure and for its evolution. The social pattern is always larger than the group that it makes possible. It includes the enemy and the guest and the morale of behavior toward him. Its mechanism of communication carries with it the possibility of conversation with others who are not members of the group. It has in it the implication of the logical universe of discourse. If symbolization can be stated in terms of the behavior of primitive communication, then every distinctively human being belongs to a possibly larger society than that within which he actually finds himself. It is this, indeed, which is implied in the rational character of the human animal. And these larger patterns afford a basis for the criticism of existing conditions and in an even unconscious way tend to realize themselves in social conduct. For social theory a great deal hinges upon the answer to the question whether society is itself psychical or whether the form of the psychical is a sort of communication which arises within primitive human behavior. Do the self and others lie within mind, or is mind itself, as psychical, a phase of experience that is an outgrowth of primitive human communication? Whether the question is stated in this form or not, it is evident that a great deal of recent social psychology has been occupied with an analysis of selves and their minds into more primitive forms of behavior. To this type of analysis Cooley's assumption of the psychical nature of society closes the door. And it commits him to a conception of society which is mental rather than scientific.

But I am unwilling to conclude a discussion of Cooley's social psychology upon a note of criticism. His successful establishment of the self and the others upon the same plane of reality in experience and his impressive study of society as the outgrowth of the association and co-operation of the primary group in its face-to-face organization are positive accomplishments for which we are profoundly indebted to his insight and constructive thought.

HUMAN NATURE AND THE SOCIAL ORDER

INTRODUCTION

HEREDITY AND INSTINCT

THE EVOLUTIONARY POINT OF VIEW—TWO CHANNELS OF LIFE—
WHAT WE GET FROM HEREDITY AND WHAT FROM SOCIETY—OUR
MODE OF LIFE DOES NOT ALTER THE HEREDITY OF OUR CHIL-
DREN—SELECTION IN HEREDITY—EUGENICS—HEREDITY AND
PROGRESS—INTERACTION OF HEREDITY AND SOCIAL ENVIRON-
MENT—ARE THEY ANTAGONISTIC?—THE TEACHABILITY OF
HUMAN HEREDITY—LONG INFANCY—TEACHABLE HEREDITY IM-
PLIES A DIVERSE AND CHANGING LIFE—WHAT IS INSTINCT?—
INSTINCTIVE EMOTION IN MAN—EXAMPLES OF INSTINCTIVE
EMOTIONAL DISPOSITION—HUMAN CONDUCT NOT TO BE EX-
PLAINED BY THE DIRECT WORKING OF INSTINCT—REASON AS
ORGANIZATION OF PLASTIC INSTINCT—HUMAN HISTORY—WHAT
IS HUMAN NATURE? DOES HUMAN NATURE CHANGE?

WE have come in recent years to look upon all
questions of human life from an evolutionary point of
view. It may be worth while to recall something of
what that phrase means.

It means, for one thing, that all our life has a history,
that nothing happens disconnectedly, that everything
we are or do is part of a current coming down from the
remote past. Every word we say, every movement
we make, every idea we have, and every feeling, is, in
one way or another, an outcome of what our predeces-

3

sors have said or done or thought or felt in past ages. There is an actual historical continuity from their life to ours, and we are constantly trying to trace this history, to see how things come about, in order that we may understand them better and may learn to bring to pass those things we regard as desirable.

It means also that if we go far enough back we find that man and the other animals have a common history, that both sprang remotely from a common ancestry in lower forms of life, and that we cannot have clear ideas of our own life except as we study it on the animal side and see how and in what respects we have risen above the condition of our cousins the horses, dogs, and apes. Life, it appears, is all one great whole, a kinship, unified by a common descent and by common principles of existence; and our part in it will not be understood unless we can see, in a general way at least, how it is related to other parts.

The stream of this life-history, whose sources are so remote and whose branchings so various, appears to flow in two rather distinct channels. Or perhaps we might better say that there is a stream and a road running along the bank—two lines of transmission. The stream is heredity or animal transmission; the road is communication or social transmission. One flows through the germ-plasm; the other comes by way of language, intercourse, and education. The road is more recent than the stream: it is an improve-

4

ment that did not exist at all in the earliest flow of animal life, but appears later as a vague trail alongside the stream, becomes more and more distinct and travelled, and finally develops into an elaborate highway, supporting many kinds of vehicles and a traffic fully equal to that of the stream itself.

How does this idea apply to the life of a given individual—of you or me, for example? His body—and his mind too, for that matter—begins in a minute, almost microscopic, bit of substance, a cell, formed by the union of cells coming from the bodies of his parents, and containing, in some way not yet understood, tendencies which reach back through his grandparents and remoter ancestors over indefinite periods of time. This is the hereditary channel of his life, and the special kind of cells in which heredity is conveyed—called the germ-plasm—are apparently the only source of those currents of being, those dispositions, capacities, potentialities, that each of us has at the beginning of his course.

The social origin of his life comes by the pathway of intercourse with other persons. It reaches him at first through his susceptibility to touches, tones of voice, gesture, and facial expression; later through his gradually acquired understanding of speech. Speech he learns from his family and playmates, who, in turn, had it from their elders, and so it goes back to the earliest human history, and farther still to the inarticulate cries of our pre-human ancestors. And it is the same with the use of tools, with music, art, religion, commerce, and whatever else he may learn to think and do. All is a social heritage from the immemorial past.

We may distinguish these two lines of history more clearly, perhaps, if we take a case where they are not parallel, where the road over which we get our social heritage has not followed the stream from which we get our animal heritage, but has switched off, as it were, from another stream. Suppose, for example, that an American family in China adopts a Chinese baby and brings it home to grow up in America. The animal life-history of that baby's past will lie in China. It will have the straight black hair, the yellowish skin and other physical traits of the Chinese people, and also any mental tendencies that may be part of their heredity. But his social past will lie in America, because he will get from the people about him the English speech and the customs, manners, and ideas that have been developed in this country. He will fall heir to the American political, religious, educational, and economic institutions; his whole mind will be an American mind, excepting only for the difference (if there is any) between his inherited aptitude to learn such things and that of other American children. The Chinese stream and the American road have come together in his life.

If there were two such babies—twins, let us say, and almost exactly alike at birth—one of whom remained in China while the other was brought to America, they would grow up alike physically, and also, probably, in temperament, as active or sluggish, thoughtful or impetuous, but would be wholly different in dress,

6

language, and ideas. In these the child bred in America would be far more like his American foster-brothers than like his twin-brother in China.

Just what is it that we get through the germ-plasm, as distinguished from what we get by social transmission? The former is evidently the main source of our bodily traits. The child of a dark race will be dark no matter in what society he grows up, and will have also whatever peculiarities as regards hair, shape of head, height, and the like belong to the racial type from which his germ-plasm comes. Nor is there any doubt, though it is not so obvious, that he gets from this source his original mental endowment. A child of feeble-minded ancestors is usually feeble-minded also, and one whose parents had unusual ability is apt to resemble them. Heredity brings us not only tendencies to a definite sort of physical development, but also capacity, aptitude, disposition, lines of teachability, or whatever else we may call the vague psychical tendencies that all of us are born with.

And from social transmission, through the environment, come all the stimulation and teaching which cause these tendencies to develop in a definite form, which lead us to speak a particular language, to develop one set of ideas or kind of ambition rather than another, to feel patriotism for America rather than for England or Italy. Everything in the way of specific function must be learned in this way, no matter what ability we have. When we say that a child is a born musician we mean, not that he can play or compose by nature alone, but that if he has the right kind of teaching he can rapidly develop power in this direction. In this sense and in no other can a man be a born lawyer, or teacher, or poet, or, if you please, a born counterfeiter or burglar. I knew a family in which the boys had a remarkable aptitude for football, several of them becoming distinguished players, but certainly unless they had all been sent to college, and to one in which football ability was prized and encouraged, this aptitude would never have been discovered.

It is an important question whether our mode of life alters the heredity that we transmit to our children, whether, for example, if I devote myself to study this fact will so affect the germ-plasm that my children are likely to have more mental capacity. The prevailing scientific opinion is that it does not, that, of two brothers, one who is uneducated, but of the same natural ability, is as likely to have bright children as one who goes to college and enters an intellectual profession. An athlete will not have stronger children because of his training.

An obvious ground for this view is that injuries or mutilations, such as the loss of a leg, are never inherited, not even if they are continued for generations, as was formerly the case with the feet-binding of certain classes of Chinese women. Nor do defects due to a non-hereditary cause, like the deafness that often follows scarlet fever, affect the offspring. In fact, notwithstanding much research, no one has been able to produce any satisfactory proof that "acquired traits,"

8

that is those due to the mode of life, are ever transmitted through the germ-plasm.

As regards the theory of the matter, it is thought
that, heredity being carried by the germ-plasm, and
this being a special kind of cells not affected by our
particular mode of life, there is no reason why the
latter should change heredity. The germ-plasm, it is
believed, bears individuals somewhat as a tree bears
fruit, but they do not react upon it; they merely carry
it and hand it on, as the apple carries the seed.

If this is true (and the evidence is so strong that we
may at least accept it as the most probable theory to
work by) it follows that we cannot improve the strictly
hereditary factor in future children by teaching their
parents, or even by bettering the life of the latter in
any or all respects. It does not follow, however, that
the germ-plasm will remain unchanged, even if we ourselves cannot change it. Apparently there is growth,
or intrinsic change of some sort, going on in all life,
and it is natural to presume that the germ-plasm is no
exception. We need not suppose that nothing takes
place in it but a mechanical recombination of ances-
tral elements: there are probably changes, but as yet
we know little of their character. If one believes, in
general, that life is mechanical and predetermined, one
will naturally apply this idea to heredity as well as
elsewhere, but if he believes that it is in some sense
free and creative, there is no reason why the hereditary current should not share in these traits.

It is possible even if our mode of life has no direct
effect upon heredity, for us to influence it by an in-

direct process known as Selection. This is based upon the fact that the germ-plasm carried by one individual may differ considerably from that carried by another, even in the same family, and varies widely as between different families, and still more widely as between different races; although all may have remotely a common ancestry. If, then, we know what sort of germ-plasm a certain individual or family or race carries, and can increase or decrease the number of children inheriting it, we can change, more or less, the proportion which this kind of heredity bears to other kinds.

An obvious case is where two contrasted races are concerned. Suppose, for example, there is a Southern county in which there are five thousand negroes and five thousand whites, and that the average number of children raised in negro and white families is about the same. Now if, in some way, you can cause the white families to raise more children, or the negroes fewer, the complexion of the county will gradually be altered. If the rate becomes as three to two in favor of the whites, there will be three white children to two black in the next generation, $\frac{3}{2} \times \frac{3}{2}$, or nine to four in the generation following, and so on in a geometrical ratio. The negroes will become a rapidly dwindling fraction of the population.

If, instead of having two distinct races in the county, we had merely the white race, in which, however, there was a considerable difference of complexion among the family stocks represented, something analogous might still take place. If the dark families were more prolific than the blonde, the population would darken, or *vice versa.* And even in the same family there might be differences in this respect which could be increased or diminished by selection. There is no doubt that, starting with a mixed population and being able to control mating and the number of children, we could in this way breed dark or light people, tall or short, blue-eyed or black-eyed, bright or dull, and indeed increase or diminish any hereditary trait ascertainable enough to be made the basis of selection.

It is believed that the conditions of life are all the time tending to cause some types of heredity to produce more children than other types, and so by an unconscious process to alter the germ-plasm in the group as a whole. For example, the frontier conditions in the early history of America probably tended to produce a physically vig rous race; not because the undergoing of hardships had any direct effect upon the germ-plasm, but because the weaker sort of people would be likely to die out under these hardships, and leave no children to inherit their weakness, while the stronger sort would leave large families and correspondingly increase the sort of germ-plasm that they carried—in other words by "natural selection" or "the survival of the fittest." This process may in time produce very great changes. The difference in color between the black and white races (which are undoubtedly sprung from a common ancestry) is plausibly explained, on the principle of natural selection, by supposing that darker skins were associated with greater power of resistance to the heat of the sun, or to the diseases of tropical climates, so that this kind of heredity would

increase in such climates; just as many species of
animals are known to develop colors that help their
survival. Most animals, including birds, are so colored as to be hard to distinguish from their environment: it is a kind of camouflage, and helps them to
escape the enemies who would otherwise devour them,
or to approach the prey which would otherwise escape
them.

It was by natural selection mainly, according to Darwin, that the various species of plants and animals
were gradually moulded to fit the conditions under
which they had to live, and any one who wishes to
know something fundamental about evolution should
read at least the first six chapters of his Origin of Species.
And in his Descent of Man one may see how he worked
out this idea in its application to the development of
the human race.

But why not make selection conscious and intelligent, and thus improve the stock of men somewhat as
we do that of domestic animals? There has, in fact,
arisen a science of Eugenics, or Race-Improvement,
seeking to stimulate the propagation of desirable types
of human heredity and prevent that of undesirable
types. There are many difficulties in this, and it is
not clear how much we may expect to accomplish, but
there is no doubt that some things can and should be
done. Scientific tests should be made of all children
to ascertain those that are feeble-minded or otherwise
hopelessly below a normal capacity, followed by a
study of their families to find whether these defects

are hereditary. If it appears that they are, the individuals having them should, as they grow older, be prevented from having children to inherit their incapacity. At present, owing to our ignorance and carelessness in this regard, large numbers of children are coming into the world with the handicap to themselves and the menace to society of an ineradicable inferiority.

On the other hand, the educated and prosperous classes show a tendency to limit the number of their children that is often spoken of as Race-Suicide. This limitation appears to be due partly to the taste for ease and luxury fostered by wealth, partly to increasing social ambition and greater desire for self-development. These latter, excellent no doubt in themselves, draw upon our means and energy, and are apt to cause us to postpone marriage or to have fewer children after marriage than we otherwise would. Since they grow with democracy, it may well be that democracy antagonizes the birth-rate.

It takes an average of nearly four children to a family to keep up the numbers of a hereditary stock, and more to maintain its proportion of an increasing population like that of the United States. This is because there must be enough not only to replace the two parents and provide for the increase, if any, but also to compensate for failure of propagation by the unmarried, the sterile, and those who die prematurely.

The upper classes are falling far short of their quota, and if we assume that they represent the abler stocks it would seem that the race is being impaired by their diminution. Is it not desirable, and perhaps practicable, to induce them to become more prolific? Even if they do not represent abler stocks than the middle class, is there not danger that the small-family tendency will pervade that class also? It has already done so in France. Many people are alarmed also by observing that the immigrant stocks in the northern and eastern states are multiplying faster than the native stocks, and that the negroes are kept from outrunning the whites only by their high death-rate. Others give their apprehensions a still wider range and see an imminent Yellow Peril in the fecundity of the oriental peoples, which threatens, they think, to put an early end to the ascendancy of the white races and of white civilization.

Although improvements in our mode of life probably do not alter heredity, it by no means follows that they are unimportant, or less important than eugenics. In fact, progress, as ordinarily understood, does not require any change in heredity, but is a development of knowledge, arts, and institutions that takes place in the social process with little or no alteration of the germ-plasm. The spread of education, the abolition of slavery, the growth of railroads, telegraphs, telephones, and automobiles, the formation of a society of nations and the abolition of war—all this kind of thing is social and may go on indefinitely with no improvement in heredity. Nevertheless better heredity would make progress more rapid, because it would give us more men of talent as leaders and a higher average of ability. And a worse heredity, such as many think we are in danger of, would hinder progress

and possibly, in time, put an end to it altogether.
Social improvement and eugenics are a team that
should be driven abreast.

When our individual life begins the two elements of
history from which it is drawn, the hereditary and the
social, merge in the new whole and cease to exist as
separable forces. Nothing that the individual is or
does can be ascribed to either alone, because everything is based on habits and experiences in which the
two are inextricably mingled. Heredity and environment, as applied to the present life of a human being,
are, in fact, abstractions; the real thing is a total organic process not separable into parts. What heredity
is, in its practical working at a given time, depends
upon the process itself, which develops some potentialities and represses others. And in like manner the
effective environment depends upon the selective and
assimilating activities of the growing organism. If
you wish to understand it the main thing to do is to
study its life-history back to its beginning in the conception and birth of the individual; beyond that you
may, if you wish, pursue still farther the germ-plasm
and the social inheritance from which it sprang.
These give us a background, like the accounts of a
man's ancestry and early surroundings in the first
chapters of his biography. But the life of William
Sykes is a thing you must study directly, and no
knowledge of heredity and environment can be more
than a help to this.*

* An old fallacy, but one constantly recurring, is that we can
in some way measure the hereditary factor in the human mind

Speech well illustrates the inextricable union of the animal and social heritages. It springs in part from the native structure of the vocal organs and from a hereditary impulse to use them which we see at work in the chattering of idiots and of the deaf and dumb. A natural sensibility to other persons and need to communicate with them also enters into it. But all articulate utterance comes by communication; it is learned from others, varies with the environment and has its source in tradition. Speech is thus a socio-biologic function. And so it is with ambition and all our socially active impulses: We are born with the need to assert ourselves, but whether we do so as hunters, warriors, fishermen, traders, politicians, or scholars, depends upon the opportunities offered us in the social process.

Evidently it is wrong, speaking generally, to regard heredity and social environment as antagonistic. They are normally complementary, each having its own work to do and neither of any use without the other.

Which is stronger? Which is more important? These are silly questions, the asking of which is sufficient proof that the asker has no clear idea of the

apart from the social or acquired factor. Thus some writers have claimed that mental tests in the army were a measure of natural intelligence, independent of social environment, and that they prove the hereditary inferiority of certain nationalities among those measured. But since the growth of the mind is altogether a social process (compare Chapter III) it is unreasonable to suppose that the outcome can be in any way independent of that process. And in fact the results of these tests can be explained quite as plausibly by differences in language, family life, education, and occupation, as by heredity.

16

INTRODUCTION

matter in hand. It is precisely as if one should ask,
Which is the more important member of the family,
the father or the mother? Both may be said to be
infinitely important, since each is indispensable; and
their functions being different in kind cannot be compared in amount.

Shall we say, then, that all discussions as to the relation between heredity and environment are futile?
By no means The fact is that, although it is plain
that they are, in general, complementary and mutually
dependent, we usually do not know precisely what
each contributes in a given case, and so may be in
doubt whether to seek improvement by working on
the germ-plasm or through social influence. It is
only with reference to general theory that the question
which is more important is silly. With reference to a
specific problem it may be quite pertinent—just as it
might be quite pertinent, as regards the troubles of a
specific family, to inquire whether you could best
reach them through the father or through the mother.
And while direct measurement of the factors, at least
where the mind is involved, is impossible, since they
have no separate existence, there may be roundabout
methods of inference which throw real light upon the
matter.

Many race questions are of this sort. There are,
for instance, great differences between the Japanese
and the Americans. Some of these, as language, religion, moral standards, are clearly social and may be
altered by education. Some, as stature, color and
shape of the eyes, are certain'y hereditary and cannot

17

be altered by education: these, however, are, in themselves, perhaps, of no great importance. But are there also, or are there not, subtle differences of temperament, mental capacity or emotional gifts, which are both hereditary and important, which render the races incapable of living together in peace, or make one of them superior to the other? We do not know the answer to this question, though it is most important that we should. It is the same with the negro question. How far is the present inferior condition of that race remediable by education and social improvement, how far is it a matter of the germ-plasm, alterable only by selection? The whole negro-white problem hinges on this question, which we cannot answer with assurance.

There is an analogous problem with reference to criminals. How far, or in just what sorts of cases, may we safely trust to educational or deterrent methods as a preventive of crime? Should we also try to prevent propagation, and, if so, when and how? And so with men of genius. We need more of them. Will education do it, or shall we follow the teaching of Galton, the founder of eugenics, who held that we must above all things induce men of great ability to have more children? And again, with reference to the rich and powerful classes. Is their ascendancy that of natural ability, of a superior breed, and so, perhaps, just and beneficial? Or is it based on social privileges in the way of education and opportunity, and hence, as many think, unfair and detrimental? Unsolved questions of this kind arise whenever we try to make out just how we may better the course of human life. At present the best we can do is to try everything

18

that seems likely to improve either the germ-plasm or the social process.

Although the transmission of heredity through the germ-plasm is much the same in man as in the other animals, there is a notable difference in the kind of traits that are transmitted, and are found to exist at birth. This difference is in teachability or plasticity. The mental outfit of the human child is above all things teachable, and therefore, of course, indefinite, consisting not of tendencies to do particular things that life calls for, but of vague aptitudes or lines of teachability that are of no practical use until they are educated. The mental outfit of the animal, on the other hand, is relatively definite and fixed, giving rise to activities which are useful with little or no teaching.

This difference is fundamental to any understanding of the relation of man to the evolutionary process, or of the relation of human nature and human life to animal nature and animal life. We need to see it with all possible clearness and to follow out its implications.

Roughly speaking, then, the heredity of the other animals is a mechanism like that of a hand-organ: it is made to play a few tunes; you can play these tunes at once, with little or no training; and you can never play any others. The heredity of man, on the other hand, is a mechanism more like that of a piano: it is not made to play particular tunes; you can do nothing at all on it without training; but a trained player can draw from it an infinite variety of music.

A newly hatched chick is able to run about and to pick up small objects of a certain size and form which prove to be food, and to sustain its life. It scarcely needs education, and I am told by a breeder that the product of the incubator, having no link with the past of their race except the germ-plasm, get along as well as those that have all a mother's care. A baby, on the other hand, takes a year to learn to walk, and many, many more years to learn the activities by which he is eventually to get his living. He has, to be sure, a definite capacity to draw nourishment from his mother, but this is only a makeshift, an animal method to help him out until his more human powers have time to develop. In general, his wonderful hereditary capacities are as ineffectual as a piano when the player begins to practise. Definite function is wholly dependent upon education.

Thus the plastic, indeterminate character of human heredity involves a long and helpless infancy; and this, in turn, is the basis of the human family, since the primary and essential function of the family is the care of children. Those species of animals in which the young are adequately prepared for life by definite heredity have no family at all, while those which more or less resemble man as regards plastic heredity, resemble him also in having some rudiments, at least, of a family. Kittens, for instance, are cared for by the mother for several months and profit in some measure by her example and instruction.

More generally, this difference as regards plasticity means that the life-activities of the animal are com-

paratively uniform and fixed, while those of man are
varied and changing. Human functions are so numerous ahd intricate that no fixed mechanism could
provide for them: they are also subject to radical
change, not only in the life of the individual but from
one generation to another. The only possible hereditary basis for them is an outfit of indeterminate capacities which can be developed and guided by experience as the needs of life require.

I see a flycatcher sitting on a dead branch, where
there are no leaves to interrupt his view. Presently
he darts toward a passing insect, hovers about him a
few seconds, catches him, or fails to do so, and returns
to his perch. That is his way of getting a living: he
has done it all his life and will go on doing it to the
end. Millions of other flycatchers on millions of other
dead branches are doing precisely the same. And this
has been the life of the species for unknown thousands
of years. They have, through the germ-plasm, a definite capacity for this—the keen eye, the swift, fluttering
movement to follow the insect, the quick, sure action
of the neck and bill to seize him—all effective with no
instruction and very little practice.

Man has a natural hunger, like the flycatcher, and a
natural mechanism of tasting, chewing, swallowing,
and digestion; but his way of getting the food varies
widely at different times of his life, is not the same
with different individuals, and often changes completely from one generation to another. The great
majority of us gain our food, after we have left the
parental nest, through what we call a job, and a job

is any activity whatever that a complex and shifting society esteems sufficiently to pay us for. It is very likely, nowadays, to last only part of our lives and to be something our ancestors never heard of. Thus whatever is most distinctively human, our adaptability, our power of growth, our arts and sciences, our social institutions and progress, is bound up with the indeterminate character of human heredity.

Of course there is no sharp line, in this matter of teachability, between man and the other animals. The activities of the latter are not wholly predetermined, and in so far as they are not there is a learning process based upon plastic heredity. The higher animals—horses, dogs, elephants, for example—are notably teachable, and may even participate in the changes of human society, as when dogs learn to draw carts, trail fugitives, guide the lost, or perform in a circus. And, on the other side, those activities of man which do not require much adaptation, such as the breathing, sucking, and crying of infants, and even walking (which is learned without instruction when the legs become strong enough), are provided for by definite heredity.

The question of the place of instinct in human life may well be considered here, since it involves not only the relation between human and animal heredity, but especially that distinction between fixed and plastic reactions to the environment that we have just discussed.

There is much disagreement upon the definition of

instinct, some confining it to definite modes of hereditary behavior, like the squirrel's burying a nut; others giving it a much wider and vaguer meaning. To inquire how this disagreement arose will throw light upon the whole matter.

Animals, as we have seen, have definite and effective modes of acting which they do not have to learn, and it was these that first attracted attention, by their contrast to human behavior, and were called instinct, as opposed to the more rational or acquired activities of man. Darwin says in his Origin of Species:

"I will not attempt any definition of instinct . . . but every one understands what is meant when it is said that instinct impels the cuckoo to migrate and to lay her eggs in other birds' nests. An action, which we ourselves require experience to enable us to perform, when performed by an animal, more especially by a very young one, without experience, and when performed by many individuals in the same way, without their knowing for what purpose it is performed, is usually said to be instinctive. But I could show that none of these characters are universal." *

Men have few instinctive actions, in this original sense of the word. But when investigators began to study our behavior from the evolutionary point of view, they saw that if not instinctive in the strict sense it had yet grown out of instinctive behavior, was historically continuous with it, and, in short, that there was no sharp line to be drawn, in this matter, between human and animal. Moreover, although our outward actions had ceased to be determined by heredity, it

* The Origin of Species, chap. viii.

seemed that we still had inward emotions and dispositions that were so determined, and had an immense
influence on our conduct. The question, then, was,
and is, whether human behavior, guided in a general
way by these hereditary emotions and dispositions,
shall be called instinctive or not.

Those who answer yes, would say that a man is
acting instinctively when he is impelled in any degree
by hunger, fear, rage, or sexual attraction, even though
his mode of expressing these impulses is quite new.
Those who say no, would mean that such action is
not instinctive because not definitely predetermined
by a hereditary mechanism. The transmission of
behavior through the germ-plasm is their test. Hence
the disagreement as to the place of instinct in human
life. If we are to give it a large place it must be used
in the former sense, that is, to mean an inner rather
than an outer process, it must be defined in terms of
motive rather than of specific action.

Perhaps a reasonable middle course would be to
avoid the word "instinct" as applied to most human
behavior, which has nothing of the fixity of animal instinct, and speak instead of "instinctive emotion,"
since the emotional side of our activity clearly includes
a hereditary element which seems to remain much the
same under the most diverse manifestations.

If we do this we shall still find that there is little
agreement as to just what instinctive emotions there
are, and how they work. The reason for this lack of
agreement is that our experience bearing upon the

question, although real and vivid, is yet elusive, hard to define and classify, subject to various interpretations. Thus the passion of love is the hackneyed topic of literature and conversation. Most of us have undergone it, have observed it in others, and are willing to impart what we know about it; yet who can say precisely what the essential phenomena are, or just what is inherited, and how this inheritance is awakened, modified, developed by experience? These are obscure questions, and perhaps always will be. There are similar questions with reference to fear, anger, grief, and the like. The student will find informing books that aim to elucidate these phases of life, analyzing and describing our modes of feeling, and tracing their probable evolution from animal instinct, but these works differ immensely in their views, and none of them is conclusive.

It is fairly clear that we have at least half a dozen well-marked types of instinctive emotional disposition that are social in that they concern directly our attitude toward other persons. I might name, as perhaps the plainest, the dispositions to anger, to fear, to maternal love, to male and female sexual love, and to the emotion of self-assertion or power. We may accept these as instinctive,

1. Because they appear to be universal in the human race, as shown by common observation, by introspection, by the evidence accumulated in literature, and by more or less scientific methods of study, such as those used by psychoanalysts. This universality

would not of itself prove them instinctive: they might be due to universal social conditions. It adds greatly, however, to the cogency of other reasons.

2. Because they are associated with physical reactions or modes of expression which can hardly be other than instinctive, many of them being practically universal among the human race and some of them found also among the apes. The clenching of the fists and teeth in rage, and the uncovering of the teeth as if to bite are an example of what I mean. Darwin investigated these in his Expression of the Emotions, but, owing to his belief that the effects of habit are inherited, he did not discriminate as clearly as we could wish between what is hereditary and what is learned from others.

3. Because they correspond to and motivate certain enduring types of function found not only in man but in other animals; because, in short, they are so deeply rooted in animal evolution that it would be strange if they were not instinctive. Human anger, for example, motivates conflict with opposing persons or other agents, being similar in function to the anger, clearly instinctive, of all the fighting animals. In the same way fear motivates escape from danger, with us as with all animals who have dangers to escape from, and so on. These instinctive emotions predetermine, not specific actions, but, in a measure, the energy that flows into actions having a certain function with reference to our environment.*

* Apparently there must be, along with the hereditary emotional disposition, some hereditary nervous mechanism to connect the emotion with the various stimuli that awaken it. Some

INTRODUCTION

Beyond such clearly ascertainable hereditary dispositions there are innumerable others, some of them, perhaps, equally clear, but most of them elusive, undefined, and disputable. Moreover, all such dispositions, including those mentioned, are rapidly developed, transformed, and interwoven by social experience, giving rise to a multitude of complex passions and sentiments which no one has satisfactorily elucidated. Indeed, as these change very considerably with changes in the social life that moulds them, it is impossible that they should be definitely and finally described. Each age and country has its own more or less peculiar modes of feeling, as it has of thinking. There is no finality in this field.*

Although instinctive emotion probably enters into everything we do, it enters in such a way that we can rarely or never explain human behavior by it alone. In human life it is not, in any considerable degree, a motive to specific behavior at all, but an impulse whose definite expression depends upon education and social situation. It does not act except through a complex, socially determined organism of thought and sentiment.

If, for example, we say "War is due to an instinct of pugnacity," we say something that includes so little regard this as a difficulty, but if so it is one for the psychologist to solve. That generalized types of function, as personal conflict, do awaken specific emotions, as anger, and are also motivated by them, is a matter of direct observation.

* Professor McDougall's Social Psychology, which appeared some years after the first edition of this book, is now well known as a standard work in the field indicated.

of the truth and ignores so much that it is practically false. War is rooted in many instinctive tendencies, all of which have been transformed by education, tradition, and organization, so that to study its sources is to study the whole process of society. This calls, above all things, for detailed historical and sociological analysis: there could hardly be anything more inimical to real knowledge or rational conduct regarding it than to ascribe it to pugnacity and let the question go at that.

Much the same may be said of the employment of a supposed gregarious instinct, or "instinct of the herd," to explain a multiplicity of phenomena, including mob-excitement, dread of isolation, conformity to fads and fashions, subservience to leaders and control by propaganda; which require, like war, a detailed study of social antecedents. This is, as Professor Findlay remarks,* "an easy, dogmatic way of explaining phenomena whose causes and effects are far more complicated than these authors would admit." Indeed I am not aware that there is any such evidence of the existence of a gregarious instinct as there is of an instinct of fear or anger; and many think the phenomena which it is used to explain may be accounted for by sympathy and suggestion, without calling in a special instinct. It seems to me to be the postulate of an individualistic psychology in search of some special motive to explain collective behavior. If you regard human nature as primarily social you need no such special motive.†

* An Introduction to Sociology, p. 72.
† The notion that collective behavior is to be attributed to

INTRODUCTION

There is, indeed, a wide-spread disposition among psychologists, psychoanalysts, biologists, economists, writers on education, and others who are interested in instinct but would gladly avoid history or sociology, to short-circuit their current of causation, leading it directly from instinct to social behavior, without following it into those intricate convolutions of social process through which, in the real world, it actually flows and by which it is transformed. This is an instance of that common fallacy, particularism, which consists in attending to only one factor in a complex whole. Social questions, because of the many factors entering into them, offer peculiar temptations to this fallacy, against which we cannot be too much on our guard.

How are we to think of reason in relation to instinct? This depends upon our view as to that question, already discussed, whether instinct means only fixed modes of behavior or whether it may include also instinctive emotion that expresses itself in plastic behavior. If we confine it to the former, then instinct and reason exclude each other, because it is the nature of reason to adapt conduct to varying conditions; but if we admit the latter, then reason and instinct may work together. Fixed instincts call for no general control: life presses a button and the hereditary mechanism does the rest. But teachable instincts imply a teacher. They must be guided, developed, co-ordi-

an "instinct of the herd" seems to owe its vogue in great part to Nietzsche, who made much use of it, in a contemptuous sense, to animate his anti-democratic philosophy.

nated, organized, so that they may work effectually; and this is the part of reason. Reason, in one aspect, is team-work in the mind; it is the mental organization required by the various and changing life of man. It takes the crude energy of the instinctive dispositions, as an officer takes his raw recruits, instructing and training them until they can work together for any end he may propose, and in any manner that the situation demands. If a man wants a wife it teaches him how, in the existing state of things, he may be able to woo and win her, and how support her when won, guiding him through a complicated course of behavior adapted to the present and yet impelled in part by hereditary emotion.

Reason, in this view, does not supplant instinct, any more than the captain supplants the private soldiers; it is a principle of higher organization, controlling and transforming instinctive energies. Indeed, reason is itself an instinctive disposition, in a large use of the term, a disposition to compare, combine, and organize the activities of the mind. Animals have it in some measure and it is unique in man only by the degree of its development: it might be compared to a common soldier emerging from the ranks, taking the lead by virtue of peculiar ability and becoming in time the commanding officer.

And human history, in distinction from animal history, is a natural outcome of those traits of human psychology that we have discussed. It is a process possible only to a species endowed with teachable

30

instinctive dispositions, organized, partly by reason, into a plastic and growing social whole. This whole, responsive to the outer world in a thousand ways, and containing also diverse and potent energies within itself, is ever putting forth new forms of life, which we describe as progress or decadence according as we think them better or worse than the old. These changes do not require any alteration in our hereditary powers. The hereditary basis, the instinctive but teachable capacities, are relatively constant, and, so far as these are concerned, there is little or no reason to think that the Teutonic stocks from which most of us are sprung are appreciably different now from what they were when Cæsar met and fought and described them. If we could substitute a thousand babies from that time for those in our own cradles, it would probably make no perceptible difference. They would grow up in our ways, driving automobiles instead of war chariots, reading the newspapers, and, in general, playing the human game as it is played to-day quite like the rest of us.

And, finally, just what do we mean by Human Nature? The phrase is used vaguely, but there are at least three meanings that can be distinguished with some precision. And as we distinguish them we may be able, at the same time, to answer the perennial question, Does Human Nature change?

It may mean, first, the strictly hereditary nature of man, borne by the germ-plasm, the formless impulses and capacities that we infer to exist at birth, but of which we have little definite knowledge because they do not manifest themselves except as a factor in social development. This nature appears to change very slowly, and we have no reason to think we are very much different at birth from our ancestors of, say, a thousand years ago.*

It may mean, second, a social nature developed in man by simple forms of intimate association or "primary groups," especially the family and neighborhood, which are found everywhere and everywhere work upon the individual in somewhat the same way. This nature consists chiefly of certain primary social sentiments and attitudes, such as consciousness of one's self in relation to others, love of approbation, resentment of censure, emulation, and a sense of social right and wrong formed by the standards of a group. This seems to me to correspond very closely to what is meant by "human nature" in ordinary speech. We mean something much more definite than hereditary disposition, which most of us know nothing about, and yet something fundamental and wide-spread if not universal in the life of man, found in ancient history and in the accounts of remote nations, as well as now and here. Thus, when we read that Joseph's brethren hated him and could not speak peaceably to him because they saw that their father loved him more than all the rest; we say, "Of course, that is human nature." This social nature is much more alterable than heredity, and if it is "pretty much the same the world over,"

* Professor E. L. Thorndike is the author of an important work on The Original Nature of Man.

as we commonly say, this is because the intimate groups in which it is formed are somewhat similar. If these are essentially changed, human nature will change with them.

There is a third sense of the phrase which is not unusual, especially in discussions which turn upon the merits or demerits of human nature. This is not easy to define, but differs from the preceding in identifying it with somewhat specific types of behavior, such as pecuniary selfishness or generosity, belligerency or peacefulness, efficiency or inefficiency, conservatism or radicalism, and the like. In other words, it departs from the generality of the idea and brings in elements that come from particular situations and institutions. Human nature, in any such sense as this, is in the highest degree changeful, because the behavior to which it gives rise varies, morally and in every other way, with the influences that act upon it. It may be selfish, inefficient, quarrelsome, conservative now, and a few years hence or in another situation generous, peaceful, efficient, and progressive; all turns upon how it is evoked and organized. Perhaps the commonest fallacy we meet in this connection is that which assumes that human nature does not change, points out respects in which it has worked deplorably, and concludes that it will always work so. An unchanging human nature, it is said, has given us wars and economic greed; it always will. On the contrary, since these things disappear or are controlled under certain conditions we may conclude that human nature, in this sense, is subject to change.

But, in the more general sense, it is a nature whose primary trait is teachability, and so does not need to change in order to be an inexhaustible source of changing conduct and institutions. We can make it work in almost any way, if we understand it, as a clever mechanic can mould to his will the universal laws of mass and motion.

CHAPTER I

SOCIETY AND THE INDIVIDUAL

AN ORGANIC RELATION—THEY ARE ASPECTS OF THE SAME THING—
THE FALLACY OF SETTING THEM IN OPPOSITION—VARIOUS
FORMS OF THIS FALLACY—FAMILIAR QUESTIONS AND HOW
THEY MAY BE ANSWERED

"SOCIETY AND THE INDIVIDUAL" is really the subject
of this whole book, and not merely of Chapter I. It
is my general aim to set forth, from various points
of view, what the individual is, considered as a member of a social whole; while the special purpose of this
chapter is only to offer a preliminary statement of
the matter, as I conceive it, afterward to be unfolded
at some length and variously illustrated.

If we accept the evolutionary point of view we are
led to see the relation between society and the individual as an organic relation. That is, we see that
the individual is not separable from the human whole,
but a living member of it, deriving his life from the
whole through social and hereditary transmission as
truly as if men were literally one body. He cannot
cut himself off; the strands of heredity and education
are woven into all his being. And, on the other hand,
the social whole is in some degree dependent upon
each individual, because each contributes something
to the common life that no one else can contribute.

35

Thus we have, in a broad sense of the word, an "organism" or living whole made up of differentiated members, each of which has a special function.

This is true of society in that large sense which embraces all humanity, and also of any specific social group. A university, for example, is an organic whole, made up of students, teachers, officials, and others. Every member is more or less dependent upon every other, because all contribute to the common life. And note that it is precisely his individuality, his functional difference from the rest, that gives each member his peculiar importance. The professor of Paleontology has a part that no one else can play; and so, less obviously, perhaps, has every teacher and student. The organic view stresses both the unity of the whole and the peculiar value of the individual, explaining each by the other. What is a football team without a quarterback? Almost as useless as a quarter-back without a team. A well-developed individual can exist only in and through a well-developed whole, and *vice versa*.

This seems a simple idea, and so it is, but it is so opposed to some of our most cherished habits of thought that we may well take time to look at it from various points of view.

A separate individual is an abstraction unknown to experience, and so likewise is society when regarded as something apart from individuals. The real thing is Human Life, which may be considered either in an individual aspect or in a social, that is to say a general, aspect; but is always, as a matter of fact, both individual and general. In other words, "society" and "individuals" do not denote separable phenomena, but are simply collective and distributive aspects of the same thing, the relation between them being like that between other expressions one of which denotes a group as a whole and the other the members of the group, such as the army and the soldiers, the class and the students, and so on. This holds true of any social aggregate, great or small; of a family, a city, a nation, a race; of mankind as a whole: no matter how extensive, complex, or enduring a group may be, no good reason can be given for regarding it as essentially different in this respect from the smallest, simplest, or most transient.

So far, then, as there is any difference between the two, it is rather in our point of view than in the object we are looking at: when we speak of society, or use any other collective term, we fix our minds upon some general view of the people concerned, while when we speak of individuals we disregard the general aspect and think of them as if they were separate. Thus "the Cabinet" may consist of President Lincoln, Secretary Stanton, Secretary Seward, and so on; but when I say "the Cabinet" I do not suggest the same idea as when I enumerate these gentlemen separately. Society, or any complex group, may, to ordinary observation, be a very different thing from all of its members viewed one by one—as a man who beheld General Grant's army from Missionary Ridge would have seen something other than he would by approaching every soldier in it. In the same way a picture is

37

made up of so many square inches of painted canvas; but if you should look at these one at a time, covering the others, until you had seen them all, you would still not have seen the picture. There may, in all such cases, be a system or organization in the whole that is not apparent in the parts. In this sense, and in no other, is there a difference between society and the individuals of which it is composed; a difference not residing in the facts themselves but existing to the observer on account of the limits of his perception. A *complete* view of society would also be a complete view of all the individuals, and *vice versa;* there would be no difference between them.

And just as there is no society or group that is not a collective view of persons, so there is no individual who may not be regarded as a particular view of social groups. He has no separate existence; through both the hereditary and the social factors in his life a man is bound into the whole of which he is a member, and to consider him apart from it is quite as artificial as to consider society apart from individuals.

If this is true there is, of course, a fallacy in that not uncommon manner of speaking which sets the social and the individual over against each other as separate and antagonistic. The word "social" appears to be used in at least three fairly distinct senses, but in none of these does it mean something that can properly be regarded as opposite to individual or personal.

In its largest sense it denotes that which pertains to the collective aspect of humanity, to society in its

38

widest and vaguest meaning. In this sense the individual and all his attributes are social, since they are all connected with the general life in one way or another, and are part of a collective development.

Again, social may mean what pertains to immediate intercourse, to the life of conversation and face-to-face sympathy—sociable, in short. This is something quite different, but no more antithetical to individual than the other; it is in these relations that individuality most obviously exists and expresses itself.

In a third sense the word means conducive to the collective welfare, and thus becomes nearly equivalent to moral, as when we say that crime or sensuality is unsocial or anti-social; but here again it cannot properly be made the antithesis of individual—since wrong is surely no more individual than right—but must be contrasted with immoral, brutal, selfish, or some other word with an ethical implication.

There are a number of expressions which are closely associated in common usage with this objectionable antithesis; such words, for instance, as individualism, socialism, particularism, collectivism.* These appear to be used with a good deal of vagueness, so that it is always in order to require that any one who employs them shall make it plain in what sense they are to be taken. I wish to make no captious objections to particular forms of expression, and so far as these can be shown to have meanings that express the facts of life I have nothing to say against them. Of the current

* Also free-will, determinism, egoism, and altruism, which involve, in my opinion, a kindred misconception.

use of individualism and socialism in antithesis to each other, about the same may be said as of the words without the *ism*. I do not see that life presents two distinct and opposing tendencies that can properly be called individualism and socialism, any more than that there are two distinct and opposing entities, society and the individual, to embody these tendencies. The phenomena usually called individualistic are always socialistic in the sense that they are expressive of tendencies growing out of the general life, and, contrariwise, the so-called socialistic phenomena have always an obvious individual aspect. These and similar terms may be used, conveniently enough, to describe theories or programmes of the day, but whether they are suitable for purposes of careful study appears somewhat doubtful. If used, they ought, it seems to me, to receive more adequate definition than they have at present.

For example, all the principal epochs of European history might be, and most of them are, spoken of as individualistic on one ground or another, and without departing from current usage of the word. The decaying Roman Empire was individualistic if a decline of public spirit and an every-man-for-himself feeling and practice constitute individualism. So also was the following period of political confusion. The feudal system is often regarded as individualistic, because of the relative independence and isolation of small political units—quite a different use of the word from the preceding—and after this come the Revival of Learning, the Renaissance, and the Reformation, which are all commonly spoken of, on still other grounds, as assertions of individualism. Then we reach the seventeenth and eighteenth centuries, sceptical, transitional, and, again, individualistic; and so to our own time, which many hold to be the most individualistic of all. One feels like asking whether a word which means so many things as this means anything whatever.

There is always some confusion of terms in speaking of opposition between an individual and society in general, even when the writer's meaning is obvious enough: it would be more accurate to say either that one individual is opposing many, or that one part of society is opposing other parts; and thus avoid confusing the two aspects of life in the same expression. When Emerson says that society is in a conspiracy against the independence of each of its members, we are to understand that any peculiar tendency represented by one person finds itself more or less at variance with the general current of tendencies organized in other persons. It is no more individual, nor any less social, in a large sense, than other tendencies represented by more persons. A thousand persons are just as truly individuals as one, and the man who seems to stand alone draws his being from the general stream of life just as truly and inevitably as if he were one of a thousand. Innovation is just as social as conformity, genius as mediocrity. These distinctions are not between what is individual and what is social, but between what is usual or established and what is exceptional or novel. In other words, wherever you find life as society there you will find life as individuality, and *vice versa*.

I think, then, that the antithesis, society *versus* the

41

individual, is false and hollow whenever used as a general or philosophical statement of human relations. Whatever idea may be in the minds of those who set these words and their derivatives over against each other, the notion conveyed is that of two separable entities or forces; and certainly such a notion is untrue to fact.

Most people not only think of individuals and society as more or less separate and antithetical, but they look upon the former as antecedent to the latter. That persons make society would be generally admitted as a matter of course; but that society makes persons would strike many as a startling notion, though I know of no good reason for looking upon the distributive aspect of life as more primary or causative than the collective aspect. The reason for the common impression appears to be that we think most naturally and easily of the individual phase of life, simply because it is a tangible one, the phase under which men appear to the senses, while the actuality of groups, of nations, of mankind at large, is realized only by the active and instructed imagination. We ordinarily regard society, so far as we conceive it at all, in a vaguely material aspect, as an aggregate of physical bodies, not as the vital whole which it is; and so, of course, we do not see that it may be as original or causative as anything else. Indeed, many look upon "society" and other general terms as somewhat mystical, and are inclined to doubt whether there is any reality back of them.

This naïve individualism of thought—which, however, does not truly see the individual any more than it does society—is reinforced by traditions in which all of us are brought up, and is so hard to shake off that it may be worth while to point out a little more definitely some of the prevalent ways of conceiving life which are permeated by it, and which any one who agrees with what has just been said may regard as fallacious. My purpose in doing this is only to make clearer the standpoint from which succeeding chapters are written, and I do not propose any thorough discussion of the views mentioned.

First, then, we have *mere individualism.* In this the distributive aspect is almost exclusively regarded, collective phases being looked upon as quite secondary and incidental. Each person is held to be a separate agent, and all social phenomena are thought of as originating in the action of such agents. The individual is the source, the independent, the only human source, of events. Although this way of looking at things has been much discredited by the evolutionary science and philosophy of recent years, it is by no means abandoned, even in theory, and practically it enters as a premise, in one shape or another, into most of the current thought of the day. It springs naturally from the established way of thinking, congenial, as I have remarked, to the ordinary material view of things and corroborated by theological and other traditions.

Next is *double causation,* or a partition of power between society and the individual, thought of as

43

separate causes. This notion, in one shape or another, is the one ordinarily met with in social and ethical discussion. It is no advance, philosophically, upon the preceding. There is the same premise of the individual as a separate, unrelated agent; but over against him is set a vaguely conceived general or collective interest and force. It seems that people are so accustomed to thinking of themselves as uncaused causes, special creators on a small scale, that when the existence of general phenomena is forced upon their notice they are likely to regard these as something additional, separate, and more or less antithetical. Our two forces contend with varying fortunes, the thinker sometimes sympathizing with one, sometimes with the other, and being an individualist or a socialist accordingly. The doctrines usually understood in connection with these terms differ, as regards their conception of the nature of life, only in taking opposite sides of the same questionable antithesis. The socialist holds it desirable that the general or collective force should win; the individualist has a contrary opinion. Neither offers any change of ground, any reconciling and renewing breadth of view. So far as breadth of view is concerned a man might quite as well be an individualist as a socialist or collectivist, the two being identical in philosophy though antagonistic in programme. If one is inclined to neither party he may take refuge in the expectation that the controversy, resting, as he may hold that it does, on a false conception of life, will presently take its proper place among the forgotten *débris* of speculation.

Thirdly we have *primitive individualism*. This expression has been used to describe the view that sociality follows individuality in time, is a later and additional product of development. This view is a variety of the preceding, and is, perhaps, formed by a mingling of individualistic preconceptions with a somewhat crude evolutionary philosophy. Individuality is usually conceived as lower in moral rank as well as precedent in time. Man *was* a mere individual, mankind a mere aggregation of such, but he had gradually become socialized, he is progressively merging into a social whole. Morally speaking, the individual is the bad, the social the good, and we must push on the work of putting down the former and bringing in the latter.

Of course the view which I regard as sound, is that individuality is neither prior in time nor lower in moral rank than sociality; but that the two have always existed side by side as complementary aspects of the same thing, and that the line of progress is from a lower to a higher type of both, not from the one to the other. If the word social is applied only to the higher forms of mental life it should, as already suggested, be opposed not to individual, but to animal, sensual, or some other word implying mental or moral inferiority. If we go back to a time when the state of our remote ancestors was such that we are not willing to call it social, then it must have been equally undeserving to be described as individual or personal; that is to say, they must have been just as inferior to us when viewed separately as when viewed collectively.

45

To question this is to question the vital unity of human life.

The life of the human species, like that of other species, must always have been both general and particular, must always have had its collective and distributive aspects. The plane of this life has gradually risen, involving, of course, both the aspects mentioned. Now, as ever, they develop as one, and may be observed united in the highest activities of the highest minds. Shakespeare, for instance, is in one point of view a unique and transcendent individual; in another he is a splendid expression of the general life of mankind: the difference is not in him but in the way we choose to look at him.

Finally, there is *the social faculty view*. This expression might be used to indicate those conceptions which regard the social as including only a part, often a rather definite part, of the individual. Human nature is thus divided into individualistic or non-social tendencies or faculties, and those that are social. Thus, certain emotions, as love, are social; others, as fear or anger, are unsocial or individualistic. Some writers have even treated the intelligence as an individualistic faculty, and have found sociality only in some sorts of emotion or sentiment.

This idea of instincts or faculties that are peculiarly social is well enough if we use this word in the sense of pertaining to conversation or immediate fellow feeling. Affection is certainly more social in this sense than fear. But if it is meant that these instincts or faculties are in themselves morally higher than others,

46

or that they alone pertain to the collective life, the view is, I think, very questionable. At any rate the opinion I hold, and expect to explain more fully in the further course of this book, is that man's psychical outfit is not divisible into the social and the non-social; but that he is all social in a large sense, is all a part of the common human life, and that his social or moral progress consists less in the aggrandizement of particular faculties or instincts and the suppression of others, than in the discipline of all with reference to a progressive organization of life which we know in thought as conscience.

Some instincts or tendencies may grow in relative importance, may have an increasing function, while the opposite may be true of others. Such relative growth and diminution of parts seems to be a general feature of evolution, and there is no reason why it should be absent from our mental development. But here as well as elsewhere most parts, if not all, are or have been functional with reference to a life collective as well as distributive; there is no sharp separation of faculties, and progress takes place rather by gradual adaptation of old organs to new functions than by disuse and decay.

To make it quite clear what the organic view involves, so far as regards theory, I will take several questions, such as I have found that people ask when discussing the relation of society and the individual, and will suggest how, as it seems to me, they may be answered.

47

HUMAN NATURE AND THE SOCIAL ORDER

1. Is not society, after all, made up of individuals, and of nothing else?

I should say, Yes. It is plain, every-day humanity, not a mysterious something else.

2. Is society anything more than the sum of the individuals?

In a sense, Yes. There is an organization, a life-process, in any social whole that you cannot see in the individuals separately. To study them one by one and attempt to understand society by putting them together will lead you astray. It is "individualism" in a bad sense of the word. Whole sciences, like political economy; great institutions, like the church, have gone wrong at this point. You must see your groups, your social processes, as the living wholes that they are.

3. Is the individual a product of society?

Yes, in the sense that everything human about him has a history in the social past. If we consider the two sources from which he draws his life, heredity and communication, we see that what he gets through the germ-plasm has a social history in that it has had to adapt itself to past society in order to survive: the traits we are born with are such as have undergone a social test in the lives of our ancestors. And what he gets from communication—language, education, and the like—comes directly from society. Even physical influences, like food and climate, rarely reach us except as modified and adapted by social conditions.

4. Can we separate the individual from society?

Only in an external sense. If you go off alone into

the wilderness you take with you a mind formed in society, and you continue social intercourse in your memory and imagination, or by the aid of books. This, and this only, keeps humanity alive in you, and just in so far as you lose the power of intercourse your mind decays. Long solitude, as in the case of sheep-herders on the Western plains, or prisoners in solitary confinement, often produces imbecility. This is especially likely to happen with the uneducated, whose memories are not well stored with material for imaginative intercourse.

At times in the history of Christianity, and of other religions also, hermits have gone to dwell in desert places, but they have usually kept up some communication with one another and with the world outside, certain of them, like St. Jerome, having been famous letter-writers. Each of them, in fact, belonged to a social system from which he drew ideals and moral support. We may suspect that St. Simeon Stylites, who dwelt for years on top of a pillar, was not unaware that his austerity was visible to others.

A castaway who should be unable to retain his imaginative hold upon human society might conceivably live the life of an intelligent animal, exercising his mind upon the natural conditions about him, but his distinctively human faculties would certainly be lost, or in abeyance.

5. Is the individual in any sense free, or is he a mere piece of society?

Yes, he is free, as I conceive the matter, but it is an organic freedom, which he works out in co-operation

49

with others, not a freedom to do things independently of society. It is team-work. He has freedom to function in his own way, like the quarter-back, but, in one way or another, he has to play the game as life brings him into it.

The evolutionary point of view encourages us to believe that life is a creative process, that we are really building up something new and worth while, and that the human will is a part of the creative energy that does this. Every individual has his unique share in the work, which no one but himself can discern and perform. Although his life flows into him from the hereditary and social past, his being as a whole is new, a fresh organization of life. Never any one before had the same powers and opportunities that you have, and you are free to use them in your own way.

It is, after all, only common sense to say that we exercise our freedom through co-operation with others. If you join a social group—let us say a dramatic club —you expect that it will increase your freedom, give your individual powers new stimulus and opportunity for expression. And why should not the same principle apply to society at large? It is through a social development that mankind has emerged from animal bondage into that organic freedom, wonderful though far from complete, that we now enjoy.

CHAPTER II

SUGGESTION AND CHOICE

THE MEANING OF THESE TERMS AND THEIR RELATION TO EACH
OTHER—INDIVIDUAL AND SOCIAL ASPECTS OF WILL OR CHOICE
—SUGGESTION AND CHOICE IN CHILDREN—THE SCOPE OF
SUGGESTION COMMONLY UNDERESTIMATED—PRACTICAL LIMITA-
TIONS UPON DELIBERATE CHOICE—ILLUSTRATIONS OF THE AC-
TION OF THE *MILIEU*—CLASS ATMOSPHERES—OUR UNCONSCIOUS-
NESS OF OUR EPOCH—THE GREATER OR LESS ACTIVITY OF
CHOICE REFLECTS THE STATE OF SOCIETY—SUGGESTIBILITY

THE antithesis between suggestion and choice is
another of those familiar ideas which are not always
so clear as they should be.

The word suggestion is used here to denote an influence that works in a comparatively mechanical or
reflex way, without calling out that higher selective
activity of the mind implied in choice or will. Thus
the hypnotic subject who performs apparently meaningless actions at the word of the operator is said to
be controlled by suggestion; so also is one who catches
up tricks of speech and action from other people without meaning to. From such instances the idea is extended to embrace any thought or action which is
mentally simple and seems not to involve choice. The
behavior of people under strong emotion is suggestive;
crowds are suggestible; habit is a kind of suggestion,
and so on.

I prefer this word to imitation, which some use in
this or a similar sense, because the latter, as ordinarily

understood, seems to cover too little in some directions and too much in others. In common use it means an action that results in visible or audible resemblance. Now, although our simple reactions to the influence of others are largely of this sort, they are by no means altogether so; the actions of a child during the first six months of life, for instance, are very little imitative in this sense; on the other hand, the imitation that produces a visible resemblance may be a voluntary process of the most complex sort imaginable, like the skilful painting of a portrait. However, it makes little difference what words we use if we have sound meanings back of them, and I am far from intending to find fault with writers, like Professor Baldwin and M. Tarde, who adopt the word and give it a wide and unusual application. For my purpose, however, it does not seem expedient to depart so far from ordinary usage.

The distinction between suggestion and choice is not, I think, a sharp opposition between separable or radically different things, but rather a way of indicating the lower and higher stages of a series. What we call choice or will appears to be an ill-defined area of more strenuous mental activity within a much wider field of activity similar in kind but less intense. It is not sharply divisible from the mass of involuntary thought. The truth is that the facts of the mind, of society, indeed of any living whole, seldom admit of sharp division, but show gradual transitions from one thing to another: there are no fences in these regions. We speak of suggestion as mechanical; but it seems

52

probable that all psychical life is selective, or, in some sense, choosing, and that the rudiments of consciousness and will may be discerned or inferred in the simplest reaction of the lowest living creature. In our own minds the comparatively simple ideas which are called suggestions are by no means single and primary, but each one is itself a living, shifting, multifarious bit of life, a portion of the fluid "stream of thought" formed by some sort of selection and synthesis out of simpler elements. On the other hand, our most elaborate and volitional thought and action is suggested in the sense that it consists not in creation out of nothing, but in a creative synthesis or reorganization of old material.

The distinction, then, is one of degree rather than of kind; and choice, as contrasted with suggestion, is, in its individual aspect, *a comparatively elaborate process of mental organization or synthesis*, of which we are reflectively aware, and which is rendered necessary by complexity in the elements of our thought. In its social aspect—for all, or nearly all, our choices relate in one way or another to the social environment—it is *an organization of comparatively complex social relations*. Precisely as the conditions about us and the ideas suggested by those conditions become intricate, are we forced to think, to choose, to define the useful and the right, and, in general, to work out the higher intellectual life. When life is simple, thought and action are comparatively mechanical or suggestive; the higher consciousness is not aroused, the reflective will has little or nothing to do; the captain stays below and the

53

inferior officers work the ship. But when life is diverse, thought is so likewise, and the mind must achieve the higher synthesis, or suffer that sense of division which is its peculiar pain. In short, the question of suggestion and choice is only another view of the question of uniformity and complexity in social relations.

Will, or choice, like all phases of mental life, may be looked at either in a particular or a general aspect; and we have, accordingly, individual will or social will, depending upon our point of view, as to whether we regard the activity singly or in a mass. But there is no real separation; they are only different phases of the same thing. Any choice that I can make is a synthesis of suggestions derived in one way or another from the general life; and it also reacts upon that life, so that my will is social as being both effect and cause with reference to it. If I buy a straw hat you may look at my action separately, as my individual choice, or as part of a social demand for straw hats, or as indicating non-conformity to a fashion of wearing some other sort of hats, and so on. There is no mystery about the matter; nothing that need puzzle any one who is capable of perceiving that a thing may look differently from different standpoints, like the post that was painted a different color on each of its four sides.

It is, I think, a mistake of superficial readers to imagine that psychologists or sociologists are trying to depreciate the will, or that there is any tendency to such depreciation in a sound evolutionary science or philosophy. The trouble with the popular view of will, derived chiefly from tradition, is not that it exaggerates its importance, which would perhaps be impossible; but, first, that it thinks of will only in the individual aspect, and does not grasp the fact—plain enough it would seem—that the act of choice is cause and effect in a general life; and, second, that it commonly overlooks the importance of involuntary forces, or at least makes them separate from and antithetical to choice—as if the captain were expected to work the ship all alone, or in opposition to the crew, instead of using them as subordinate agents. There is little use in arguing abstractly points like these; but if the reader who may be puzzled by them will try to free himself from metaphysical formulæ, and determine to *see* the facts as they are, he will be in a way to get some healthy understanding of the matter.*

* It should easily be understood that one who agrees with what was said in the preceding chapter about the relation between society and the individual, can hardly entertain the question whether the individual will is free or externally determined. This question assumes as true what he holds to be false, namely, that the particular aspect of mankind is separable from the collective aspect. The idea underlying it is that of an isolated fragment of life, the will, on the one hand, and some great mass of life, the environment, on the other; the question being which of these two antithetical forces shall be master. If one, then the will is free; if the other, then it is determined. It is as if each man's mind were a castle besieged by an army, and the question were whether the army should make a breach and capture the occupants. It is hard to see how this way of conceiving the matter could arise from a direct observation of actual social relations. Take, for instance, the case of a member of Congress, or of any other group of reasoning, feeling, and mutually influencing creatures. Is he free in relation to the rest of the body or do they control him? The question appears senseless. He is influenced by them and also exerts an influence upon them. While he is certainly not apart from their power, he is controlled,

By way of illustrating these general statements I shall first offer a few remarks concerning suggestion and choice in the life of children, and then go on to discuss their working in adult life and upon the career as a whole.

There appears to be quite a general impression that children are far more subject to control through suggestion or mechanical imitation than grown-up people are; in other words, that their volition is less active. I am not at all sure that this is the case: their choices are, as a rule, less stable and consistent than ours,

if we use that word, *through* his own will and not in spite of it. And it seems plain enough that a relation similar in kind holds between the individual and the nation, or between the individual and humanity in general. If you think of human life as a whole and of each individual as a member and not a fragment, as, in my opinion, you must if you base your thoughts on a direct study of society and not upon metaphysical or theological preconceptions, the question whether the will is free or not is seen to be meaningless. The individual will appears to be a specialized part of the general life, more or less divergent from other parts and possibly contending with them; but this very divergence is a part of its function—just as a member of Congress serves that body by urging his particular opinions—and in a large view does not separate but unites it to life as a whole. It is often necessary to consider the individual with reference to his opposition to other persons, or to prevailing tendencies, and in so doing it may be convenient to speak of him as separate from and antithetical to the life about him: but this separateness and opposition are incidental, like the right hand pulling against the left to break a string, and there seems to be no sufficient warrant for extending it into a general or philosophical proposition.

There may be some sense in which the question of the freedom of the will is still of interest; but it seems to me that the student of social relations may well pass it by as one of those scholastic controversies which are settled, if at all, not by being decided one way or the other, but by becoming obsolete.

56

their minds have less definiteness of organization, so that their actions appear less rational and more externally determined; but on the other hand they have less of the mechanical subjection to habit that goes with a settled character. Choice is a process of growth, of progressive mental organization through selection and assimilation of the materials which life presents, and this process is surely never more vigorous than in childhood and youth. It can hardly be doubted that the choosing and formative vigor of the mind is greater under the age of twenty-five than after: the will of middle age is stronger in the sense that it has more momentum, but it has less acceleration, runs more on habit, and so is less capable of fresh choice.

I am distrustful of that plausible but possibly illusive analogy between the mind of the child and the mind of primitive man, which, in this connection, would suggest a like simplicity and inertness of thought in the two. Our children achieve in a dozen years a mental development much above that of savages, and supposing that they do, in some sense, recapitulate the progress of the race, they certainly cover the ground at a very different rate of speed, which involves a corresponding intensity of mental life. After the first year certainly, if not from birth, they share our social order, and we induct them so rapidly into its complex life that their minds have perhaps as much novelty and diversity to synthetize as ours do.

Certainly one who begins to observe children with a vague notion that their actions, after the first few

months, are almost all mechanically imitative, is
likely to be surprised. I had this notion, derived,
perhaps without much warrant, from a slight acquaintance with writings on child-study current previous
to 1893, when my first child was born. He was a boy
—I will call him R.—in whom imitativeness, as ordinarily understood, happened to be unusually late in
its development. Until he was more than two years
and a half old all that I noticed that was obviously
imitative, in the sense of a visible or audible repetition of the acts of others, was the utterance of about
six words that he learned to say during his second year.
It is likely that very close observation, assisted by
the clearer notion of what to look for that comes by
experience, would have discovered more: but no more
was obvious to ordinary expectant attention. The
obvious thing was his constant use of experiment and
reflection, and the slow and often curious results that
he attained in this manner. At two and a half he had
learned, for instance, to use a fork quite skilfully. The
wish to use it was perhaps an imitative impulse, in a
sense, but his methods were original and the outcome
of a long course of independent and reflective experiment. His skill was the continuation of a dexterity
previously acquired in playing with long pins, which
he ran into cushions, the interstices of his carriage,
etc. The fork was apparently conceived as an interesting variation upon the hatpin, and not, primarily,
as a means of getting food or doing what others did.
In creeping or walking, at which he was very slow,
partly on account of a lame foot, he went through a

similar series of devious experiments, which apparently had no reference to what he saw others do.

He did not begin to talk—beyond using the few words already mentioned—until over two years and eight months old; having previously refused to interest himself in it, although he understood others as well, apparently, as any child of his age. He preferred to make his wants known by grunts and signs; and instead of delighting in imitation he evidently liked better a kind of activity that was only indirectly connected with the suggestions of others.

I frequently tried to produce imitation, but almost wholly without success. For example, when he was striving to accomplish something with his blocks I would intervene and show him, by example, how, as I thought, it might be done, but these suggestions were invariably, so far as I remember or have recorded, received with indifference or protest. He liked to puzzle it out quietly for himself, and to be shown how to do a thing often seemed to destroy his interest in it. Yet he would profit by observation of others in his own fashion, and I sometimes detected him making use of ideas to which he seemed to pay no attention when they were first presented. In short, he showed that aversion, which minds of a pondering, constructive turn perhaps always show, to anything which suddenly and crudely broke in upon his system of thought. At the same time that he was so backward in the ordinary curriculum of childhood, he showed in other ways, which it is perhaps unnecessary to describe, that comparison and reflection were well developed. This

59

preoccupation with private experiment and reflection, and reluctance to learn from others, were undoubtedly a cause of his slow development, particularly in speech, his natural aptitude for which appeared in a good enunciation and a marked volubility as soon as he really began to talk.

Imitation came all at once: he seemed to perceive quite suddenly that this was a short cut to many things, and took it up, not in a merely mechanical or suggestive way, but consciously, intelligently, as a means to an end. The imitative act, however, was often an end in itself, an interesting exercise of his constructive faculties, pursued at first without much regard to anything beyond. This was the case with the utterance of words, and, later, with spelling, with each of which he became fascinated for its own sake and regardless of its use as a means of communication.

In a second child, M., a girl, I was able to observe the working of a mind of a different sort, and of a much more common type as regards imitation. When two months and seven days old she was observed to make sounds in reply to her mother when coaxed with a certain pitch and inflection of voice. These sounds were clearly imitative, since they were seldom made at other times, but not mechanically so. They were produced with every appearance of mental effort and of delight in its success. Only vocal imitations, of this rudimentary sort, were observed until eight months was nearly reached, when the first manual imitation, striking a button-hook upon the back of a chair, was noticed. This action had been performed experimentally before, and the imitation was merely a repetition suggested by seeing her mother do it, or perhaps by hearing the sound. After this the development of imitative activity proceeded much in the usual way, which has often been described.

In both of these cases I was a good deal impressed with the idea that the life of children, as compared with that of adults, is less determined in a merely suggestive way, and involves more will and choice, than is commonly supposed. Imitation, in the sense of visible or audible repetition, was not so omnipresent as I had expected, and when present seemed to be in great part rational and voluntary rather than mechanical. It is very natural to assume that to do what some one else does requires no mental effort; but this, as applied to little children, is, of course, a great mistake. They cannot imitate an act except by learning how to do it, any more than grown-up people can, and for a child to learn a word may be as complicated a process as for an older person to learn a difficult piece on the piano. A novel imitation is not at all mechanical, but a strenuous voluntary activity, accompanied by effort and followed by pleasure in success. All sympathetic observers of children must be impressed, I imagine, by the evident mental stress and concentration which often accompanies their endeavors, whether imitative or not, and is followed, as in adults, by the appearance of relief when the action has come off successfully.*

* The imitativeness of children is stimulated by the imitativeness of parents. A baby cannot hit upon any sort of a

The "imitative instinct" is sometimes spoken of as if it were a mysterious something that enabled the child to perform involuntarily and without preparation acts that are quite new to him. It will be found difficult, if one reflects upon the matter, to conceive what could be the nature of an instinct or hereditary tendency, not to do a definite thing previously performed by our ancestors—as is the case with ordinary instinct—but to do *anything*, within vague limits, which happened to be done within our sight or hearing. This doing of new things without definite preparation, *either in heredity or experience*, would seem to involve something like special creation in the mental and nervous organism: and the imitation of children has no such character. It is quite evidently an acquired power, and if the act imitated is at all complex the learning process involves a good deal of thought and will. If there is an imitative instinct it must, apparently, be something in the way of a taste for repetition, which stimulates the learning process without, however, having any tendency to dispense with it. The taste for repetition seems, in fact, to exist, at least in most children, but even this may be sufficiently explained as a phase of the general mental tendency to act upon uncontradicted ideas. It is a doctrine now generally taught by psychologists that

noise, but the admiring family, eager for communication, will imitate it again and again, hoping to get a repetition. They are usually disappointed, but the exercise probably causes the child to notice the likeness of the sounds and so prepares the way for imitation. It is perhaps safe to say that up to the end of the first year the parents are more imitative than the child.

62

the idea of an action is itself a motive to that action, and tends intrinsically to produce it unless something intervenes to prevent. This being the case, it would appear that we must always have some impulse to do what we see done, provided it is something we understand sufficiently to be able to form a definite idea of doing it.* 1 am inclined to the view that it is unnecessary to assume, in man, a special imitative instinct, but that, "as Preyer and others have shown in the case of young children, mimicry arises mainly from pleasure in activity as such, and not from its peculiar quality as imitation." † An intelligent child imitates because he has faculties crying for employment, and imitation is a key that lets them loose: he needs to do things and imitation gives him things to do. An indication that sensible resemblance to the acts of others is not the main thing sought is seen in such cases as the following: M. had a trick of raising her hands above her head, which she would perform, when in the mood for it, either imitatively, when some one else did it, or in response to the words "How big is M.?" but she responded more readily in the second or non-imitative way than in the other. This example well illustrates the reason for my preference of the word suggestion over imitation to describe these simple re-

* "In like manner any act or expression is a stimulus to the nerve-centres that perceive or understand it. Unless this action is inhibited by the will, or by counter-stimulation, they must discharge themselves in movements that more or less closely copy the originals."—Giddings, Principles of Sociology, 110.

† H. M. Stanley, The Evolutionary Psychology of Feeling, p. 53.

actions. In this case the action performed had no sort of resemblance to the form of words "How big is M.?" that started it, and could be called imitative only in a recondite sense. All that is necessary is that there should be a suggestion, that something should be presented that is connected in the child's mind with the action to be produced. Whether this connection is by sensible resemblance or not seems immaterial.

There seems to be some opposition between imitation of the visible, external kind, and reflection. Children of one sort are attracted by sensible resemblance and so are early and conspicuously imitative. If this is kept up in a mechanical way after the acts are well learned, and at the expense of new efforts, it would seem to be a sign of mental apathy, or even defect, as in the silly mimicry of some idiots. Those of another sort are preoccupied by the subtler combinations of thought which do not, as a rule, lead to obvious imitation. Such children are likely to be backward in the development of active faculties, and slow to observe except where their minds are specially interested. They are also, if I may judge by R., slow to interpret features and tones of voice, guileless and unaffected, just because of this lack of keen personal perceptions, and not quickly sympathetic.

Accordingly, it is not at all clear that children are, on the whole, any more given to imitation of the mechanical sort, any more suggestible, than adults. They appear so to us chiefly, perhaps, for two reasons. In the first place, we fail to realize the thought, the will, the effort, they expend upon their imitations. They do things that have become mechanical to us, and we assume that they are mechanical to them, though closer observation and reflection would show us the contrary. These actions are largely daring experiments, strenuous syntheses of previously acquired knowledge, comparable in quality to our own most earnest efforts, and not to the thoughtless routine of our lives. We do not see that their echoing of the words they hear is often not a silly repetition, but a difficult and instructive exercise of the vocal apparatus. Children imitate much because they are growing much, and imitation is a principal means of growth. This is true at any age; the more alive and progressive a man is the more actively he is admiring and profiting by his chosen models.

A second reason is that adults imitate at longer range, as it were, so that the imitative character of their acts is not so obvious. They come into contact with more sorts of persons, largely unknown to one another, and have access to a greater variety of suggestions in books. Accordingly they present a deceitful appearance of independence simply because we do not see their models.

Though we may be likely to exaggerate the difference between children and adults as regards the sway of suggestive influences, there is little danger of our overestimating the importance of these in the life of mankind at large. The common impression among those who have given no special study to the matter appears to be that suggestion has little part in the mature life of a rational being; and though the control of involuntary impulses is recognized in tricks of speech and manner, in fads, fashions, and the like, it is not perceived to touch the more important points of conduct. The fact, however, is that the main current of our thought is made up of impulses absorbed without deliberate choice from the life about us, or else arising from hereditary instinct, or from habit; while the function of higher thought and of will is to organize and apply these impulses. To revert to an illustration already suggested, the voluntary is related to the involuntary very much as the captain of a ship is related to the seamen and subordinate officers. Their work is not altogether of a different sort from his, but is of a lower grade in a mental series. He supplies the higher sort of co-ordination, but the main bulk of the activity is of the mentally lower order.

The chief reason why popular attention should fix itself upon voluntary thought and action, and tend to overlook the involuntary, is that choice is acutely conscious, and so must, from its very nature, be the focus of introspective thought. Because he *is* an individual, a specialized, contending bit of psychical force, a man very naturally holds his will, in its individual aspect, to be of supreme moment. If we did not feel a great importance in the things we do we could not will to do them. And in the life of other people voluntary action seems supreme, for very much the same reasons that it does in our own. It is always in the foreground, active, obvious, intrusive, the thing that creates differences and so fixes the attention.

We notice nothing except through contrast; and accordingly the mechanical control of suggestion, affecting all very much alike, is usually unperceived. As we do not notice the air, precisely because it is always with us, so, for the same reason, we do not notice a prevailing mode of dress. In like manner we are ignorant of our local accent and bearing, and are totally unaware, for the most part, of all that is common to our time, our country, our customary environment. Choice is a central area of light and activity upon which our eyes are fixed; while the unconscious is a dark, illimitable background enveloping this area. Or, again, choice is like the earth, which we unconsciously assume to be the principal part of creation, simply because it is the centre of our interest and the field of our exertions.

The practical limitations upon the scope of choice arise, first, from its very nature as a selective and organizing agent, working upon comparatively simple or suggestive ideas as its raw material, and, second, from the fact that it absorbs a great deal of vital energy. Owing to the first circumstance its activity is always confined to points where there is a competition of ideas. So long as an idea is uncontradicted, not felt to be in any way inconsistent with others, we take it as a matter of course. It is a truth, though hard for us to realize, that if we had lived in Dante's time we should have believed in a material Hell, Purgatory, and Paradise, as he did, and that our doubts of this, and of many other things which his age did not question, have nothing to do with our natural intelligence, but are made possible and necessary by competing ideas which the growth of knowledge has enabled us to form. Our particular minds or wills are members of a slowly growing whole, and at any given moment are limited in scope by the state of the whole, and especially of those parts of the whole with which they are in most active contact. Our thought is never isolated, but always some sort of a response to the influences around us, so that we can hardly have thoughts that are not in some way aroused by communication. Will—free will if you choose—is thus a co-operative whole, not an aggregation of disconnected fragments, and the freedom of the individual is freedom under law, like that of the good citizen, not anarchy. We learn to speak by the exercise of will, but no one, I suppose, will assert that an infant who hears only French is free to learn English. Where suggestions are numerous and conflicting we feel the need to choose; to make these choices is the function of will, and the result of them is a step in the progress of life, an act of freedom or creation, if you wish to call it so; but where suggestion is single, as with religious dogma in ages of faith, we are very much at its mercy. We do not perceive these limitations, because there is no point of vantage from which we can observe and measure the general state of thought; there is nothing to compare it with. Only when it begins to change, when competing suggestions enter our minds and we get new points of view from which we can look back upon it, do we begin to notice its power over us.*

The exhausting character of choice, of making up one's mind, is a matter of common experience. In some way the mental synthesis, this calling in and reducing to order the errant population of the mind, draws severely upon the vital energy, and one of the invariable signs of fatigue is a dread of making decisions and assuming responsibility. In our complicated life the will can, in fact, manage only a small part of the competing suggestions that are within our reach. What we are all forced to do is to choose a field of action which for some reason we look upon as specially interesting or important, and exercise our choice in that; in other matters protecting ourselves, for the most part, by some sort of mechanical control—some accepted personal authority, some local

* Goethe, in various places, contrasts modern art and literature with those of the Greeks in respect to the fact that the former express individual characteristics, the latter those of a race and an epoch. Thus in a letter to Schiller—No. 631 of the Goethe-Schiller correspondence—he says of Paradise Lost, "In the case of this poem, as with all modern works of art, it is in reality the individual that manifests itself that awakens the interest."

Can there be some illusion mixed with the truth of this idea? Is it not the case that the nearer a thing is to our habit of thought the more clearly we see the individual, and the more vaguely, if at all, the universal? And would not an ancient Greek, perhaps, have seen as much of what was peculiar to each artist, and as little of what was common to all, as we do in a writer of our own time? The principle is much the same as that which makes all Chinamen look pretty much alike to us: we see the type because it is so different from what we are used to, but only one who lives within it can fully perceive the differences among individuals.

69

custom, some professional tradition, or the like. Indeed, to know where and how to narrow the activity of the will in order to preserve its tone and vigor for its most essential functions, is a great part of knowing how to live. An incontinent exercise of choice wears people out, so that many break down and yield even essentials to discipline and authority in some form; while many more wish, at times, to do so and indulge themselves, perhaps, in Thomas à Kempis, or "The Christian's Secret of a Happy Life." Not a few so far exhaust the power of self-direction as to be left drifting at the mercy of undisciplined passions. There are many roads to degeneracy, and persons of an eager, strenuous nature not infrequently take this one.

A common instance of the insidious power of *milieu* is afforded by the transition from university education to getting a living. At a university one finds himself, if he has any vigor of imagination, in one of the widest environments the world can afford. He has access to the suggestions of the richest minds of all times and countries, and has also, or should have, time and encouragement to explore, in his own way, this spacious society. It is his business to think, to aspire, and grow; and if he is at all capable of it he does so. Philosophy and art and science and the betterment of mankind are real and living interests to him, largely because he is in the great stream of higher thought that flows through libraries. Now let him graduate and enter, we will say, upon the

lumber business at Kawkawlin. Here he finds the
scope of existence largely taken up with the details
of this industry—wholesome for him in some ways,
but likely to be overemphasized. These and a few
other things are repeated over and over again, dinned
into him, everywhere assumed to be the solid things
of life, so that he must believe in them; while the
rest grows misty and begins to lose hold upon him.
He cannot make things seem real that do not enter
into his experience, and if he resists the narrowing
environment it must be by keeping touch with a
larger world, through books or other personal intercourse, and by the exercise of imagination. Marcus
Aurelius told himself that he was free to think what
he chose, but it appears that he realized this freedom
by keeping books about him that suggested the kind
of thoughts he chose to think; and it is only in some
such sense as this implies that the assertion is true.
When the palpable environment does not suit us we
can, if our minds are vigorous enough, build up a
better one out of remembered material; but we must
have material of some sort.

It is easy to feel the effect of surroundings in such
cases as this, because of the sharp and definite change,
and because the imagination clings to one state long
after the senses are subdued to the other; but it is not
so with national habits and sentiments, which so completely envelop us that we are for the most part unaware of them. The more thoroughly American a
man is the less he can perceive Americanism. He
will embody it; all he does, says, or writes, will be full

71

of it; but he can never truly see it, simply because he has no exterior point of view from which to look at it. If he goes to Europe he begins to get by contrast some vague notion of it, though he will never be able to see just what it is that makes futile his attempts to seem an Englishman, a German, or an Italian. Our appearance to other peoples is like one's own voice, which one never hears quite as others hear it, and which sounds strange when it comes back from the phonograph.

There is nothing more important to understand, or less understood, than the class atmospheres in which nearly all of us live. We usually believe that the way we look upon social and economic questions is the natural way, the American way, the right way, not perceiving that it is a way imposed upon us by suggestions which, flowing in upon us from the people with whom we associate, determine the premises of our thought. There is something rather alarming, to one who wishes to see his country united, in the self-complacent ignorance which men in one class show regarding the ideas and feelings of their fellow citizens in another. It is rare to find among business or professional men any real comprehension of the struggles and aspirations of the hand-working class, while the contemptuous attitude of the native toward the immigrant, or the white toward the negro, is inevitably answered by resentment on the other side. The basis of these misunderstandings is the lack of real communication. We mean well but unless we understand one another good meanings are ineffective. The press, which ought to interpret social classes to each other, is itself divided on class lines, and the papers and magazines which the well-to-do man reads confirm him in his class bias, while the hand-worker feeds his upon labor and socialist publications. Nor do the common schools, for the most part, give the children instruction which prepares them for large and sympathetic views.

One result of all this is that it is easy, in times of excitement, for propagandists to arouse dangerous suspicions and hostilities of one class against another—as was shown during the trying period immediately following the Great War. If we are to have friendly co-operation, among classes or among nations, we must begin by having more understanding.

The control of those larger movements of thought and sentiment that make a historical epoch is still less conscious, more inevitable. Only the imaginative student, in his best hours, can really free himself —and that only in some respects—from the limitations of his time and see things from a height. For the most part the people of other epochs seem strange, outlandish, or a little insane. We can scarcely rid ourselves of the impression that the way of life we are used to is the normal, and that other ways are eccentric. Doctor Sidis holds that the people of the Middle Ages were in a quasi-hypnotic state, and instances the crusades, dancing manias, and the like.* But the question is, would not our own time,

* See the latter chapters of his Psychology of Suggestion.

viewed from an equal distance, appear to present the signs of abnormal suggestibility? Will not the intense preoccupation with material production, the hurry and strain of our cities, the draining of life into one channel, at the expense of breadth, richness, and beauty, appear as mad as the crusades, and perhaps of a lower type of madness? Could anything be more indicative of a slight but general insanity than the aspect of the crowd on the streets of Chicago?

An illustration of this unconsciousness of what is distinctive in our time is the fact that those who participate in momentous changes have seldom any but the vaguest notion of their significance. There is perhaps no time in the history of art that seems to us now so splendid, so dramatic, as that of the sudden rise of Gothic architecture in northern France, and the erection of the church of St. Denis at Paris was its culmination: yet Professor C. E. Norton, speaking of the Abbot Suger, who erected it, and of his memoirs, says, "Under his watchful and intelligent oversight the church became the most splendid and the most interesting building of the century; but of the features that gave it special interest, that make it one of the most important monuments of mediæval architecture, neither Suger, in his account of it, nor his biographer, nor any contemporary writer, says a single word." *
To Suger and his time the Gothic, it would seem, was simply a new and improved way of building a church, a technical matter with which he had little concern, except to see that it was duly carried out

* See Harper's Magazine, vol. 79, p. 770.

according to specifications. It was developed by draughtsmen and handicraftsmen, mostly nameless, who felt their own thrill of constructive delight as they worked, but had no thought of historical glory. It is no doubt the same in our own time, and Mr. Bryce has noted with astonishment the unconsciousness or indifference of those who founded cities in western America, to the fact that they were doing something that would be memorable and influential for ages.*

I have already said, or implied, that the activity of the will reflects the state of the social order. A constant and strenuous exercise of volition implies complexity in the surrounding life from which suggestions come, while in a simple society choice is limited in scope and life is comparatively mechanical. It is the variety of social intercourse or, what comes to the same thing, the character of social organization, that determines the field of choice; and accordingly there is a tendency for the scope of the will to increase with that widening and intensification of life that is so conspicuous a feature of recent history. This change is bound up with the extension and diffusion of communication, opening up innumerable channels by which competing suggestions may enter the mind. We are still dependent upon environment—life is always a give and take with surrounding conditions— but environment is becoming very wide, and in the case of imaginative persons may extend itself to almost any ideas that the past or present life of the race has

* See The American Commonwealth, vol. ii, p. 705.

brought into being. This brings opportunity for congenial choice and characteristic personal growth, and at the same time a good deal of distraction and strain. There is more and more need of stability, and of a vigorous rejection of excessive material, if one would escape mental exhaustion and degeneracy. Choice is like a river; it broadens as it comes down through history—though there are always banks—and the wider it becomes the more persons drown in it. Stronger and stronger swimming is required, and types of character that lack vigor and self-reliance are more and more likely to go under.

The aptitude to yield to impulse in a mechanical or reflex way is called suggestibility. As might be expected, it is subject to great variations in different persons, and in the same person under different conditions. Abnormal suggestibility has received much study, and there is a great body of valuable literature relating to it. I wish in this connection only to recall a few well-known principles which the student of normal social life needs to have in mind.

As would naturally follow from our analysis of the relation between suggestion and choice, suggestibility is simply the absence of the controlling and organizing action of the reflective will. This function not being properly performed, thought and action are disintegrated and fly off on tangents; the captain being disabled the crew breaks up into factions, and discipline goes to pieces. Accordingly, whatever weakens the reason, and thus destroys the breadth and symmetry of consciousness, produces some form of suggestibility. To be excited is to be suggestible, that is to become liable to yield impulsively to an idea in harmony with the exciting emotion. An angry man is suggestible as regards denunciation, threats, and the like, a jealous one as regards suspicions, and similarly with any passion.

The suggestibility of crowds is a peculiar form of that limitation of choice by the environment already discussed. We have here a very transient environment which owes its power over choice to the vague but potent emotion so easily generated in dense aggregates. The thick humanity is in itself exciting, and the will is further stupefied by the sense of insignificance, by the strangeness of the situation, and by the absence, as a rule, of any separate purpose to maintain an independent momentum. A man is like a ship in that he cannot guide his course unless he has way on. If he drifts he will shift about with any light air; and the man in the crowd is usually drifting, is not pursuing any settled line of action in which he is sustained by knowledge and habit. This state of mind, added to intense emotion directed by some series of special suggestions, is the source of the wild and often destructive behavior of crowds and mobs, as well as of a great deal of heroic enthusiasm. An orator, for instance, first unifying and heightening the emotional state of his audience by some humorous or pathetic incident, will be able, if tolerably skilful, to do pretty much as he pleases with them, so long as he does not go against their settled habits of thought.

77

Anger, always a ready passion, is easily aroused, appeals to resentment being the staples of much popular oratory, and under certain conditions readily expresses itself in stoning, burning, and lynching. And so with fear: General Grant, in describing the battle of Shiloh, gives a picture of several thousand men on a hill-side in the rear, incapable of moving, though threatened to be shot for cowardice where they lay. Yet these very men, calmed and restored to their places, were among those who heroically fought and won the next day's battle. They had been restored to the domination of another class of suggestions, namely, those implied in military discipline.*

Suggestibility from exhaustion or strain is a rather common condition with many of us. Probably all eager brain workers find themselves now and then in a state where they are "too tired to stop." The over-wrought mind loses the healthy power of casting off its burden, and seems capable of nothing but going on and on in the same painful and futile course. One may know that he is accomplishing nothing, that work done in such a state of mind is always bad work, and that "that way madness lies," but yet be too weak to resist, chained to the wheel of his thought so that he must wait till it runs down. And such a state, however induced, is the opportunity for all sorts of undisciplined impulses, perhaps some gross passion, like anger, dread, the need of drink, or the like.

According to Mr. Tylor,† fasting, solitude, and

---

* Memoirs of U. S. Grant, vol. i, p. 344.
† See his Primitive Culture, vol. ii, p. 372.

physical exhaustion by dancing, shouting, or flagellation are very generally employed by savage peoples to bring on abnormal states of mind of which suggestibility—the sleep of choice, and control by some idea from the subconscious life—is always a trait. The visions and ecstasies following the fastings, watchings, and flagellations of Christian devotees of an earlier time seem ʋo belong, psychologically, in much the same category.

It is well known that suggestibility is limited by habit, or, more accurately stated, that habit is itself a perennial source of suggestions that set bounds and conditions upon the power of fresh suggestions. A total abstainer will resist the suggestion to drink, a modest person will refuse to do anything indecent, and so on. People are least liable to yield to irrational suggestions, to be stampeded with the crowd, in matters with which they are familiar, so that they have habits regarding them. The soldier, in his place in the ranks and with his captain in sight, will march forward to certain death, very likely without any acute emotion whatever, simply because he has the habits that constitute discipline; and so with firemen, policemen, sailors, brakemen, physicians, and many others who learn to deal with life and death as calmly as they read a newspaper. It is all in the day's work.

As regards the greater or less suggestibility of different persons there is, of course, no distinct line between the normal and the abnormal; it is simply a matter of the greater or less efficiency of the higher mental organization. Most people, perhaps, are so far suggestible that they make no energetic and persistent attempt to interpret in any broad way the elements of life accessible to them, but receive the stamp of some rather narrow and simple class of suggestions to which their allegiance is yielded. There are innumerable people of much energy but sluggish intellect, who will go ahead—as all who have energy must do—but what direction they take is a matter of the opportune suggestion. The humbler walks of religion and philanthropy, for instance, the Salvation Army, the village prayer-meeting, and the city mission, are full of such. They do not reason on general topics, but believe and labor. The intellectual travail of the time does not directly touch them. At some epoch in the past, perhaps in some hour of emotional exaltation, something was printed on their minds to remain there till death, and be read and followed daily. To the philosopher such people are fanatics; but their function is as important as his. They are repositories of moral energy—which he is very likely to lack—they are the people who brought in Christianity and have kept it going ever since. And this is only one of many comparatively automatic types of mankind. Rationality, in the sense of a patient and open-minded attempt to think out the general problems of life, is, and perhaps always must be, confined to a small minority even of the most intelligent populations.

CHAPTER III

SOCIABILITY AND PERSONAL IDEAS

AIM OF THIS CHAPTER—THE SOCIABILITY OF CHILDREN—IMAGI-
NARY CONVERSATION AND ITS SIGNIFICANCE—THE NATURE OF
THE IMPULSE TO COMMUNICATE—THERE IS NO SEPARATION
BETWEEN REAL AND IMAGINARY PERSONS—NOR BETWEEN
THOUGHT AND INTERCOURSE—THE STUDY AND INTERPRETATION
OF EXPRESSION BY CHILDREN—THE SYMBOL OR SENSUOUS
NUCLEUS OF PERSONAL IDEAS—PERSONAL ATMOSPHERE—PER-
SONAL PHYSIOGNOMY IN ART AND LITERATURE—IN THE IDEA
OF SOCIAL GROUPS—SENTIMENT IN PERSONAL IDEAS—THE
PERSONAL IDEA IS THE IMMEDIATE SOCIAL REALITY—SOCIETY
MUST BE STUDIED IN THE IMAGINATION—THE POSSIBLE REALITY
OF INCORPOREAL PERSONS—THE MATERIAL NOTION OF PERSON-
ALITY CONTRASTED WITH THE NOTION BASED ON A STUDY OF
PERSONAL IDEAS—SELF AND OTHER IN PERSONAL IDEAS—
PERSONAL OPPOSITION—FURTHER ILLUSTRATION AND DEFENSE
OF THE VIEW OF PERSONS AND SOCIETY HERE SET FORTH

In this chapter I hope to show something of the origin and growth of social ideas and feelings in the mind of the individual, and also something of the nature of society as we may find it implied in these ideas and feelings. If it appears that the human mind is social, that society is mental, and that, in short, society and the mind are aspects of the same whole, these conclusions will be no more than a development of the propositions advanced in the first chapter.

To any but a mother a new-born child hardly seems human. It appears rather to be a strange little animal, wonderful indeed, exquisitely finished even to the finger-nails; mysterious, awakening a fresh sense of our ignorance of the nearest things of life, but not friendly, not lovable. It is only after some days that a kindly nature begins to express itself and to grow into something that can be sympathized with and personally cared for. The earliest signs of it are chiefly certain smiles and babbling sounds, which are a matter of fascinating observation to any one interested in the genesis of social feeling.

Spasmodic smiles or grimaces occur even during the first week of life, and at first seem to mean nothing in particular. I have watched the face of an infant a week old while a variety of expressions, smiles, frowns, and so on, passed over it in rapid succession: it was as if the child were rehearsing a repertory of emotional expression belonging to it by instinct. So soon as they can be connected with anything definite these rudimentary smiles appear to be a sign of satisfaction. Mrs. Moore says that her child smiled on the sixth day "when comfortable,"* and that this "never occurred when the child was known to be in pain." Preyer notes a smile on the face of a sleeping child, after nursing, on the tenth day.† They soon begin to connect themselves quite definitely with sensible objects, such as bright color, voices, movements, and fondling. At the same time the smile gradually develops from a grimace into a subtler, more human expression, and Doctor Perez,

* K. C. Moore, The Mental Development of a Child, p. 37.
† The Senses and the Will, p. 295.

who seems to have studied a large number of children, says that all whom he observed smiled, when pleased, by the time they were two months old.* When a child is, say, five months old, no doubt can remain, in most cases, that the smile has become an expression of pleasure in the movements, sounds, touches, and general appearance of other people. It would seem, however, that personal feeling is not at first clearly differentiated from pleasures of sight, sound, and touch of other origin, or from animal satisfactions having no obvious cause. Both of my children expended much of their early sociability on inanimate objects, such as a red Japanese screen, a swinging lamp, a bright door-knob, an orange, and the like, babbling and smiling at them for many minutes at a time; and M., when about three months old and later, would often lie awake laughing and chattering in the dead of night. The general impression left upon one is that the early manifestations of sociability indicate less fellow feeling than the adult imagination likes to impute, but are expressions of a pleasure which persons excite chiefly because they offer such a variety of stimuli to sight, hearing, and touch; or, to put it otherwise, kindliness, while existing almost from the first, is vague and undiscriminating, has not yet become fixed upon its proper objects, but flows out upon all the pleasantness the child finds about him, like that of St. Francis, when, in his "Canticle of the Sun," he addresses the sun and the moon, stars, winds, clouds, fire, earth, and water, as brothers and sisters.

* See his First Three Years of Childhood, p. 13.

Indeed, there is nothing about personal feeling which sharply marks it off from other feeling; here as elsewhere we find no fences, but gradual transition, progressive differentiation.

I do not think that early smiles are imitative. I observed both my children carefully to discover whether they smiled in response to a smile, and obtained negative results when they were under ten months old. A baby does not smile by imitation, but because he is pleased; and what pleases him in the first year of life is usually some rather obvious stimulus to the senses. If you wish a smile you must earn it by acceptable exertion; it does no good to smirk. The belief that many people seem to have that infants respond to smiling is possibly due to the fact that when a grown-up person appears, both he and the infant are likely to smile, each at the other; but although the smiles are simultaneous one need not be the cause of the other, and many observations lead me to think that it makes no difference to the infant whether the grown-up person smiles or not. He has not yet learned to appreciate this rather subtle phenomenon.

At this and at all later ages the delight in companionship so evident in children may be ascribed partly to specific social emotion or sentiment, and partly to a need of stimulating suggestions to enable them to gratify their instinct for various sorts of mental and physical activity. The influence of the latter appears in their marked preference for active persons, for grown-up people who will play with them—provided they do so with tact—and especially for other children. It is the same throughout life; alone one is like fireworks without a match: he cannot set himself off, but is a victim of *ennui*, the prisoner of some tiresome train of thought that holds his mind simply by the absence of a competitor. A good companion brings release and fresh activity, the primal delight in a fuller existence. So with the child: what excitement when visiting children come! He shouts, laughs, jumps about, produces his playthings and all his accomplishments. He needs to express himself, and a companion enables him to do so. The shout of another boy in the distance gives him the joy of shouting in response.

But the need is for something more than muscular or sensory activities. There is also a need of feeling, an overflowing of personal emotion and sentiment, set free by the act of communication. By the time a child is a year old the social feeling that at first is indistinguishable from sensuous pleasure has become much specialized upon persons, and from that time onward to call it forth by reciprocation is a chief aim of his life. Perhaps it will not be out of place to emphasize this by transcribing two or three notes taken from life.

"M. will now [eleven months old] hold up something she has found, *e.g.*, the petal of a flower, or a little stick, demanding your attention to it by grunts and squeals. When you look and make some motion or exclamation she smiles."

"R. [four years old] talks all day long, to real companions, if they will listen, if not to imaginary ones. As I sit on the steps this morning he seems to wish me to share his every thought and sensation. He describes everything he does, although I can see it, saying, 'Now I'm digging up little stones,' etc. I must look at the butterfly, feel of the fuzz on the clover stems, and try to squawk on the dandelion stems. Meanwhile he is reminded of what happened some other time, and he gives me various anecdotes of what he and other people did and said. He thinks aloud. If I seem not to listen he presently notices it and will come up and touch me, or bend over and look up into my face."

"R. [about the same time] is hilariously delighted and excited when he can get any one to laugh or wonder with him at his pictures, etc. He himself always shares by anticipation, and exaggerates the feeling he expects to produce. When B. was calling, R., with his usual desire to entertain guests, brought out his pull-book, in which pulling a strip of pasteboard transforms the picture. When he prepared to work this he was actually shaking with eagerness—apparently in anticipation of the coming surprise."

"I watch E. and R. [four and a half years old] playing McGinty on the couch and guessing what card will turn up. R. is in a state of intense excitement which breaks out in boisterous laughter and all sorts of movements of the head and limbs. He is full of an emotion which has very little to do with mere curiosity or surprise relating to the card."

I take it that the child has by heredity a generous capacity and need for social feeling, rather too vague and plastic to be given any specific name like love. It is not so much any particular personal emotion or sentiment as the undifferentiated material of many: perhaps sociability is as good a word for it as any.

And this material, like all other instinct, allies itself with social experience to form, as time goes on, a growing and diversifying body of personal thought, in which the phases of social feeling developed correspond, in some measure, to the complexity of life itself. It is a process of organization, involving progressive differentiation and integration, such as we see everywhere in nature.

In children and in simple-minded adults, kindly feeling may be very strong and yet very naïve, involving little insight into the emotional states of others. A child who is extremely sociable, bubbling over with joy in companionship, may yet show a total incomprehension of pain and a scant regard for disapproval and punishment that does not take the form of a cessation of intercourse. In other words, there is a sociability that asks little from others except bodily presence and an occasional sign of attention, and often learns to supply even these by imagination. It seems nearly or quite independent of that power of interpretation which is the starting-point of true sympathy. While both of my children were extremely sociable, R. was not at all sympathetic in the sense of having quick insight into others' states of feeling.

Sociability in this simple form is an innocent, unself-conscious joy, primary and unmoral, like all simple emotion. It may shine with full brightness from the faces of idiots and imbeciles, where it sometimes alternates with fear, rage, or lust. A visitor to an institution where large numbers of these classes are collected will be impressed, as I have been, with the fact that they are as a rule amply endowed with those

87

kindly impulses which some appear to look upon as almost the sole requisite for human welfare. It is a singular and moving fact that there is a class of cases, mostly women, I think, in whom kindly emotion is so excitable as to be a frequent source of hysterical spasms, so that it has to be discouraged by frowns and apparent harshness on the part of those in charge. The chief difference between normal people and imbeciles in this regard is that, while the former have more or less of this simple kindliness in them, social emotion is also elaborately compounded and worked up by the mind into an indefinite number of complex passions and sentiments, corresponding to the relations and functions of an intricate life.

When left to themselves children continue the joys of sociability by means of an imaginary playmate. Although all must have noticed this who have observed children at all, only close and constant observation will enable one to realize the extent to which it is carried on. It is not an occasional practice, but, rather, a necessary form of thought, flowing from a life in which personal communication is the chief interest and social feeling the stream in which, like boats on a river, most other feelings float. Some children appear to live in personal imaginations almost from the first month; others occupy their minds in early infancy mostly with solitary experiments upon blocks, cards, and other impersonal objects, and their thoughts are doubtless filled with the images of these. But, in either case, after a child learns to talk and the social world in all its wonder and provocation opens on his mind, it floods his imagination so that all his thoughts are conversations. He is never alone. Sometimes the inaudible interlocutor is recognizable as the image of a tangible playmate, sometimes he appears to be purely imaginary. Of course each child has his own peculiarities. R., beginning when about three years of age, almost invariably talked aloud while he was playing alone—which, as he was a first child, was very often the case. Most commonly he would use no form of address but "you," and perhaps had no definite person in mind. To listen to him was like hearing one at the telephone; though occasionally he would give both sides of the conversation. At times again he would be calling upon some real name, Esyllt or Dorothy, or upon "Piggy," a fanciful person of his own invention. Every thought seemed to be spoken out. If his mother called him he would say, "I've got to go in now." Once when he slipped down on the floor he was heard to say, "Did you tumble down? No. *I* did."

The main point to note here is that these conversations are not occasional and temporary effusions of the imagination, but are the naïve expression of a socialization of the mind that is to be permanent and to underlie all later thinking. The imaginary dialogue passes beyond the thinking aloud of little children into something more elaborate, reticent, and sophisticated; but it never ceases. Grown people, like children, are usually unconscious of these dialogues; as we get older we cease, for the most part, to carry them on out loud, and some of us practise a good deal of apparently solitary meditation and experiment. But, speaking broadly, it is true of adults as of children, that the mind lives in perpetual conversation. It is one of those things that we seldom notice just because they are so familiar and involuntary; but we can perceive it if we try to. If one suddenly stops and takes note of his thoughts at some time when his mind has been running free, as when he is busy with some simple mechanical work, he will be likely to find them taking the form of vague conversations. This is particularly true when one is somewhat excited with reference to a social situation. If he feels under accusation or suspicion in any way he will probably find himself making a defense, or perhaps a confession, to an imaginary hearer. A guilty man confesses "to get the load off his mind"; that is to say, the excitement of his thought cannot stop there but extends to the connected impulses of expression and creates an intense need to tell somebody. Impulsive people often talk out loud when excited, either "to themselves," as we say when we can see no one else present, or to any one whom they can get to listen. Dreams also consist very largely of imaginary conversations; and, with some people at least, the mind runs in dialogue during the half-waking state before going to sleep. There are many other familiar facts that bear the same interpretation—such, for instance, as that it is much easier for most people to compose in the form of letters or dialogue than in any other; so that literature of this kind has been common in all ages.

SOCIABILITY AND PERSONAL IDEAS

Goethe, in giving an account of how he came to write Werther as a series of letters, discusses the matter with his usual perspicuity, and lets us see how habitually conversational was his way of thinking. Speaking of himself in the third person, he says: "Accustomed to pass his time most pleasantly in society, he changed even solitary thought into social converse, and this in the following manner: He had the habit, when he was alone, of calling before his mind any person of his acquaintance. This person he entreated to sit down, walked up and down by him, remained standing before him, and discoursed with him on the subject he had in mind. To this the person answered as occasion required, or by the ordinary gestures signified his assent or dissent—in which every man has something peculiar to himself. The speaker then continued to carry out further that which seemed to please the guest, or to condition and define more closely that of which he disapproved; and finally was polite enough to give up his own notion. . . . How nearly such a dialogue is akin to a written correspondence is clear enough; only in the latter one sees returned the confidence one has bestowed, while in the former one creates for himself a confidence which is new, ever-changing, and unreturned." * 'Accustomed to pass his time most pleasantly in society, he changed even solitary thought into social converse," is not only a particular but a general truth, more or less applicable to all thought. The fact is that language, developed by the race through personal intercourse

* Oxenford's Translation, vol. i, p. 501.

and imparted to the individual in the same way, can never be dissociated from personal intercourse in the mind; and since higher thought involves language, it is always a kind of imaginary conversation. The word and the interlocutor are correlative ideas.

The impulse to communicate is not so much a result of thought as it is an inseparable part of it. They are like root and branch, two phases of a common growth, so that the death of one presently involves that of the other. Psychologists now teach that every thought involves an active impulse as part of its very nature; and this impulse, with reference to the more complex and socially developed forms of thought, takes the shape of a need to talk, to write, and so on; and if none of these is practicable, it expends itself in a wholly imaginary communication.

Montaigne, who understood human nature as well, perhaps, as any one who ever lived, remarks: "There is no pleasure to me without communication: there is not so much as a sprightly thought comes into my mind that it does not grieve me to have produced alone, and that I have no one to tell it to." * And it was doubtless because he had many such thoughts which no one was at hand to appreciate, that he took to writing essays. The uncomprehended of all times and peoples have kept diaries for the same reason. So, in general, a true creative impulse in literature or art is, in one aspect, an expression of this simple, childlike need to think aloud or *to* somebody; to define and vivify

* See his Essay on Vanity.

thought by imparting it to an imaginary companion; by developing that communicative element which belongs to its very nature, and without which it cannot live and grow. Many authors have confessed that they always think of some person when they write, and I am inclined to believe that this is always more or less definitely the case, though the writer himself may not be aware of it. Emerson somewhere says that "the man is but half himself; the other half is his expression," and this is literally true. The man comes to be through some sort of expression, and has no higher existence apart from it; overt or imaginary it takes place all the time.

Men apparently solitary, like Thoreau, are often the best illustrations of the inseparability of thought and life from communication. No sympathetic reader of his works, I should say, can fail to see that he took to the woods and fields not because he lacked sociability, but precisely because his sensibilities were so keen that he needed to rest and protect them by a peculiar mode of life, and to express them by the indirect and considerate method of literature. No man ever labored more passionately to communicate, to give and receive adequate expression, than he did. This may be read between the lines in all his works, and is recorded in his diary. "I would fain communicate the wealth of my life to men, would really give them what is most precious in my gift. I would secrete pearls with the shell-fish and lay up honey with the bees for them. I will sift the sunbeams for the public good. I know no riches I would keep back.

I have no private good unless it be my peculiar ability to serve the public. This is the only individual property. Each one may thus be innocently rich. I enclose and foster the pearl till it is grown. I wish to communicate those parts of my life which I would gladly live again." * This shows, I think, a just notion of the relation between the individual and society, privacy and publicity. There is, in fact, a great deal of sound sociology in Thoreau.

Since, therefore, the need to impart is of this primary and essential character, we ought not to look upon it as something separable from and additional to the need to think or to be; it is only by imparting that one is enabled to think or to be. Every one, in proportion to his natural vigor, necessarily strives to communicate to others that part of his life which he is trying to unfold in himself. It is a matter of self-preservation, because without expression thought cannot live. Imaginary conversation—that is, conversation carried on without the stimulus of a visible and audible response—may satisfy the needs of the mind for a long time. There is, indeed, an advantage to a vigorously constructive and yet impressible imagination in restricting communication; because in this way ideas are enabled to have a clearer and more independent development than they could have if continually disturbed by criticism or opposition. Thus artists, men of letters, and productive minds of all sorts often find it better to keep their productions to themselves until they are fully matured. But, after

* Early Spring in Massachusetts, p. 232.

all, the response must come sooner or later or thought itself will perish. The imagination, in time, loses the power to create an interlocutor who is not corroborated by any fresh experience. If the artist finds no appreciator for his book or picture he will scarcely be able to produce another.

People differ much in the vividness of their imaginative sociability. The more simple, concrete, dramatic, their habit of mind is, the more their thinking is carried on in terms of actual conversation with a visible and audible interlocutor. Women, as a rule, probably do this more vividly than men, the unlettered more vividly than those trained to abstract thought, and the sort of people we call emotional more vividly than the impassive. Moreover, the interlocutor is a very mutable person, and is likely to resemble the last strong character we have been in contact with. I have noticed, for instance, that when I take up a book after a person of decided and interesting character has been talking with me I am likely to hear the words of the book in his voice. The same is true of opinions, moral standards, and the like, as well as of physical traits. In short, the interlocutor, who is half of all thought and life, is drawn from the accessible environment.

It is worth noting here that there is no separation between real and imaginary persons; indeed, to be imagined is to become real, in a social sense, as I shall presently point out. An invisible person may easily be more real to an imaginative mind than a visible one; sensible presence is not necessarily a matter of the first importance. A person can be real to us only in the degree in which we imagine an inner life which exists in us, for the time being, and which we refer to him. The sensible presence is important chiefly in stimulating us to do this. All real persons are imaginary in this sense. If, however, we use imaginary in the sense of illusory, an imagination not corresponding to fact, it is easy to see that visible presence is no bar to illusion. Thus I meet a stranger on the steamboat who corners me and tells me his private history. I care nothing for it, and he half knows that I do not; he uses me only as a lay figure to sustain the agreeable illusion of sympathy, and is talking to an imaginary companion quite as he might if I were elsewhere. So likewise good manners are largely a tribute to imaginary companionship, a make-believe of sympathy which it is agreeable to accept as real, though we may know, when we think, that it is not. To conceive a kindly and approving companion is something that one involuntarily tries to do, in accordance with that instinctive hedonizing inseparable from all wholesome mental processes, and to assist in this by at least a seeming of friendly appreciation is properly regarded as a part of good breeding. To be always sincere would be brutally to destroy this pleasant and mostly harmless figment of the imagination.

Thus the imaginary companionship which a child of three or four years so naïvely creates and expresses is something elementary and almost omnipresent in the thought of a normal person. In fact, thought and personal intercourse may be regarded as merely aspects of the same thing: we call it personal intercourse when the suggestions that keep it going are received through faces or other symbols present to the senses; reflection when the personal suggestions come through memory and are more elaborately worked over in thought. But both are mental, both are personal. Personal images, as they are connected with nearly all our higher thought in its inception, remain inseparable from it in memory. The mind is not a hermit's cell, but a place of hospitality and intercourse. We have no higher life that is really apart from other people. It is by imagining them that our personality is built up; to be without the power of imagining them is to be a low-grade idiot; and in the measure that a mind is lacking in this power it is degenerate. Apart from this mental society there is no wisdom, no power, justice, or right, no higher existence at all. The life of the mind is essentially a life of intercourse.

Let us now consider somewhat more carefully the way in which ideas of people grow up in the mind, and try to make out, as nearly as we can, their real nature and significance.

The studies through which the child learns, in time, to interpret personal expression are very early begun. On her twelfth day M. was observed to get her eyes upon her mother's face; and after gazing for some time at it she seemed attracted to the eyes, into which she looked quite steadily. From the end of the first month this face study was very frequent and long-continued. Doubtless any one who notices infants could multiply indefinitely observations like the following:

"M., in her eighth week, lies in her mother's lap gazing up at her face with a frown of fixed and anxious attention. Evidently the play of the eyes and lips, the flashing of the teeth, and the wrinkles of expression are the object of her earnest study. So also the coaxing noises which are made to please her."

"She now [four months and twenty-one days old] seems to fix her attention almost entirely upon the eyes, and will stare at them for a minute or more with the most intent expression."

The eye seems to receive most notice. As Perez says: "The eye is one of the most interesting and attractive of objects; the vivacity of the pupil set in its oval background of white, its sparkles, its darts of light, its tender looks, its liquid depths, attract and fascinate a young child. . . ." * The mouth also gets much attention, especially when in movement; I have sometimes noticed a child who is looking into the eyes turn from them to the mouth when the person commences to talk: the flashing of the teeth then adds to its interest. The voice is also the object of close observation. The intentness with which a child listens to it, the quickness with which he learns to distinguish different voices and different inflections of the same voice, and the fact that vocal imitation precedes other sorts, all show this. It cannot fail to strike the observer that observation of these traits is not merely casual, but a strenuous study,

* The First Three Years of Childhood, p. 77.

often accompanied by a frown of earnest attention. The mind is evidently aroused, something important is going on, something conscious, voluntary, eager. It would seem likely that this something is the storing up, arrangement, and interpretation of those images of expression which remain throughout life the starting-point of personal imaginations.

The wrinkles about the eyes and mouth, which are perhaps the most expressive parts of the countenance, would not be so noticeable at first as the eyes, the lips, and the teeth, but they are always in the field of vision, and in time their special significance as a seat of expression comes to be noticed and studied. M. appeared to understand a smile sufficiently to be pleased by it about the end of the tenth month. The first unequivocal case of smiling in response to a smile was noticed on the twenty-sixth day of this month. Even at this age smiling is not imitative in the sense of being a voluntary repetition of the other's action, but appears to be merely an involuntary expression of pleasure. Facial expression is one of the later things to be imitated, for the reason, apparently, that the little child cannot be aware of the expression of his own countenance as he can hear his own voice or see his own hands; and therefore does not so soon learn to control it and to make it a means of voluntary imitation. He learns this only when he comes to study his features in the looking-glass. This children do as early as the second year, when they may be observed experimenting before the mirror with all sorts of gestures and grimaces.

The interpretation of a smile, or of any sort of facial expression, is apparently learned much as other things are. By constant study of the face from the first month the child comes, in time, to associate the wrinkles that form a smile with pleasant experiences —fondling, coaxing, offering of playthings or of the bottle, and so on. Thus the smile comes to be recognized as a harbinger of pleasure, and so is greeted with a smile. Its absence, on the other hand, is associated with inattention and indifference. Toward the end of the fifth month M., on one occasion, seemed to notice the change from a smile to a frown, and stopped smiling herself. However, a number of observations taken in the tenth month show that even then it was doubtful whether she could be made to smile merely by seeing some one else do it; and, as I say, the first unequivocal case was noticed toward the end of this month.

Such evidence as we have from the direct observation of children does not seem to me to substantiate the opinion that we have a definite instinctive sensibility to facial expression. Whatever hereditary element there is I imagine to be very vague, and incapable of producing definite phenomena without the aid of experience. I experimented upon my own and some other children with frowns, attempts at ferocity, and pictures of faces, as well as with smiles—in order to elicit instinctive apprehension of expression, but during the first year these phenomena seemed to produce no definite effect. At about fifteen months M. appeared to be dismayed by a savage expression as-

100

sumed while playing with her, and at about the same period became very sensitive to frowns. The impression left upon me was that after a child learns to expect a smiling face as the concomitant of kindness, he is puzzled, troubled, or startled when it is taken away, and moreover learns by experience that frowns and gravity mean disapproval and opposition. I imagine that children fail to understand any facial expression that is quite new to them. An unfamiliar look, an expression of ferocity for example, may excite vague alarm simply because it is strange; or, as is very likely with children used to kind treatment, this or any other contortion of the face may be welcomed with a laugh on the assumption that it is some new kind of play. I feel sure that observation will dissipate the notion of any *definite* instinctive capacity to interpret the countenance.

I might also mention, as having some bearing upon this question of definite hereditary ideas, that my children did not show that instinctive fear of animals that some believe to be implanted in us. R., the elder, until about three years of age, delighted in animals, and when taken to the menagerie regarded the lions and tigers with the calmest interest; but later, apparently as a result of rude treatment by a puppy, became exceedingly timid. M. has never, so far as I know, shown any fear of any animal.

As regards sounds, there is no doubt of a vague instinctive susceptibility, at least to what is harsh—sharp, or plaintive. Children less than a month old will show pain at such sounds. A harsh cry, or a

101

sharp sound like that of a tin horn, will sometimes make them draw down the mouth and cry even during the first week.

Darwin records that in one of his children sympathy "was clearly shown at six months and eleven days by his melancholy face, with the corners of his mouth well depressed, when his nurse pretended to cry." * Such manifestations are probably caused rather by the plaintive voice than by facial expression; at any rate, I have never been able to produce them by the latter alone.

Some believe that young children have an intuition of personal character quicker and more trustworthy than that of grown people. If this were so it would be a strong argument in favor of the existence of a congenital instinct which does not need experience and is impaired by it. My own belief is that close observation of children under two years of age will lead to the conclusion that personal impressions are developed by experience. Yet it is possibly true that children three years old or more are sometimes quicker and more acute judges of some traits, such as sincerity and good will, than grown people. In so far as it is a fact it may perhaps be explained in this way. The faces that children see and study are mostly full of the expression of love and truth. Nothing like it occurs in later life, even to the most fortunate. These images, we may believe, give rise in the child's mind to a more or less definite ideal of what a true and kindly face should be, and this ideal he uses

* See his Biographical Sketch of an Infant, Mind, vol. 2, p. 289.

with great effect in detecting what falls short of it. He sees that there is something wrong with the false smile; it does not fit the image in his mind; some lines are not there, others are exaggerated. He does not understand what coldness and insincerity are, but their expression puzzles and alarms him, merely because it is not what he is used to. The adult loses this clear, simple ideal of love and truth, and the sharp judgment that flows from it. His perception becomes somewhat vulgarized by a flood of miscellaneous experience, and he sacrifices childish spontaneity to wider range and more complex insight, valuing and studying many traits of which the child knows nothing. It will not be seriously maintained that, on the whole, we know people better when we are children than we do later.

I put forward these scanty observations for what little they may be worth, and not as disproving the existence of special instincts in which Darwin and other great observers have believed. I do not maintain that there is no hereditary aptitude to interpret facial expression—there must be some sort of an instinctive basis to start from—but I think that it develops gradually and in indistinguishable conjunction with knowledge gained by experience.

Apparently, then, voice, facial expression, gesture, and the like, which later become the vehicle of personal impressions and the sensible basis of sympathy, are attractive at first chiefly for their sensuous variety and vividness, very much as other bright, moving, sounding things are attractive; and the interpreta-

103

tion of them comes gradually by the interworking of instinct and observation. This interpretation is nothing other than the growth, in connection with these sensuous experiences, of a system of ideas that we associate with them. The interpretation of an angry look, for instance, consists in the expectation of angry words and acts, in feelings of resentment or fear, and so on; in short, it is our whole mental reaction to this sign It may consist in part of sympathetic states of mind, that is of states of mind that we suppose the other to experience also; but it is not confined to such. These ideas that enrich the meaning of the symbol—the resentment or fear, for instance—have all, no doubt, their roots in instinct; we are born with the crude raw material of such feelings And it is precisely in the act of communication, in social contact of some sort, that this material grows, that it gets the impulses that give it further definition, refinement, organization. It is by intercourse with others that we expand our inner experience. In other words, and this is the point of the matter, the personal idea consists at first and in all later development, of a sensuous element or symbol with which is connected a more or less complex body of thought and sentiment; the whole social in genesis, formed by a series of communications.

What do we think of when we think of a person? Is not the nucleus of the thought an image of the sort just mentioned, some ghost of characteristic expression? It may be a vague memory of lines around the mouth and eyes, or of other lines indicating pose, carriage, or gesture; or it may be an echo of some tone or inflection of the voice. I am unable, perhaps, to call up any distinct outline of the features of my best friend, of my own mother, or my child; but I can see a smile, a turn of the eyelid, a way of standing or sitting, indistinct and flitting glimpses, but potent to call up those past states of feeling of which personal memories are chiefly formed. The most real thing in physical presence is not height, nor breadth, nor the shape of the nose or forehead, nor that of any other comparatively immobile part of the body, but it is something in the plastic, expressive features: these are noticed and remembered because they tell us what we most care to know.

The judgment of personal character seems to take place in much the same way. We estimate a man, I think, by imagining what he would do in various situations. Experience supplies us with an almost infinite variety of images of men in action, that is of impressions of faces, tones, and the like, accompanied by certain other elements making up a situation. When we wish to judge a new face, voice, and form, we unconsciously ask ourselves where they would fit; we try them in various situations, and if they fit, if we can think of them as doing the things without incongruity, we conclude that we have that kind of a man to deal with. If I can imagine a man intimidated, I do not respect him; if I can imagine him lying, I do not trust him; if I can see him receiving, comprehending, resisting men and disposing them

105

in accordance with his own plans, I ascribe executive ability to him; if I can think of him in his study patiently working out occult problems, I judge him to be a scholar; and so on. The symbol before us reminds us of some other symbol resembling it, and this brings with it a whole group of ideas which constitutes our personal impression of the new man.*

The power to make these judgments is intuitive, imaginative, not arrived at by ratiocination, but it is dependent upon experience. I have no belief in the theory, which I have seen suggested, that we unconsciously imitate other people's expression, and then judge of their character by noting how we feel when we look like them. The men of uncommon insight into character are usually somewhat impassive in countenance and not given to facial imitation. Most of us become to some extent judges of the character of dogs, so that we can tell by the tone of a dog's bark whether he is a biting dog or only a barking dog. Surely imitation can have nothing to do with this; we do not imitate the dog's bark to learn whether he is serious or not; we observe, remember, and imagine; and it seems to me that we judge people in much the same way.

That which we usually speak of as "personality," in a somewhat external sense, is a sort of atmosphere, having its source in habitual states of feeling, which each of us unconsciously communicates through facial

* A good way to interpret a man's face is to ask one's self how he would look saying "I" in an emphatic manner. This seems to help the imagination in grasping what is most essential and characteristic in him.

106

and vocal expression. If one is cheerful, confident, candid, sympathetic, he awakens similar feelings in others, and so makes a pleasant and favorable impression; while gloom, reserve, indifference to what others are feeling, and the like, have an opposite effect. We cannot assume or conceal these states of feeling with much success; the only way to appear to be a certain sort of person is actually to become that sort of person by cultivating the necessary habits. We impart what we are without effort or consciousness, and rarely impart anything else.

These visible and audible signs of personality, these lines and tones whose meaning is impressed upon us by the intense and constant observation of our childhood, are also a chief basis of the communication of impressions in art and literature.

This is evidently the case in those arts which imitate the human face and figure. Painters and illustrators give the most minute study to facial expression, and suggest various sentiments by bits of light and shade so subtle that the uninitiated cannot see what or where they are, although their effect is everything as regards the depiction of personality. It is the failure to reproduce them that makes the emptiness of nearly all copies of famous painting or sculpture that represents the face. Perhaps not one person in a thousand, comparing the "Mona Lisa" or the "Beatrice Cenci" with one of the mediocre copies generally standing near them, can point out where the painter of the latter has gone amiss; yet the difference is like that between life and a wax image.

The chief fame of some painters rests upon their power to portray and suggest certain rare kinds of feeling. Thus the people of Fra Angelico express to the eye the higher love, described in words by St. Paul and Thomas à Kempis. It is a distinctly human and social sentiment; his persons are nearly always in pairs, and, in his Paradise for instance, almost every face among the blest is directed in rapture toward some other face. Other painters, as Botticelli and Perugino—alike in this respect though not in most—depict a more detached sort of sentiment; and their people look out of the picture in isolated ecstasy or meditation.

Sculpture appeals more to reminiscence of attitude, facial expression being somewhat subordinate, though here also the difference between originals and copies is largely in the lines of the eyes and mouth, too delicate to be reproduced by the mechanical instruments which copy broader outlines quite exactly.

As to literature, it is enough to recall the fact that words allusive to traits of facial expression, and especially to the eye, are the immemorial and chosen means of suggesting personality.* To poetry, which seeks the sensuous nucleus of thought, the eye is very generally the person; as when Shakespeare says:

> "When in disgrace with fortune and men's eyes,
> I all alone beweep my outcast state . . ."

or Milton:

> "Thy rapt soul sitting in thine eyes."

Only four words—"heart," "love," "man," "world"—take up more space in the index of "Familiar Quotations" than "eye."

108

Poetry, however, usually refrains from minute description of expression, a thing impossible in words, and strikes for a vivid, if inexact, impression, by the use of such phrases as "a fiery eye," "a liquid eye," and "The poet's eye in a fine frenzy rolling." *

We also get from every art a personal impression that does not come from the imitation of features and tones, nor from a description of these in words, but is the personality of the author himself, subtly communicated by something that we interpret as signs of his state of mind. When one reads Motley's histories he gets a personal impression not only of the Prince of Orange or Alexander of Parma, but also of Mr. Motley; and the same is true or may be true of any work of art, however "objective" it may be. What we call style, when we say "The style is the man," is the equivalent, in the artist's way of doing things, of those visible and audible traits of the form and voice by which we judge people who are bodily present.† "Every work of genius," says John Burroughs, "has its own physiognomy—sad, cheerful, frowning, yearning, determined, meditative." Just as we are glad of the presence of certain forms and faces, because of the mood they put us in, so we are glad of

* On the fear of (imaginary) eyes see G. Stanley Hall's study of Fear in The American Journal of Psychology, vol. 8, p. 147.

† Two apparently opposite views are current as to what style is. One regards it as the distinctive or characteristic in expression, that which marks off a writer or other artist from all the rest; according to the other, style is mastery over the common medium of expression, as language or the technique of painting or sculpture. These are not so inconsistent as they seem. Good style is both; that is, a significant personality expressed in a workmanlike manner.

the physiognomy of certain writers in their books, quite apart from the intellectual content of what they say; and this is the subtlest, most durable, most indispensable charm of all. Every lover of books has authors whom he reads over and over again, whom he cares for as persons and not as sources of information, who are more to him, possibly, than any person he sees. He continually returns to the cherished companion and feeds eagerly upon his thought. It is because there is something in the book which he needs, which awakens and directs trains of thought that lead him where he likes to be led. The thing that does this is something personal and hard to define; it is in the words and yet not in any definite information that they convey. It is rather an attitude, a way of feeling, communicated by a style faithful to the writer's mind. Some people find pleasure and profit, for example, in perusing even the somewhat obscure and little inspired portions of Goethe's writings, like the "Campaign in France"; it would perhaps be impossible to tell why, further than by saying that they get the feeling of something calm, free, and onward which is Goethe himself, and not to be had elsewhere.

And so any one who practises literary composition, even of a pedestrian sort, will find at least one reward for his pains in a growing insight into the personality of great writers. He will come to feel that such a word was chosen or such a sentence framed in just that way, under the influence of such a purpose or sentiment, and by putting these impressions together, will presently arrive at some personal acquaintance with any author whose character and aims are at all congenial with his own.

We feel this more in literature than in any other art, and more in prose of an intimate sort than in any other kind of literature. The reason appears to be that writing, particularly writing of a familiar kind, like letters and autobiographies, is something which we all practise in one way or another, and which we can, therefore, interpret; while the methods of other arts are beyond our imaginations. It is easy to share the spirit of Charles Lamb writing his Letters, or of Montaigne dictating his Essays, or of Thackeray discoursing in the first person about his characters; because they merely did what all of us do, only did it better. On the other hand, Michelangelo, or Wagner, or Shakespeare—except in his sonnets—remains for most of us personally remote and inconceivable. But a painter, or a composer, or a sculptor, or a poet, will always get an impression of personality, of style, from another artist of the same sort, because his experience enables him to feel the subtle indications of mood and method. Mr. Frith, the painter, says in his autobiography that a picture "will betray the real character of its author; who, in the unconscious development of his peculiarities, constantly presents to the initiated signs by which an infallible judgment may be pronounced on the painter's mind and character." *
In fact, it is true of any earnest career that a man expresses his character in his work, and that another

* P. 493.

man of similar aims can read what he expresses. We see in General Grant's Memoirs, how an able commander feels the personality of an opponent in the movements of his armies, imagines what he will do in various exigencies, and deals with him accordingly.

These personal impressions of a writer or other artist may or may not be accompanied by a vague imagination of his visible appearance. Some persons have so strong a need to think in connection with visual images that they seem to form no notion of personality without involuntarily imagining what the person looks like; while others can have a strong impression of feeling and purpose that seems not to be accompanied by any visual picture. There can be no doubt, however, that sensible images of the face, voice, etc., usually go with personal ideas. Our earliest personal conceptions grow up about such images; and they always remain for most of us the principal means of getting hold of other people. Naturally, they have about the same relative place in memory and imagination as they do in observation. Probably, if we could get to the bottom of the matter, it would be found that our impression of a writer is always accompanied by some idea of his sensible appearance, is always associated with a physiognomy, even when we are not aware of it. Can any one, for example, read Macaulay and think of a soft and delicately inflected voice? I imagine not: these periods must be connected with a sonorous and somewhat mechanical utterance; the sort of person that speaks softly and with delicate inflections would have written otherwise. On the other hand, in reading Robert Louis Stevenson it is impossible, I should say, not to get the impression of a sensitive and flexible speech. Such impressions are mostly vague and may be incorrect, but for sympathetic readers they exist and constitute a real, though subtle, physiognomy.

Not only the idea of particular persons but that of social groups seems to have a sensible basis in these ghosts of expression. The sentiment by which one's family, club, college, state, or country is realized in his mind is stimulated by vague images, largely personal. Thus the spirit of a college fraternity seems to come back to me through a memory of the old rooms and of the faces of friends. The idea of country is a rich and various one and has connected with it many sensuous symbols—such as flags, music, and the rhythm of patriotic poetry—that are not directly personal; but it is chiefly an idea of personal traits that we share and like, as set over against others that are different and repugnant. We think of America as the land of freedom, simplicity, cordiality, equality, and so on, in antithesis to other countries which we suppose to be otherwise—and we think of these traits by imagining the people that embody them. For countless school-children patriotism begins in sympathy with our forefathers in resistance to the hateful oppression and arrogance of the British, and this fact of early training largely accounts for the perennial popularity of the anti-British side in international questions. Where the country has a permanent ruler to typify it his image is doubtless a chief element in the patriotic idea. On the other hand, the impulse which we feel to personify country, or anything else that awakens strong emotion in us, shows our imaginations to be so profoundly personal that deep feeling almost inevitably connects itself with a personal image. In short, group sentiment, in so far as it is awakened by definite images, is only a variety of personal sentiment. A sort of vague agitation, however, is sometimes produced by mere numbers. Thus public opinion is sometimes thought of as a vast impersonal force, like a great wind, though ordinarily it is conceived simply as the opinion of particular persons, whose expressions or tones are more or less definitely imagined.

In the preceding I have considered the rise of personal ideas chiefly from the point of view of the visual or auditory element in them—the personal symbol or vehicle of communication; but of course there is a parallel growth in feeling. An infant's states of feeling may be supposed to be nearly as crude as his ideas of the appearance of things; and the process that gives form, variety, and coherence to the latter does the same for the former. It is precisely the act of intercourse, the stimulation of the mind by a personal symbol, which gives a formative impulse to the vague mass of hereditary feeling-tendency, and this impulse, in turn, results in a larger power of interpreting the symbol. It is not to be supposed, for instance, that such feelings as generosity, respect, mortification, emu-

114

lation, the sense of honor, and the like, are an original endowment of the mind. Like all the finer and larger mental life these arise in conjunction with communication and could not exist without it. It is these finer modes of feeling, these intricate branchings or differentiations of the primitive trunk of emotion, to which the name sentiments is usually applied. Personal sentiments are correlative with personal symbols, the interpretation of the latter meaning nothing more than that the former are associated with them; while the sentiments, in turn, cannot be felt except by the aid of the symbols. If I see a face and feel that here is an honest man, it means that I have, in the past, achieved through intercourse an idea of honest personality, with the visual elements of which the face before me has something in common, so that it calls up this socially achieved sentiment. And moreover in knowing this honest man my idea of honest personality will be enlarged and corrected for future use. Both the sentiment and its visual associations will be somewhat different from what they were.

Thus no personal sentiment is the exclusive product of any one influence, but all is of various origin and has a social history. The more clearly one can grasp this fact the better, at least if I am right in supposing that a whole system of wrong thinking results from overlooking it and assuming that personal ideas are separable and fragmentary elements in the mind. Of this I shall say more presently. The fact I mean is that expressed by Shakespeare, with reference to love, or loving friendship, in his thirty-first sonnet:

115

"Thy bosom is endeared with all hearts,
  Which I by lacking have supposed dead,
And there reigns love, and all love's loving parts,
  And all those friends which I thought buried.

.   .   .   .

Thou art the grave where buried love doth live,
  Hung with the trophies of my lovers gone,
Who all their parts of me to thee did give;
  That due of many now is thine alone:
Their images I loved I view in thee,
And thou (all they) hast all the all of me."

In this sonnet may be discerned, I think, a true theory of personal sentiment, quite accordant with the genetic point of view of modern psychology, and very important in the understanding of social relations.

Facial expression, tone of voice, and the like, the sensible nucleus of personal and social ideas, serve as the handle, so to speak, of such ideas, the principal substance of which is drawn from the region of inner imagination and sentiment. The personality of a friend, as it lives in my mind and forms there a part of the society in which I live, is simply a group or system of thoughts associated with the symbols that stand for him. To think of him is to revive some part of the system—to have the old feeling along with the familiar symbol, though perhaps in a new connection with other ideas. The real and intimate thing in him is the thought to which he gives life, the feeling his presence or memory has the power to suggest. This clings about the sensible imagery, the personal symbols already discussed, because the latter have served as bridges by which we have entered other minds and therein enriched our own. We have laid up stores, but we always need some help to get at them in order that we may use and increase them; and this help commonly consists in something visible or audible, which has been connected with them in the past and now acts as a key by which they are unlocked. Thus the face of a friend has power over us in much the same way as the sight of a favorite book, of the flag of one's country, or the refrain of an old song; it starts a train of thought, lifts the curtain from an intimate experience. And his presence does not consist in the pressure of his flesh upon a neighboring chair, but in the thoughts clustering about some symbol of him, whether the latter be his tangible person or something else. If a person is more his best self in a letter than in speech, as sometimes happens, he is more truly present to me in his correspondence than when I see and hear him. And in most cases a favorite writer is more with us in his book than he ever could have been in the flesh; since, being a writer, he is one who has studied and perfected this particular mode of personal incarnation, very likely to the detriment of any other. I should like as a matter of curiosity to see and hear for a moment the men whose works I admire; but I should hardly expect to find further intercourse particularly profitable.

The world of sentiment and imagination, of all finer and warmer thought, is chiefly a personal world—that is, it is inextricably interwoven with personal symbols. If you try to think of a person you will find that what you really think is chiefly sentiments which you connect with his image; and, on the other hand, if you try to recall a sentiment you will find, as a rule, that it will not come up except along with symbols of the persons who have suggested it. To think of love, gratitude, pity, grief, honor, courage, justice, and the like, it is necessary to think of people by whom or toward whom these sentiments may be entertained.* Thus justice may be recalled by thinking of Washington, kindness by Lincoln, honor by Sir Philip Sidney, and so on. The reason for this, as already intimated, is that sentiment and imagination are generated, for the most part, in the life of communication, and so belong with personal images by original and necessary association, having no separate existence except in our forms of speech. The ideas that such words as modesty and magnanimity stand for could never have been formed apart from social intercourse, and indeed are nothing other than remembered aspects of such intercourse. To live this higher life, then, we must live with others, by the aid of their visible presence, by reading their words, or by recalling in imagination these or other symbols of them. To lose our hold upon them—as, for example, by long isolation or by the decay of the imagination in disease or old age—is to lapse into a life of sensation and crude instinct.

So far as the study of immediate social relations is concerned the personal idea is the real person. That

* With me, at least, this is the case. Some whom I have consulted find that certain sentiments—for instance, pity— may be directly suggested by the word, without the mediation of a personal symbol. This hardly affects the argument, as it will not be doubted that the sentiment was in its inception associated with a personal symbol.

is to say, it is in this alone that one man exists for another, and acts directly upon his mind. My association with you evidently consists in the relation between my idea of you and the rest of my mind. If there is something in you that is wholly beyond this and makes no impression upon me it has no social reality in this relation. *The immediate social reality is the personal idea;* nothing, it would seem, could be much more obvious than this.

Society, then, in its immediate aspect, *is a relation among personal ideas.* In order to have society it is evidently necessary that persons should get together somewhere; and they get together only as personal ideas in the mind. Where else? What other possible *locus* can be assigned for the real contact of persons, or in what other form can they come in contact except as impressions or ideas formed in this common *locus?* Society exists in my mind as the contact and reciprocal influence of certain ideas named "I," Thomas, Henry, Susan, Bridget, and so on. It exists in your mind as a similar group, and so in every mind. Each person is immediately aware of a particular aspect of society: and so far as he is aware of great social wholes, like a nation or an epoch, it is by embracing in this particular aspect ideas or sentiments which he attributes to his countrymen or contemporaries in their collective aspect. In order to see this it seems to me only necessary to discard vague modes of speech which have no conceptions back of them that will bear scrutiny, and look at the facts as we know them in experience.

Yet most of us, perhaps, will find it hard to assent to the view that the social person is a group of sentiments attached to some symbol or other characteristic element, which keeps them together and from which the whole idea is named. The reason for this reluctance I take to be that we are accustomed to talk and think, so far as we do think in this connection, as if a person were a material rather than a psychical fact. Instead of basing our sociology and ethics upon what a man really is as part of our mental and moral life, he is vaguely and yet grossly regarded as a shadowy material body, a lump of flesh, and not as an ideal thing at all. But surely it is only common sense to hold that the social and moral reality is that which lives in our imaginations and affects our motives. As regards the physical it is only the finer, more plastic and mentally significant aspects of it that imagination is concerned with, and with them chiefly as a nucleus or centre of crystallization for sentiment. Instead of perceiving this we commonly make the physical the dominant factor, and think of the mental and moral only by a vague analogy to it.

Persons and society must, then, be studied primarily in the imagination. It is surely true, *prima facie*, that the best way of observing things is that which is most direct; and I do not see how any one can hold that we know persons directly except as imaginative ideas in the mind. These are perhaps the most vivid things in our experience, and as observable as anything else, though it is a kind of observation in which accuracy has not been systematically cultivated. The observation of the physical aspects, however important, is for social purposes quite subsidiary: there is no way of weighing or measuring men which throws more than a very dim side-light on their personality. The physical factors most significant are those elusive traits of expression already discussed, and in the observation and interpretation of these physical science is only indirectly helpful. What, for instance, could the most elaborate knowledge of his weights and measures, including the anatomy of his brain, tell us of the character of Napoleon? Not enough, I take it, to distinguish him with certainty from an imbecile. Our real knowledge of him is derived from reports of his conversation and manner, from his legislation and military dispositions, from the impression made upon those about him and by them communicated to us, from his portraits and the like; all serving as aids to the imagination in forming a system that we call by his name. I by no means aim to discredit the study of man or of society with the aid of physical measurements, such as those of psychological laboratories; but I think that these methods are indirect and ancil-. lary in their nature and are most useful when employed in connection with a trained imagination.

I conclude, therefore, that the imaginations which people have of one another are the *solid facts* of society, and that to observe and interpret these must be a chief aim of sociology. I do not mean merely that society must be studied *by* the imagination—that is true of all investigations in their higher reaches—but

121

that the *object* of study is primarily an imaginative idea or group of ideas in the mind, that we have to imagine imaginations. The intimate grasp of any social fact will be found to require that we divine what men think of one another. Charity, for instance, is not understood without imagining what ideas the giver and recipient have of each other; to grasp homicide we must, for one thing, conceive how the offender thinks of his victim and of the administrators of the law; the relation between the employing and hand-laboring classes is first of all a matter of personal attitude which we must apprehend by sympathy with both, and so on. In other words, we want to get at motives, and motives spring from personal ideas. There is nothing particularly novel in this view; historians, for instance, have always assumed that to understand and interpret personal relations was their main business; but apparently the time is coming when this will have to be done in a more systematic and penetrating manner then in the past. Whatever may justly be urged against the introduction of frivolous and disconnected "personalities" into history, the understanding of persons is the aim of this and all other branches of social study.

It is important to face the question of persons who have no corporeal reality, as for instance the dead, characters of fiction or the drama, ideas of the gods and the like. Are these real people, members of society? I should say that in so far as we imagine them they are. Would it not be absurd to deny social reality to Robert Louis Stevenson, who is so much alive in many minds and so potently affects important phases of thought and conduct? He is certainly more real in this practical sense than most of us who have not yet lost our corporeity, more alive, perhaps, than he was before he lost his own, because of his wider influence. And so Colonel Newcome, or Romola, or Hamlet is real to the imaginative reader with the realest kind of reality, the kind that works directly upon his personal character. And the like is true of the conceptions of supernatural beings handed down by the aid of tradition among all peoples. What, indeed, would society be, or what would any one of us be, if we associated only with corporeal persons and insisted that no one should enter our company who could not show his power to tip the scales and cast a shadow?

On the other hand, a corporeally existent person is not socially real unless he is imagined. If the nobleman thinks of the serf as a mere animal and does not attribute to him a human way of thinking and feeling, the latter is not real to him in the sense of acting personally upon his mind and conscience. And if a man should go into a strange country and hide himself so completely that no one knew he was there, he would evidently have no social existence for the inhabitants.

In saying this I hope I do not seem to question the independent reality of persons or to confuse it with personal ideas. The man is one thing and the various ideas entertained about him are another; but

123

the latter, the personal idea, is the immediate social reality, the thing in which men exist for one another, and work directly upon one another's lives.· Thus any study of society that is not supported by a firm grasp of personal ideas is empty and dead—mere doctrine and not knowledge at all.

I believe that the vaguely material notion of personality, which does not confront the social fact at all but assumes it to be the analogue of the physical fact, is a main source of fallacious thinking about ethics, politics, and indeed every aspect of social and personal life. It seems to underlie all four of the ways of conceiving society and the individual alleged in the first chapter to be false. If the person is thought of primarily as a separate material form, inhabited by thoughts and feelings conceived by analogy to be equally separate, then the only way of getting a society is by adding on a new principle of socialism, social faculty, altruism, or the like. But if you start with the idea that the social person is primarily a fact in the mind, and observe him there, you find at once that he has no existence apart from a mental whole of which all personal ideas are members, and which is a particular aspect of society. Every one of these ideas, as we have seen, is the outcome of our experience of all the persons we have known, and is only a special aspect of our general idea of mankind.

To many people it would seem mystical to say that persons, as we know them, are not separable and mutually exclusive, like physical bodies, so that what is part of one cannot be part of another, but that they interpenetrate one another, the same element pertaining to different persons at different times, or even at the same time: yet this is a verifiable and not very abstruse fact.* The sentiments which make up the largest and most vivid part of our idea of any person are not, as a rule, peculiarly and exclusively his, but each one may be entertained in conjunction with other persons also. It is, so to speak, at the point of intersection of many personal ideas, and may be reached through any one of them. Not only Philip Sidney but many other people call up the sentiment of honor, and likewise with kindness, magnanimity, and so on. Perhaps these sentiments are never precisely the same in any two cases, but they are nearly enough alike to act in about the same manner upon our motives, which is the main thing from a practical point of view. Any kindly face will arouse friendly feeling, any suffering child awaken pity, any brave man inspire respect. A sense of justice, of something being due to a man as such, is potentially a part of the idea of every man I know. All such feelings are a cumulative product of social experience and do not belong exclusively to any one personal

* This idea that social persons are not mutually exclusive but composed largely of common elements is implied in Professor William James's doctrine of the Social Self and set forth at more length in Professor James Mark Baldwin's Social and Ethical Interpretations of Mental Development. Like other students of social psychology I have received much instruction and even more helpful provocation from the latter brilliant and original work. To Professor James my obligation is perhaps greater still.

symbol. A sentiment, if we consider it as something in itself, is vaguely, indeterminately personal; it may come to life, with only slight variations, in connection with any one of many symbols; whether it is referred to one or to another, or to two or more at once, is determined by the way one's thoughts arrange themselves, by the connection in which the sentiment is suggested.

As regards one's self in relation to other people, I shall have more to say in a later chapter; but I may say here that there is no view of the self, that will bear examination, which makes it altogether distinct, in our minds, from other persons. If it includes the whole mind, then, of course, it includes all the persons we think of, all the society which lives in our thoughts. If we confine it to a certain part of our thought with which we connect a distinctive emotion or sentiment called self-feeling, as I prefer to do, it still includes the persons with whom we feel most identified. *Self and other do not exist as mutually exclusive social facts*, and phraseology which implies that they do, like the antithesis egoism *versus* altruism, is open to the objection of vagueness, if not of falsity.* It seems to me that the classification of

* I distinguish, of course, between egotism, which is an English word of long standing, and egoism, which was, I believe, somewhat recently introduced by moralists to designate, in antithesis to altruism, certain theories or facts of ethics. I do not object to these words as names of theories, but as purporting to be names of facts of conduct I do, and have in mind more particularly their use by Herbert Spencer in his Principles of Psychology and other works. As used by Spencer they seem to me valid

impulses as altruistic and egoistic, with or without a third class called, perhaps, ego-altruistic, is empty; and I do not see how any other conclusion can result from a concrete study of the matter. There is no class of altruistic impulses specifically different from other impulses: all our higher, socially developed sentiments are indeterminately personal, and may be associated with self-feeling, or with whatever personal symbol may happen to arouse them. Those feelings which are merely sensual and have not been refined into sentiments by communication and imagination are not so much egoistic as merely animal: they do not pertain to social persons, either first or second, but belong in a lower stratum of thought. Sensuality is not to be confused with the social self. As I shall try to show later we do not think "I" except with reference to a complementary thought of other persons; it is an idea developed by association and communication.

from a physiological standpoint only, and fallacious when employed to describe mental, social, or moral facts. The trouble is, as with his whole system, that the physiological aspect of life is expounded and assumed, apparently, to be the only aspect that science can consider. Having ventured to find fault with Spencer, I may be allowed to add that I have perhaps learned as much from him as from any other writer. If only his system did not appear at first quite so complete and final, one might more easily remain loyal to it in spite of its deficiencies. But when these latter begin to appear its very completeness makes it seem a sort of a prison-wall which one must break down to get out.

My views regarding Spencer's sociology are given at some length in an article published in The American Journal of Sociology for September, 1920.

I shall try to show the nature of egotism and selfishness in Chapter VI.

The egoism-altruism way of speaking falsifies the facts at the most vital point possible by assuming that our impulses relating to persons are separable into two classes, the I impulses and the You impulses, in much the same way that physical persons are separable; whereas a primary fact throughout the range of sentiment is a fusion of persons, so that the impulse belongs not to one or the other, but precisely to the common ground that both occupy, to their intercourse or mingling. Thus the sentiment of gratitude does not pertain to me as against you, nor to you as against me, but springs right from our union, and so with all personal sentiment. Special terms like egoism and altruism are presumably introduced into moral discussions for the more accurate naming of facts. But I cannot discover the facts for which these are supposed to be names. The more I consider the matter the more they appear to be mere fictions of analogical thought. If you have no definite idea of personality or self beyond the physical idea, you are naturally led to regard the higher phases of thought, which have no evident relation to the body, as in some way external to the first person or self. Thus instead of psychology, sociology, or ethics we have a mere shadow of physiology.

Pity is typical of the impulses ordinarily called altruistic; but if one thinks of the question closely it is hard to see how this adjective is especially applicable to it. Pity is not aroused exclusively by images or symbols of other persons, as against those of one's self. If I think of my own body in a pitiable condition I am perhaps as likely to feel pity as if I think of some one else in such a condition.* At any rate, self-pity is much too common to be ignored. Even if the sentiment were aroused only by symbols of other persons it would not necessarily be non-egoistic. "A father pitieth his children," but any searching analysis will show that he incorporates the children into his own imaginative self. And, finally, pity is not necessarily moral or good, but is often mere "self-indulgence," as when it is practised at the expense of justice and true sympathy. A "wounding pity," to use a phrase of Mr. Stevenson's, is one of the commonest forms of objectionable sentiment. In short, pity is a sentiment like any other, having in itself no determinate personality, as first or second, and no determinate moral character: personal reference and moral rank depend upon the conditions under which it is suggested. The reason that it strikes us as appropriate to call pity "altruistic" apparently is that it often leads directly and obviously to helpful practical activity, as toward the poor or the sick. But "altruistic" is used to imply something more than kindly or benevolent, some radical psychological or moral distinction between this sentiment or class of sentiments and others called egoistic, and this distinction appears not to exist. All social sentiments are altruistic in the sense that they involve reference to another person; few are so in the sense that they

* Some may question whether we can pity ourselves in this way. But it seems to me that we avoid self-pity only by not vividly imagining ourselves in a piteous plight; and that if we do so imagine ourselves the sentiment follows quite naturally.

exclude the self. The idea of a division on this line appears to flow from a vague presumption that personal ideas must have a separateness answering to that of material bodies.

I do not mean to deny or depreciate the fact of personal opposition; it is real and most important, though it does not rest upon any such essential and, as it were, material separateness as the common way of thinking implies. At a given moment personal symbols may stand for different and opposing tendencies; thus the missionary may be urging me to contribute to his cause, and, if he is skilful, the impulses he awakens will move me in that direction; but if I think of my wife and children and the summer outing I had planned to give them from my savings, an opposite impulse appears. And in all such cases the very fact of opposition and the attention thereby drawn to the conflicting impulses gives emphasis to them, so that common elements are overlooked and the persons in the imagination seem separate and exclusive.

In such cases, however, the harmonizing or moralizing of the situation consists precisely in evoking or appealing to the common element in the apparently conflicting personalities, that is to some sentiment of justice or right. Thus I may say to myself, "I can afford a dollar, but ought not, out of consideration for my family, to give more," and may be able to imagine all parties accepting this view of the case.

Opposition between one's self and some one else is also a very real thing; but this opposition, instead of coming from a separateness like that of material bodies, is, on the contrary, dependent upon a measure of community between one's self and the disturbing other, so that the hostility between one's self and a social person may always be described as hostile sympathy. And the sentiments connected with opposition, like resentment, pertain neither to myself, considered separately, nor to the symbol of the other person, but to ideas including both. I shall discuss these matters at more length in subsequent chapters; the main thing here is to note that personal opposition does not involve mechanical separateness, but arises from the emphasis of inconsistent elements in ideas having much in common.

The relations to one another and to the mind of the various persons one thinks of might be rudely pictured in some such way as this. Suppose we conceive the mind as a vast wall covered with electric-light bulbs, each of which represents a possible thought or impulse whose presence in our consciousness may be indicated by the lighting up of the bulb. Now each of the persons we know is represented in such a scheme, not by a particular area of the wall set apart for him, but by a system of hidden connections among the bulbs which causes certain combinations of them to be lit up when his characteristic symbol is suggested. If something presses the button corresponding to my friend A, a peculiarly shaped figure appears upon the wall; when that is released and B's button is pressed another figure appears, including perhaps many of the same lights, yet unique as a whole though not in

131

its parts; and so on with as many people as you please. It should also be considered that we usually think of a person in relation to some particular social situation, and that those phases of him that bear on this situation are the only ones vividly conceived. To recall some one is commonly to imagine how this or that idea would strike him, what he would say or do in our place, and so on. Accordingly, only some part, some appropriate and characteristic part, of the whole figure that might be lighted up in connection with a man's symbol, is actually illuminated.

To introduce the self into this illustration we might say that the lights near the centre of the wall were of a particular color—say red—which faded, not too abruptly, into white toward the edges. This red would represent self-feeling, and other persons would be more or less colored by it according as they were or were not intimately identified with our cherished activities. In a mother's mind, for instance, her child would lie altogether in the inmost and reddest area. Thus the same sentiment may belong to the self and to several other persons at the same time. If a man and his family are suffering from his being thrown out of work, his apprehension and resentment will be part of his idea of each member of his family, as well as part of his self-idea and of the idea of people whom he thinks to blame.

I trust it will be plain that there is nothing fantastic, unreal, or impractical about this way of conceiving people, that is by observing them as facts of the imagination. On the contrary, the fantastic, unreal, and practically pernicious way is the ordinary and traditional one of speculating upon them as shadowy bodies, without any real observation of them as mental facts. It is the man as imagined that we love or hate, imitate, or avoid, that helps or harms us, that moulds our wills and our careers. What is it that makes a person real to us; is it material contact or contact in the imagination? Suppose, for instance, that on suddenly turning a corner I collide with one coming from the opposite direction: I receive a slight bruise, have the breath knocked out of me, exchange conventional apologies, and immediately forget the incident. It takes no intimate hold upon me, means nothing except a slight and temporary disturbance in the animal processes. Now suppose, on the other hand, that I take up Froude's Cæsar, and presently find myself, under the guidance of that skilful writer, imagining a hero whose body long ago turned to clay. He is alive in my thought: there is perhaps some notion of his visible presence, and along with this the awakening of sentiments of audacity, magnanimity, and the like, that glow with intense life, consume my energy, make me resolve to be like Cæsar in some respect, and cause me to see right and wrong and other great questions as I conceive he would have seen them. Very possibly he keeps me awake after I go to bed—every boy has lain awake thinking of book people. My whole after life will be considerably affected by this experience, and yet this is a contact that takes place only in the imagination. Even as regards the physical organism it is immeasurably

133

more important, as a rule, than the material collision. A blow in the face, if accidental and so not disturbing to the imagination, affects the nerves, the heart, and the digestion very little, but an injurious word or look may cause sleepless nights, dyspepsia, or palpitation. It is, then, the personal idea, the man in the imagination, the real man of power and fruits, that we need primarily to consider, and he appears to be somewhat different from the rather conventional and material man of traditionary social philosophy.

According to this view of the matter society is simply the collective aspect of personal thought. Each man's imagination, regarded as a mass of personal impressions worked up into a living, growing whole, is a special phase of society; and Mind or Imagination as a whole, that is human thought considered in the largest way as having a growth and organization extending throughout the ages, is the *locus* of society in the widest possible sense.

It may be objected that society in this sense has no definite limits, but seems to include the whole range of experience. That is to say, the mind is all one growth, and we cannot draw any distinct line between personal thought and other thought. There is probably no such thing as an idea that is wholly independent of minds other than that in which it exists; through heredity, if not through communication, all is connected with the general life, and so in some sense social. What are spoken of above as personal ideas are merely those in which the connection with other persons is most direct and apparent.

This objection, however, applies to any way of defining society, and those who take the material standpoint are obliged to consider whether houses, factories, domestic animals, tilled land, and so on are not really parts of the social order. The truth, of course, is that all life hangs together in such a manner that any attempt to delimit a part of it is artificial. Society is rather a phase of life than a thing by itself; it is life regarded from the point of view of personal intercourse. And personal intercourse may be considered either in its primary aspects, such as are treated in this book, or in secondary aspects, such as groups, institutions, or processes. Sociology, I suppose, is the science of these things.

CHAPTER IV

SYMPATHY OR UNDERSTANDING AS AN ASPECT OF SOCIETY

THE MEANING OF SYMPATHY AS HERE USED—ITS RELATION TO
THOUGHT, SENTIMENT, AND SOCIAL EXPERIENCE—THE RANGE
OF SYMPATHY IS A MEASURE OF PERSONALITY, *e. g.*, OF POWER,
OF MORAL RANK, AND OF SANITY—A MAN'S SYMPATHIES RE-
FLECT THE STATE OF THE SOCIAL ORDER—SPECIALIZATION AND
BREADTH—SYMPATHY REFLECTS SOCIAL PROCESS IN THE
MINGLING OF LIKENESS WITH DIFFERENCE—ALSO IN THAT IT
IS A PROCESS OF SELECTION GUIDED BY FEELING—THE MEAN-
ING OF LOVE IN SOCIAL DISCUSSION—LOVE IN RELATION TO
SELF—THE STUDY OF SYMPATHY REVEALS THE VITAL UNITY
OF HUMAN LIFE

THE growth of personal ideas through intercourse, described in the preceding chapter, implies a growing power of sympathy, of entering into and sharing the minds of other persons. To converse with another, through words, looks, or other symbols, means to have more or less understanding or communion with him, to get on common ground and partake of his ideas and sentiments. If one uses sympathy in this connection—and it is perhaps the most available word—one has to bear in mind that it denotes the sharing of any mental state that can be communicated, and has not the special implication of pity or other "tender emotion" that it very commonly carries in ordinary speech.* This emotionally colorless usage

* Sympathy in the sense of compassion is a specific emotion or sentiment, and has nothing necessarily in common with sympathy in the sense of communion. It might be thought, perhaps, that

136

is, however, perfectly legitimate, and is, I think, more common in classical English literature than any other. Thus Shakespeare, who uses sympathy five times, if we may trust the Shakespeare Phrase Book, never means by it the particular emotion of compassion, but either the sharing of a mental state, as when he speaks of "sympathy in choice," or mere resemblance, as when Iago mentions the lack of "sympathy in years, manners, and beauties" between Othello and

compassion was one form of the sharing of feeling; but this appears not to be the case. The sharing of painful feeling may precede and cause compassion, but is not the same with it. When I feel sorry for a man in disgrace, it is, no doubt, in most cases, because I have imaginatively partaken of his humiliation; but my compassion for him is not the thing that is shared, but is something additional, a comment on the shared feeling. I may imagine how a suffering man feels—sympathize with him in that sense—and be moved not to pity but to disgust, contempt, or perhaps admiration. Our feeling makes all sorts of comments on the imagined feeling of others. Moreover it is not essential that there should be any real understanding in order that compassion may be felt. One may compassionate a worm squirming on a hook, or a fish, or even a tree. As between persons pity, while often a helpful and healing emotion, leading to kindly acts, is sometimes indicative of the absence of true sympathy. We all wish to be understood, at least in what we regard as our better aspects, but few of us wish to be pitied except in moments of weakness and discouragement. To accept pity is to confess that one falls below the healthy standard of vigor and self-help. While a real understanding of our deeper thought is rare and precious, pity is usually cheap, many people finding an easy pleasure in indulging it, as one may in the indulgence of grief, resentment, or almost any emotion. It is often felt by the person who is its object as a sort of an insult, a back-handed thrust at self-respect, the unkindest cut of all. For instance, as between richer and poorer classes in a free country a mutually respecting antagonism is much healthier than pity on the one hand and dependence on the other, and is, perhaps, the next best thing to fraternal feeling.

137

Desdemona. This latter sense is also one which must be excluded in our use of the word, since what is here meant is an active process of mental assimilation, not mere likeness.

In this chapter sympathy, in the sense of understanding or personal insight, will be considered chiefly with a view to showing something of its nature as a phase or member of the general life of mankind.

The content of it, the matter understood, is chiefly thought and sentiment, in distinction from mere sensation or crude emotion. I do not venture to say that these latter cannot be shared, but certainly they play a relatively small part in the communicative life. Thus although to get one's finger pinched is a common experience, it is impossible, to me at least, to recall the sensation when another person has his finger pinched. So when we say that we feel sympathy for a person who has a headache, we mean that we pity him, not that we share the headache. There is little true communication of physical pain, or anything of that simple sort. The reason appears to be that as ideas of this kind are due to mere physical contacts, or other simple stimuli, in the first instance, they are and remain detached and isolated in the mind, so that they are unlikely to be recalled except by some sensation of the sort originally associated with them. If they become objects of thought and conversation, as is likely to be the case when they are agreeable, they are by that very process refined into sentiments. Thus when the pleasures of the table are

138

discussed the thing communicated is hardly the sensation of taste but something much subtler, although partly based upon that. Thought and sentiment are from the first parts or aspects of highly complex and imaginative personal ideas, and of course may be reached by anything which recalls any part of those ideas. They are aroused by personal intercourse because in their origin they are connected with personal symbols. The sharing of a sentiment ordinarily comes to pass by our perceiving one of these symbols or traits of expression which has belonged with the sentiment in the past and now brings it back. And likewise with thought: it is communicated by words, and these are freighted with the net result of centuries of intercourse. Both spring from the general life of society and cannot be separated from that life, nor it from them.

It is not to be inferred that we must go through the same visible and tangible experiences as other people before we can sympathize with them. On the contrary, there is only an indirect and uncertain connection between one's sympathies and the obvious events—such as the death of friends, success or failure in business, travels, and the like—that one has gone through. Social experience is a matter of imaginative, not of material, contacts; and there are so many aids to the imagination that little can be judged as to one's experience by the merely external course of his life. An imaginative student of a few people and of books often has many times the range of comprehension that the most varied career can give to a duller mind; and a man of genius, like Shakespeare, may cover almost the whole range of human sentiment in his time, not by miracle, but by a marvellous vigor and refinement of imagination. The idea that seeing life means going from place to place and doing a great variety of obvious things is an illusion natural to dull minds.

One's range of sympathy is a measure of his personality, indicating how much or how little of a man he is. It is in no way a special faculty, but a function of the whole mind to which every special faculty contributes, so that what a person is and what he can understand or enter into through the life of others are very much the same thing. We often hear people described as sympathetic who have little mental power, but are of a sensitive, impressionable, quickly responsive type of mind. The sympathy of such a mind always has some defect corresponding to its lack of character and of constructive force. A strong, deep understanding of other people implies mental energy and stability; it is a work of persistent, cumulative imagination which may be associated with a comparative slowness of direct sensibility. On the other hand, we often see the union of a quick sensitiveness to immediate impressions with an inability to comprehend what has to be reached by reason or constructive imagination.

Sympathy is a requisite to social power. Only in so far as a man understands other people and thus enters into the life around him has he any effective

140

existence; the less he has of this the more he is a mere animal, not truly in contact with human life. And if he is not in contact with it he can of course have no power over it. This is a principle of familiar application, and yet one that is often overlooked, practical men having, perhaps, a better grasp of it than theorists. It is well understood by men of the world that effectiveness depends at least as much upon address, *savoir-faire*, tact, and the like, involving sympathetic insight into the minds of other people, as upon any more particular faculties. There is nothing more practical than social imagination; to lack it is to lack everything. All classes of persons need it—the mechanic, the farmer, and the tradesman, as well as the lawyer, the clergyman, the railway president, the politician, the philanthropist, and the poet. Every year thousands of young men are preferred to other thousands and given positions of more responsibility largely because they are seen to have a power of personal insight which promises efficiency and growth. Without "caliber," which means chiefly a good imagination, there is no getting on much in the world. The strong men of our society, however much we may disapprove of the particular direction in which their sympathy is sometimes developed or the ends their power is made to serve, are very human men, not at all the abnormal creatures they are sometimes asserted to be. I have met a fair number of such men, and they have generally appeared, each in his own way, to be persons of a certain scope and breadth that marked them off from the majority.

141

A person of definite character and purpose who comprehends our way of thought is sure to exert power over us. He cannot altogether be resisted; because, if he understands us, he can make us understand him, through the word, the look, or other symbol, which both of us connect with the common sentiment or idea; and thus by communicating an impulse he can move the will. Sympathetic influence enters into our system of thought as a matter of course, and affects our conduct as surely as water affects the growth of a plant. The kindred spirit can turn on a system of lights, to recur to the image of the last chapter, and so transform the mental illumination. This is the nature of all authority and leadership, as I shall try to explain more fully in another chapter.

Again, sympathy, in the broad sense in which it is here used, underlies also the moral rank of a man and goes to fix our estimate of his justice and goodness. The just, the good, or the right under any name is of course not a thing by itself, but is a finer product wrought up out of the various impulses that life affords, and colored by them. Hence no one can think and act in a way that strikes us as right unless he feels, in great part, the same impulses that we do. If he shares the feelings that seem to us to have the best claims, it naturally follows, if he is a person of stable character, that he does them justice in thought and action. To be upright, public-spirited, patriotic, charitable, generous, and just implies that a man has a broad personality which feels the urgency of sympathetic or imaginative motives that in narrower minds are weak or lacking. He has achieved the higher sentiments, the wider range of personal thought. And so far as we see in his conduct that he feels such motives and that they enter into his decisions, we are likely to call him good. What is it to do good, in the ordinary sense? Is it not to help people to enjoy and to work, to fulfil the healthy and happy tendencies of human nature; to give play to children, education to youth, a career to men, a household to women, and peace to old age? And it is sympathy that makes a man wish and need to do these things. One who is large enough to live the life of the race will feel the impulses of each class as his own, and do what he can to gratify them as naturally as he eats his dinner. The idea that goodness is something apart from ordinary human nature is pernicious; it is only an ampler expression of that nature.

On the other hand, all badness, injustice, or wrong is, in one of its aspects, a lack of sympathy. If a man's action is injurious to interests which other men value, and so impresses them as wrong, it must be because, at the moment of action, he does not feel those interests as they do. Accordingly the wrong-doer is either a person whose sympathies do not embrace the claims he wrongs, or one who lacks sufficient stability of character to express his sympathies in action. A liar, for instance, is either one who does not feel strongly the dishonor, injustice, and confusion of lying, or one who, feeling them at times, does not retain the feeling in decisive moments. And so a brutal person may be such either in a dull or chronic way, which

143

does not know the gentler sentiments at any time, or in a sudden and passionate way which perhaps alternates with kindness.

Much the same may be said regarding mental health in general; its presence or absence may always be expressed in terms of sympathy. The test of sanity which every one instinctively applies is that of a certain tact or feeling of the social situation, which we expect of all right-minded people and which flows from sympathetic contact with other minds. One whose words and bearing give the impression that he stands apart and lacks intuition of what others are thinking is judged as more or less absent-minded, queer, dull, or even insane or imbecile, according to the character and permanence of the phenomenon. The essence of insanity, from the social point of view (and, it would seem, the only final test of it) is a confirmed lack of touch with other minds in matters upon which men in general are agreed; and imbecility might be defined as a general failure to compass the more complex sympathies.

A man's sympathies as a whole reflect the social order in which he lives, or rather they are a particular phase of it. Every group of which he is really a member, in which he has any vital share, must live in his sympathy; so that his mind is a microcosm of so much of society as he truly belongs to. Every social phenomenon, we need to remember, is simply a collective view of what we find distributively in particular persons—public opinion is a phase of the judgments of individuals; traditions and institutions live in the thought of particular men, social standards of right do not exist apart from private consciences, and so on. Accordingly, so far as a man has any vital part in the life of a time or a country, that life is imaged in those personal ideas or sympathies which are the impress of his intercourse.

So, whatever is peculiar to our own time implies a corresponding peculiarity in the sympathetic life of each one of us. Thus the age, at least in the more intellectually active parts of life, is strenuous, characterized by the multiplication of points of personal contact through enlarged and accelerated communication. The mental aspect of this is a more rapid and multitudinous flow of personal images, sentiments, and impulses. Accordingly there prevails among us an animation of thought that tends to lift men above sensuality; and there is also possible a choice of relations that opens to each mind a more varied and congenial development than the past afforded. On the other hand, these advantages are not without their cost; the intensity of life often becomes a strain, bringing to many persons an over-excitation which weakens or breaks down character; as we see in the increase of suicide and insanity, and in many similar phenomena. An effect very generally produced upon all except the strongest minds appears to be a sort of superficiality of imagination, a dissipation and attenuation of impulses, which watches the stream of personal imagery go by like a procession, but lacks the power to organize and direct it.

The different degrees of urgency in personal impressions are reflected in the behavior of different classes of people. Every one must have noticed that he finds more real openness of sympathy in the country than in the city—though perhaps there is more of a superficial readiness in the latter—and often more among plain, hand-working people than among professional and business men. The main reason for this, I take it, is that the social imagination is not so hard worked in the one case as in the other. In the mountains of North Carolina the hospitable inhabitants will take in any stranger and invite him to spend the night; but this is hardly possible upon Broadway; and the case is very much the same with the hospitality of the mind. If one sees few people and hears a new thing only once a week, he accumulates a fund of sociability and curiosity very favorable to eager intercourse; but if he is assailed all day and every day by calls upon feeling and thought in excess of his power to respond, he soon finds that he must put up some sort of a barrier. Sensitive people who live where life is insistent take on a sort of social shell whose function is to deal mechanically with ordinary relations and preserve the interior from destruction. They are likely to acquire a conventional smile and conventional phrases for polite intercourse, and a cold mask for curiosity, hostility, or solicitation. In fact, a vigorous power of resistance to the numerous influences that in no way make for the substantial development of his character, but rather tend to distract and demoralize him, is a primary need of one who lives in the more active portions of present society, and the loss of this power by strain is in countless instances the beginning of mental and moral decline. There are times of abounding energy when we exclaim with Schiller,

> "Seid willkommen, Millionen,
> Diesen Kuss der ganzen Welt!"

but it is hardly possible or desirable to maintain this attitude continuously. Universal sympathy is impracticable; what we need is better control and selection, avoiding both the narrowness of our class and the dissipation of promiscuous impressions. It is well for a man to open out and take in as much of life as he can organize into a consistent whole, but to go beyond that is not desirable. In a time of insistent suggestion, like the present, it is fully as important to many of us to know when and how to restrict the impulses of sympathy as it is to avoid narrowness. And this is in no way inconsistent, I think, with that modern democracy of sentiment—also connected with the enlargement of communication—which deprecates the limitation of sympathy by wealth or position. Sympathy must be selective, but the less it is controlled by conventional and external circumstances, such as wealth, and the more it penetrates to the essentials of character, the better. It is this liberation from convention, locality, and chance, I think, that the spirit of the time calls for.

Again, the life of this age is more diversified than life ever was before, and this appears in the mind of

147

the person who shares it as a greater variety of interests and affiliations. A man may be regarded as the point of intersection of an indefinite number of circles representing social groups, having as many arcs passing through him as there are groups. This diversity is connected with the growth of communication, and is another phase of the general enlargement and variegation of life. Because of the greater variety of imaginative contacts it is impossible for a normally open-minded individual not to lead a broader life, in some respects at least, than he would have led in the past. Why is it, for instance, that such ideas as brotherhood and the sentiment of equal right are now so generally extended to all classes of men? Primarily, I think, because all classes have become imaginable, by acquiring power and means of expression. He whom I imagine without antipathy becomes my brother. If we feel that we must give aid to another, it is because that other lives and strives in our imaginations, and so is a part of ourselves. The shallow separation of self and other in common speech obscures the extreme simplicity and naturalness of such feelings. If I come to imagine a person suffering wrong it is not "altruism" that makes me wish to right that wrong, but simple human impulse. He is my life, as really and immediately as anything else. His symbol arouses a sentiment which is no more his than mine.

Thus we lead a wider life; and yet it is also true that there is demanded of us a more distinct specialization than has been required in the past. The complexity of society takes the form of organization, that is, of a growing unity and breadth sustained by the co-operation of differentiated parts, and the man of the age must reflect both the unity and the differentiation; he must be more distinctly a specialist and at the same time more a man of the world.

It seems to many a puzzling question whether, on the whole, the breadth or the specialization is more potent in the action of modern life upon the individual; and by insisting on one aspect or the other it is easy to frame an argument to show either that personal life is becoming richer or that man is getting to be a mere cog in a machine.* I think, however, that these two tendencies are not really opposite but complementary; that it is not a case of breadth *versus* specialization, but, in the long run at least, of breadth *plus* specialization to produce a richer and more various humanity. There are many evils connected with the sudden growth in our day of new social structures, and the subjection of a part of the people to a narrow and deadening routine is one of them, but I think that a healthy specialization has no tendency to bring this about. On the contrary, it is part of a liberating development. The narrow specialist is a bad specialist; and we shall learn that it is a mistake to produce him.

* Much of what is ordinarily said in this connection indicates a confusion of the two ideas of specialization and isolation. These are not only different but, in what they imply, quite opposite and inconsistent. Speciality implies a whole to which the special part has a peculiar relation, while isolation implies that there is no whole.

In an organized life isolation cannot succeed, and a right specialization does not isolate. There is no such separation between special and general knowledge or efficiency as is sometimes supposed. In what does the larger knowledge of particulars consist if not in perceiving their relation to wholes? Has a student less general knowledge because he is familiar with a specialty, or is it not rather true that in so far as he knows one thing well it is a window through which he sees things in general?

There is no way to penetrate the surface of life but by attacking it earnestly at a particular point. If one takes his stand in a field of corn when the young plants have begun to sprout, all the plants in the field will appear to be arranged in a system of rows radiating from his feet; and no matter where he stands the system will appear to centre at that point. It is so with any standpoint in the field of thought and intercourse; to possess it is to have a point of vantage from which the whole may, in a particular manner, be apprehended. It is surely a matter of common observation that a man who knows no one thing intimately has no views worth hearing on things in general. The farmer philosophizes in terms of crops, soils, markets, and implements, the mechanic generalizes his experience of wood and iron, the seaman reaches similar conclusions by his own special road; and if the scholar keeps pace with these it must be by an equally virile productivity. It is a common opinion that breadth of culture is a thing by itself, to be imparted by a particular sort of studies, as, for

instance, the classics, modern languages, and so on.
And there is a certain practical truth in this, owing,
I think, to the fact that certain studies are taught in
a broad or cultural way, while others are not. But
the right theory of the matter is that speciality and
culture are simply aspects of the same healthy mental
growth, and that any study is cultural when taught
in the best way. And so the humblest careers in life
may involve culture and breadth of view, if the in-
cumbent is trained, as he should be, to feel their larger
relations.

A certain sort of writers often assume that it is the
tendency of our modern specialized production to
stunt the mind of the workman by a meaningless routine; but fair opportunities of observation and some
practical acquaintance with machinery and the men
who use it lead me to think that this is not the *general* fact. On the contrary, it is precisely the broad
or cultural traits of general intelligence, self-reliance,
and adaptability that make a man at home and efficient in the midst of modern machinery, and it is
because the American workman has these traits in a
comparatively high degree that he surpasses others
in the most highly specialized production. One who
goes into our shops will find that the intelligent and
adaptive workman is almost always preferred and
gets higher wages; and if there are large numbers
employed upon deadening routine it is partly because
there is unfortunately a part of our population whose
education makes them unfit for anything else. The
type of mechanic which a complex industrial system

requires, and which it is even now, on the whole, evolving, is one that combines an intimate knowledge of particular tools and processes with an intelligent apprehension of the system in which he works. If he lacks the latter he requires constant oversight and so becomes a nuisance. Any one acquainted with such matters knows that "gumption" in workmen is fully as important and much harder to find than mere manual skill; and that those who possess it are usually given superior positions. No doubt there are cases in which intelligence seems to have passed out of the man into the machine, leaving the former a mere "tender"; but I think these are not representative of the change as a whole.* And if we pass from tools to personal relations we shall find that the specialized production so much deprecated is only one phase of a wider general life, a life of comparative freedom, intelligence, education, and opportunity, whose general effect is to enlarge the individual.

The idea of a necessary antagonism between specialization and breadth seems to me an illusion of the same class as that which opposes the individual to the social order. First one aspect and then another

* It may well be thought that the vast development, since this passage was written, of the automatic tool and of the mechanized labor that goes with it, corroborates the views I opposed. I can only say that I believe that the question of the effect of mechanical development upon the worker is still undetermined, that some of the factors now at work—such as the supply of low-grade immigrant labor—are probably transitory, and that it is unlikely that, in the long run, human intelligence can be superfluous.

is looked at in artificial isolation, and it is not perceived that we are beholding but one thing, after all.

Not only does the sympathetic life of a man reflect and imply the *state* of society, but we may also discern in it some inkling of those processes, or principles of change, that we see at large in the general movement of mankind. This is a matter rather beyond the scope of this book; but a few illustrations will show, in a general way, what I mean.

The act of sympathy follows the general law that nature works onward by mixing like and unlike, continuity and change; and so illustrates the same principle that we see in the mingling of heredity with variation, specific resemblance with a differentiation of sexes and of individuals, tradition with discussion, inherited social position with competition, and so on. The likeness in the communicating persons is necessary for comprehension, the difference for interest. We cannot feel strongly toward the totally unlike because it is unimaginable, unrealizable; nor yet toward the wholly like because it is stale—identity must always be dull company. The power of other natures over us lies in a stimulating difference which causes excitement and opens communication, in ideas similar to our own but not identical, in states of mind attainable but not actual. If one has energy he soon wearies of any habitual round of activities and feelings, and his organism, competent to a larger life, suffers pains of excess and want at the same time. The key to the situation is another person who can start a new circle of activities and give the faculties concerned with the old a chance to rest. As Emerson has remarked, we come into society to be played upon. "Friendship," he says again, "requires that rare mean betwixt likeness and unlikeness, that piques each with the presence of power and of consent in the other party. . . . Let him not cease an instant to be himself. The only joy I have in his being mine is that the *not mine* is *mine*. . . . There must be very two before there can be very one." * So Goethe, speaking of Spinoza's attraction for him, remarks that the closest unions rest on contrast; † and it is well known that such a contrast was the basis of his union with Schiller, "whose character and life," he says, "were in complete contrast to my own." ‡ Of course, some sorts of sympathy are especially active in their tendency, like the sympathy of vigorous boys with soldiers and sea-captains; while others are comparatively quiet, like those of old people renewing common memories. It is vivid and elastic where the tendency to growth is strong, reaching out toward the new, the onward, the mysterious; while old persons, the undervitalized and the relaxed or wearied prefer a mild sociability, a comfortable companionship in habit; but even with the latter there must always be a stimulus given, something new suggested or something forgotten recalled, not merely a resemblance of thought but a "resembling difference."

* See his Essay on Friendship.
† Lewes's Life of Goethe, vol. i, p. 282.
‡ Goethe, Biographische Einzelheiten, Jacobi.

And sympathy between man and woman, while it is very much complicated with the special instinct of sex, draws its life from this same mixture of mental likeness and difference. The love of the sexes is above all a need, a need of new life which only the other can unlock.

> "Ich musst' ihn lieben, weil mit ihm mein Leben
> Zum Leben ward, wie ich es nie gekannt," *

says the princess in Tasso; and this appears to express a general principle. Each sex represents to the other a wide range of fresh and vital experience inaccessible alone. Thus the woman usually stands for a richer and more open emotional life, the man for a stronger mental grasp, for control and synthesis. Alfred without Laura feels dull, narrow, and coarse, while Laura on her part feels selfish and hysterical.

Again, sympathy is selective, and thus illustrates a phase of the vital process more talked about at present than any other. To go out into the life of other people takes energy, as every one may see in his own experience; and since energy is limited and requires some special stimulus to evoke it, sympathy becomes active only when our imaginations are reaching out after something we admire or love, or in some way feel the need to understand and make our own. A healthy mind, at least, does not spend much energy on things that do not, in some way, contribute to its de-

* "I had to love him, for with him my life grew to such life as I had never known."—Act 3, sc. 2.

velopment: ideas and persons that lie wholly aside from the direction of its growth, or from which it has absorbed all they have to give, necessarily lack interest for it and so fail to awaken sympathy. An incontinent response to every suggestion offered indicates the breaking down of that power of inhibition or refusal that is our natural defense against the reception of material we cannot digest, and looks toward weakness, instability, and mental decay. So with persons from whom we have nothing to gain, in any sense, whom we do not admire, or love, or fear, or hate, and who do not even interest us as psychological problems or objects of charity, we can have no sympathy except of the most superficial and fleeting sort. I do not overlook the fact that a large class of people suffer a loss of human breadth and power by falling into a narrow and exclusive habit of mind; but at the same time personality is nothing unless it has character, individuality, a distinctive line of growth, and to have this is to have a principle of rejection as well as reception in sympathy.

Social development as a whole, and every act of sympathy as a part of that development, is guided and stimulated in its selective growth by feeling. The outgoing of the mind into the thought of another is always, it would seem, an excursion in search of the congenial; not necessarily of the pleasant, in the ordinary sense, but of that which is fitting or congruous with our actual state of feeling. Thus we would not call Carlyle or the Book of Job pleasant exactly, yet we have moods in which these writers, however lacking in amenity, seem harmonious and attractive.

In fact, our mental life, individual and collective, is truly a never finished work of art, in the sense that we are ever striving, with such energy and materials as we possess, to make of it a harmonious and congenial whole. Each man does this in his own peculiar way, and men in the aggregate do it for human nature at large, each individual contributing to the general endeavor. There is a tendency to judge every new influence, as the painter judges every fresh stroke of his brush, by its relation to the whole achieved or in contemplation, and to call it good or ill according to whether it does or does not make for a congruous development. We do this for the most part instinctively, that is, without deliberate reasoning; something of the whole past, hereditary and social, lives in our present state of mind, and welcomes or rejects the suggestions of the moment. There is always some profound reason for the eagerness that certain influences arouse in us, through which they tap our energy and draw us in their direction, so that we cling to and augment them, growing more and more in their sense. Thus if one likes a book, so that he feels himself inclined to take it down from time to time and linger in the companionship of the author, he may be sure he is getting something that he needs, though it may be long before he discovers what it is. It is quite evident that there must be, in every phase of mental life, an æsthetic impulse to preside over selection.

In common thought and speech sympathy and love are closely connected; and in fact, as most frequently used, they mean somewhat the same thing, the sympathy ordinarily understood being an affectionate sympathy and the love a sympathetic affection. I have already suggested that sympathy is not dependent upon any particular emotion, but may, for instance, be hostile as well as friendly; and it might also be shown that affection, though it stimulates sympathy and so usually goes with it, is not inseparable from it, but may exist in the absence of the mental development which true sympathy requires. Whoever has visited an institution for the care of idiots and imbeciles must have been struck by the exuberance with which the milk of human kindness seems to flow from the hearts of these creatures. If kept quiet and otherwise properly cared for they are mostly as amiable as could be wished, fully as much so, apparently, as persons of normal development; while at the same time they offer little or no resistance to other impulses, such as rage and fear, that sometimes possess them. Kindliness seems to exist primarily as an animal instinct, so deeply rooted that mental degeneracy, which works from the top down, does not destroy it until the mind sinks to the lower grades of idiocy.

However, the excitant of love, in all its finer aspects, is a felt possibility of communication, a dawning of sympathetic renewal. We grow by influence, and where we feel the presence of an influence that is enlarging or uplifting, we begin to love. Love is the normal and usual accompaniment of the healthy expansion of human nature by communion; and in turn is the stimulus to more communion. It seems not to be a special emotion in quite the same way that anger, grief, fear, and the like are, but something more primary and general, the stream, perhaps, of which these and many other sentiments are special channels or eddies.

Love and sympathy, then, are two things which, though distinguishable, are very commonly found together, each being an instigator of the other; what we love we sympathize with, so far as our mental development permits. To be sure, it is also true that when we hate a person, with an intimate, imaginative, human hatred, we enter into his mind, or sympathize—any strong interest will arouse the imagination and create some sort of sympathy—but affection is a more usual stimulus.

Love, in this sense of kindly sympathy, may have all degrees of emotional intensity and of sympathetic penetration, from a sort of passive good-nature, not involving imagination or mental activity of any sort, up to an all-containing human enthusiasm, involving the fullest action of the highest faculties, and bringing with it so strong a conviction of complete good that the best minds have felt and taught that God is love. Thus understood, it is not any specific sort of emotion, at least not that alone, but a general out-flowing of the mind and heart, accompanied by that gladness that the fullest life carries with it. When the apostle John says that God is love, and that every one that loveth knoweth God, he evidently means something more than personal affection, something

159

that knows as well as feels, that takes account of all special aspects of life and is just to all.

Ordinary personal affection does not fill our ideal of right or justice, but encroaches, like all special impulses. It is not at all uncommon to wrong one person out of affection for another. If, for instance, I am able to procure a desirable position for a friend, it may well happen that there is another and a fitter man, whom I do not know or do not care for, from whose point of view my action is an injurious abuse of power. It is evident that good can be identified with no simple emotion, but must be sought in some wider phase of life that embraces all points of view. So far as love approaches this comprehensiveness it tends toward justice, because the claims of all live and are adjusted in the mind of him who has it.

> "Love's hearts are faithful but not fond,
> Bound for the just but not beyond."

Thus love of a large and symmetrical sort, not merely a narrow tenderness, implies justice and right, since a mind that has the breadth and insight to feel this will be sure to work out magnanimous principles of conduct.

It is in some such sense as this, as an expansion of human nature into a wider life, that I can best understand the use of the word love in the writings of certain great teachers, for instance in such passages as the following:

"What is Love, and why is it the chief good, but because it is an overpowering enthusiasm? . . . He who is in love

160

is wise and is becoming wiser, sees newly every time he looks at the object beloved, drawing from it with his eyes and his mind those virtues which it possesses." *

"A great thing is love, ever a great good; which alone makes light all the heavy and bears equally every inequality. For its burden is not a burden, and it makes every bitter sweet and savory. . . . Love would be arisen, not held down by anything base. Love would be free, and alienated from every worldly affection, that its intimate desire may not be hindered, that it may not become entangled through any temporal good fortune, nor fall through any ill. There is nothing sweeter than love, nothing braver, nothing higher, nothing broader, nothing joyfuller, nothing fuller or better in heaven or on earth, since love is born of God, nor can rest save in God above all created things.

"He that loves, flies, runs, and is joyful; is free and not restrained. He gives all for all and has all in all, since he is at rest above all in the one highest good from which every good flows and proceeds. He regards not gifts, but beyond all good things turns to the giver. Love oft knows not the manner, but its heat is more than every manner. Love feels no burden, regards not labors, strives toward more than it attains, argues not of impossibility, since it believes that it may and can all things. Therefore it avails for all things, and fulfils and accomplishes much where one not a lover falls and lies helpless." †

The sense of joy, of freshness, of youth, and of the indifference of circumstances, that comes with love, seems to be connected with its receptive, outgoing nature. It is the fullest life, and when we have it we feel happy because our faculties are richly em-

* Emerson, Address on The Method of Nature.
† De Imitatione Christi, part iii, chap. 5, pars. 3 and 4. Dante, in the Divina Commedia, means by love (*amore*), creative passion in all its forms.

ployed; young because reception is the essence of youth, and indifferent to conditions because we feel by our present experience that welfare is independent of them. It is when we have lost our hold upon this sort of happiness that we begin to be anxious about security and comfort, and to take a distrustful and pessimistic attitude toward the world in general.

In the literature of the feelings we often find that love and self are set over against each other, as by Tennyson when he says:

"Love took up the harp of life and smote on all the chords
    with might;
  Smote the chord of self, that, trembling, passed in music
    out of sight."

Let us consider for a moment whether, or in what sense, this antithesis is a just one.

As regards its relation to self we may, perhaps, distinguish two kinds of love, one of which is mingled with self-feeling and the other is not. The latter is a disinterested, contemplative joy, in feeling which the mind loses all sense of its private existence; while the former is active, purposeful, and appropriative, rejoicing in its object with a sense of being one with it as against the rest of the world.

In so far as one feels the disinterested love, that which has no designs with reference to its object, he has no sense of "I" at all, but simply exists in something to which he feels no bounds. Of this sort, for instance, seem to be the delight in natural beauty, in the landscape and the shining sea, the joy and rest of art—so long as we have no thought of production or criticism—and the admiration of persons regarding whom we have no intentions, either of influence or imitation. It appears to be the final perfection of this unspecialized joy that the Buddhist sages seek in Nirvana. Love of this sort obliterates that idea of separate personality whose life is always unsure and often painful. One who feels it leaves the precarious self; his boat glides out upon a wider stream; he forgets his own deformity, weakness, shame, or failure, or if he thinks of them it is to feel free of them, released from their coil. No matter what you and I may be, if we can comprehend that which is fair and great we may still have it, may transcend ourselves and go out into it. It carries us beyond the sense of all individuality, either our own or others', into the feeling of universal and joyous life. The "I," the specialized self, and the passions involved with it, have a great and necessary part to play, but they afford no continuing city; they are so evidently transient and insecure that the idealizing mind cannot rest in them, and is glad to forget them at times and to go out into a life joyous and without bounds in which thought may be at peace.

But love that plans and strives is always in some degree self-love. That is, self-feeling is correlated with individualized, purposeful thought and action, and so begins to spring up as soon as love lingers upon something, forms intentions, and begins to act. The love of a mother for her child is appropriative, as is apparent from the fact that it is capable of jealousy.

163

Its characteristic is not selflessness, by any means, but the association of self-feeling with the idea of *her* child. It is no more selfless in its nature than the ambitions of a man, and may or may not be morally superior; the idea that it involves self-abnegation seems to spring from the crudely material notion of personality which assumes that other persons are external to the self. And so of all productive, specialized love. I shall say more of the self in the next chapter, but my belief is that it is impossible to cherish and strive for special purposes without having self-feeling about them; without becoming more or less capable of resentment, pride, and fear regarding them. The imaginative and sympathetic aims that are commonly spoken of as self-renunciation are more properly an enlargement of the self, and by no means destroy, though they may transform, the "I." A wholly selfless love is mere contemplation, an escape from conscious speciality, and a dwelling in undifferentiated life. It sees all things as one and makes no effort.

These two sorts of love are properly complementary, one corresponding to production and giving each of us a specialized intensity and effectiveness, while in the other we find enlargement and relief. They are indeed closely bound together and each contributory to the other. The self and the special love that goes with it seem to grow by a sort of crystallization about them of elements from the wider life. The man first loves the woman as something transcendent, divine, or universal, which he dares not think of appropriating; but presently he begins to claim her as *his* in antithesis to the rest of the world, and to have hopes, fears, and resentments regarding her; the painter loves beauty contemplatively, and then tries to paint it; the poet delights in his visions, and then tries to tell them, and so on. It is necessary to our growth that we should be capable of delighting in that upon which we have no designs, because we draw our fresh materials from this region. The sort of self-love that is harmful is one that has hardened about a particular object and ceased to expand. On the other hand, it seems that the power to enter into universal life depends upon a healthy development of the special self. "Willst du in's Unendliche schreiten," said Goethe, "geh nur im Endlichen nach allen Seiten." That which we have achieved by special, selfful endeavor becomes a basis of inference and sympathy, which gives a wider reach to our disinterested contemplation. While the artist is trying to paint he forfeits the pure joy of contemplation; he is strenuous, anxious, vain, or mortified; but when he ceases trying he will be capable, just because of this experience, of a fuller appreciation of beauty in general than he was before. And so of personal affection; the winning of wife, home, and children involves constant self-assertion, but it multiplies the power of sympathy. We cannot, then, exalt one of these over the other; what would seem desirable is that the self, without losing its special purpose and vigor, should keep expanding, so that it should tend to include more and more of what is largest and highest in the general life.

It appears, then, that sympathy, in the sense of mental sharing or communication, is by no means a simple matter, but that so much enters into it as to suggest that by the time we thoroughly understood one sympathetic experience we should be in a way to understand the social order itself. An act of communication is a particular aspect of the whole which we call society, and necessarily reflects that of which it is a characteristic part. To come into touch with a friend, a leader, an antagonist, or a book, is an act of sympathy; but it is precisely in the totality of such acts that society consists. Even the most complex and rigid institutions may be looked upon as consisting of innumerable personal influences or acts of sympathy, organized, in the case of institutions, into a definite and continuing whole by means of some system of permanent symbols, such as laws, constitutions, sacred writings, and the like, in which personal influences are preserved. And, turning the matter around, we may look upon every act of sympathy as a particular expression of the history, institutions, and tendencies of the society in which it takes place. Every influence which you or I can receive or impart will be characteristic of the race, the country, the epoch, in which our personalities have grown up.

The main thing here is to bring out the *vital* unity of every phase of personal life, from the simplest interchange of a friendly word to the polity of nations or of hierarchies. The common idea of the matter is crudely mechanical—that there are persons as there are bricks, and societies as there are walls. A person, or some trait of personality or of intercourse, is held to be the element of society, and the latter is formed by the aggregation of these elements. Now there is no such thing as an element of society in the sense that a brick is the element of a wall; this is a mechanical conception quite inapplicable to vital phenomena. I should say that living wholes have aspects but not elements.

In the Capitoline Museum at Rome is a famous statue of Venus, which, like many works of this kind, is ingeniously mounted upon a pivot, so that one who wishes to study it can place it at any angle with reference to the light that he may prefer. Thus he may get an indefinite number of views, but in every view what he really observes, so far as he observes intelligently, is the whole statue in a particular aspect. Even if he fixes his attention upon the foot, or the great toe, he sees this part, if he sees it rightly, in relation to the work as a whole. And it seems to me that the study of human life is analogous in character. It is expedient to divide it into manageable parts in some way; but this division can only be a matter of aspects, not of elements. The various chapters of this book, for instance, do not deal with separable subjects, but merely with phases of a common subject, and the same is true of any work in psychology, history, or biology.

CHAPTER V

THE SOCIAL SELF—1. THE MEANING OF "I"

THE "EMPIRICAL SELF"—"I" AS A STATE OF FEELING—ITS RE-
LATION TO THE BODY—AS A SENSE OF POWER OR CAUSATION—
AS A SENSE OF SPECIALITY OR DIFFERENTIATION IN A SOCIAL
LIFE—WHEN THE BODY IS "I"; INANIMATE OBJECTS—THE RE-
FLECTED OR LOOKING-GLASS "I"—"I" IS ROOTED IN THE PAST
AND VARIES WITH SOCIAL CONDITIONS—ITS RELATION TO HABIT
—TO DISINTERESTED LOVE—HOW CHILDREN LEARN THE
MEANING OF "I"—THE SPECULATIVE OR METAPHYSICAL "I"
IN CHILDREN—THE LOOKING-GLASS "I" IN CHILDREN—THE
SAME IN ADOLESCENCE—"I" IN RELATION TO SEX—SIMPLICITY
AND AFFECTATION—SOCIAL SELF-FEELING IS UNIVERSAL—THE
GROUP SELF OR "WE"

IT is well to say at the outset that by the word
"self" in this discussion is meant simply that which
is designated in common speech by the pronouns of
the first person singular, "I," "me," "my," "mine,"
and "myself." "Self" and "ego" are used by metaphysicians and moralists in many other senses, more
or less remote from the "I" of daily speech and thought,
and with these I wish to have as little to do as possible.
What is here discussed is what psychologists call the
empirical self, the self that can be apprehended or
verified by ordinary observation. I qualify it by the
word social not as implying the existence of a self
that is not social—for I think that the "I" of common
language always has more or less distinct reference
to other people as well as the speaker—but because

168

I wish to emphasize and dwell upon the social aspect of it.

Although the topic of the self is regarded as an abstruse one this abstruseness belongs chiefly, perhaps, to the metaphysical discussion of the "pure ego"—whatever that may be—while the empirical self should not be very much more difficult to get hold of than other facts of the mind. At any rate, it may be assumed that the pronouns of the first person have a substantial, important, and not very recondite meaning, otherwise they would not be in constant and intelligible use by simple people and young children the world over. And since they have such a meaning why should it not be observed and reflected upon like any other matter of fact? As to the underlying mystery, it is no doubt real, important, and a very fit subject of discussion by those who are competent, but I do not see that it is a *peculiar* mystery. I mean that it seems to be simply a phase of the general mystery of life, not pertaining to "I" more than to any other personal or social fact; so that here as elsewhere those who are not attempting to penetrate the mystery may simply ignore it. If this is a just view of the matter, "I" is merely a fact like any other.

The distinctive thing in the idea for which the pronouns of the first person are names is apparently a characteristic kind of feeling which may be called the my-feeling or sense of appropriation. Almost any sort of ideas may be associated with this feeling, and so come to be named "I" or "mine," but the feeling, and that alone it would seem, is the determining factor in the matter. As Professor James says in his admirable discussion of the self, the words "me" and "self" designate "all the things which have the power to produce in a stream of consciousness excitement of a certain peculiar sort." * This view is very fully set forth by Professor Hiram M. Stanley, whose work, "The Evolutionary Psychology of Feeling," has an extremely suggestive chapter on self-feeling.

I do not mean that the feeling aspect of the self is necessarily more important than any other, but that it is the immediate and decisive sign and proof of what "I" is; there is no appeal from it; if we go behind it it must be to study its history and conditions, not to question its authority. But, of course, this study of history and conditions may be quite as profitable as the direct contemplation of self-feeling. What I would wish to do is to present each aspect in its proper light.

The emotion or feeling of self may be regarded as instinctive, and was doubtless evolved in connection with

* "*The words* ME, *then, and* SELF, *so far as they arouse feeling and connote emotional worth, are* OBJECTIVE *designations meaning* ALL THE THINGS *which have the power to produce in a stream of consciousness excitement of a certain peculiar sort.*" Psychology, i., p. 319. A little earlier he says: "*In its widest possible sense,* however, *a man's self is the sum total of all he* CAN *call his,* not only his body and his psychic powers, but his clothes and his house, his wife and children, his ancestors and friends, his reputation and works, his lands and horses and yacht and bank-account. All these things give him the same emotions." *Idem,* p. 291.

So Wundt says of "Ich": "Es ist ein *Gefühl,* nicht eine Vorstellung, wie es häufig genannt wird." Grundriss der Psychologie, 4 Auflage, S. 265.

THE MEANING OF " I "

its important function in stimulating and unifying the special activities of individuals.* It is thus very profoundly rooted in the history of the human race and apparently indispensable to any plan of life at all similar to ours. It seems to exist in a vague though vigorous form at the birth of each individual, and, like other instinctive ideas or germs of ideas, to be defined and developed by experience, becoming associated, or rather incorporated, with muscular, visual, and other sensations; with perceptions, apperceptions, and conceptions of every degree of complexity and of infinite variety of content; and, especially, with personal ideas. Meantime the feeling itself does not remain unaltered, but undergoes differentiation and refinement just as does any other sort of crude innate feeling. Thus, while retaining under every phase its characteristic tone or flavor, it breaks up into innumerable self-sentiments. And concrete self-feeling, as it exists in mature persons, is a whole made up of these various sentiments, along with a good deal of primitive emotion not thus broken up. It partakes fully of the general development of the mind, but never loses that peculiar gusto of appropriation that causes us to name a thought with a first-personal pronoun. The other contents of the self-idea are of little use, apparently, in defining it, because they are so extremely various. It would be no more futile, it seems to me, to attempt to define fear by enumerating the things

* It is, perhaps, to be thought of as a more general instinct, of which anger, etc., are differentiated forms, rather than as standing by itself.

that people are afraid of, than to attempt to define "I" by enumerating the objects with which the word is associated. Very much as fear means primarily a state of feeling, or its expression, and not darkness, fire, lions, snakes, or other things that excite it, so "I" means primarily self-feeling, or its expression, and not body, clothes, treasures, ambition, honors, and the like, with which this feeling may be connected. In either case it is possible and useful to go behind the feeling and inquire what ideas arouse it and why they do so, but this is in a sense a secondary investigation.

Since "I" is known to our experience primarily as a feeling, or as a feeling-ingredient in our ideas, it cannot be described or defined without suggesting that feeling. We are sometimes likely to fall into a formal and empty way of talking regarding questions of emotion, by attempting to define that which is in its nature primary and indefinable. A formal definition of self-feeling, or indeed of any sort of feeling, must be as hollow as a formal definition of the taste of salt, or the color red; we can expect to know what it is only by experiencing it. There can be no final test of the self except the way we feel; it is that toward which we have the "my" attitude. But as this feeling is quite as familiar to us and as easy to recall as the taste of salt or the color red, there should be no difficulty in understanding what is meant by it. One need only imagine some attack on his "me," say ridicule of his dress or an attempt to take away his property or his child, or his good name by slander,

172

and self-feeling immediately appears. Indeed, he need only pronounce, with strong emphasis, one of the self-words, like "I" or "my," and self-feeling will be recalled by association. Another good way is to enter by sympathy into some self-assertive state of mind depicted in literature; as, for instance, into that of Coriolanus when, having been sneered at as a "boy of tears," he cries out:

> "Boy! . . .
> If you have writ your annals true, 'tis there,
> That, like an eagle in a dovecote, I
> Fluttered your Volscians in Corioli;
> Alone I did it.—Boy!"

Here is a self indeed, which no one can fail to feel, though he might be unable to describe it. What a ferocious scream of the outraged ego is that "I" at the end of the second line!

So much is written on this topic that ignores self-feeling and thus deprives "self" of all vivid and palpable meaning, that I feel it permissible to add a few more passages in which this feeling is forcibly expressed. Thus in Lowell's poem, "A Glance Behind the Curtain," Cromwell says:

> "I, perchance,
> Am one raised up by the Almighty arm
> To witness some great truth to all the world."

And his Columbus, on the bow of his vessel, soliloquizes:

> "Here am I, with no friend but the sad sea,
> The beating heart of this great enterprise,
> Which, without me, would stiffen in swift death."

And so the "I am the way" which we read in the New Testament is surely the expression of a sentiment not very different from these. In the following we have a more plaintive sentiment of self:

Philoctetes.—And know'st thou not, O boy, whom thou dost
             see?
Neoptolemus.—How can I know a man I ne'er beheld?
Philoctetes.—And didst thou never hear my name, nor fame
             Of these my ills, in which I pined away?
Neoptolemus.—Know that I nothing know of what thou
             ask'st.
Philoctetes.—O crushed with many woes, and of the Gods
             Hated am I, of whom, in this my woe,
             No rumor travelled homeward, nor went forth
             Through any clime of Hellas.*

We all have thoughts of the same sort as these, and yet it is possible to talk so coldly or mystically about the self that one begins to forget that there is, really, any such thing.

But perhaps the best way to realize the naïve meaning of "I" is to listen to the talk of children playing together, especially if they do not agree very well. They use the first person with none of the conventional self-repression of their elders, but with much emphasis and variety of inflection, so that its emotional animus is unmistakable.

Self-feeling of a reflective and agreeable sort, an appropriative zest of contemplation, is strongly suggested by the word "gloating." To gloat, in this sense, is as much as to think "mine, mine, mine,"

* Plumptre's Sophocles, p. 352.

with a pleasant warmth of feeling. Thus a boy gloats over something he has made with his scroll-saw, over the bird he has brought down with his gun, or over his collection of stamps or eggs; a girl gloats over her new clothes, and over the approving words or looks of others; a farmer over his fields and his stock; a business man over his trade and his bank-account; a mother over her child; the poet over a successful quatrain; the self-righteous man over the state of his soul; and in like manner every one gloats over the prosperity of any cherished idea.

I would not be understood as saying that self-feeling is clearly marked off in experience from other kinds of feeling; but it is, perhaps, as definite in this regard as anger, fear, grief, and the like. To quote Professor James, "The emotions themselves of self-satisfaction and abasement are of a unique sort, each as worthy to be classed as a primitive emotional species as are, for example, rage or pain." * It is true here, as wherever mental facts are distinguished, that there are no fences, but that one thing merges by degrees into another. Yet if "I" did not denote an idea much the same in all minds and fairly distinguishable from other ideas, it could not be used freely and universally as a means of communication.

As many people have the impression that the verifiable self, the object that we name with "I," is usually the material body, it may be well to say that this impression is an illusion, easily dispelled by any one

* Psychology, i, p. 307.

who will undertake a simple examination of facts. It is true that when we philosophize a little about "I" and look around for a tangible object to which to attach it, we soon fix upon the material body as the most available *locus;* but when we use the word naïvely, as in ordinary speech, it is not very common to think of the body in connection with it; not nearly so common as it is to think of other things. There is no difficulty in testing this statement, since the word "I" is one of the commonest in conversation and literature, so that nothing is more practicable than to study its meaning at any length that may be desired. One need only listen to ordinary speech until the word has occurred, say, a hundred times, noting its connections, or observe its use in a similar number of cases by the characters in a novel. Ordinarily it will be found that in not more than ten cases in a hundred does "I" have reference to the body of the person speaking. It refers chiefly to opinions, purposes, desires, claims, and the like, concerning matters that involve no thought of the body. *I* think or feel so and so; *I* wish or intend so and so; *I* want this or that; are typical uses, the self-feeling being associated with the view, purpose, or object mentioned. It should also be remembered that "my" and "mine" are as much the names of the self as "I," and these, of course, commonly refer to miscellaneous possessions.

I had the curiosity to attempt a rough classification of the first hundred "I's" and "me's" in Hamlet, with the following results. The pronoun was used in

176

connection with perception, as "I hear," "I see," fourteen times; with thought, sentiment, intention, etc., thirty-two times; with wish, as "I pray you," six times; as speaking—"I'll speak to it"—sixteen times; as spoken to, twelve times; in connection with action, involving perhaps some vague notion of the body, as "I came to Denmark," nine times; vague or doubtful, ten times; as equivalent to bodily appearance—"No more like my father than I to Hercules"— once. Some of the classifications are arbitrary, and another observer would doubtless get a different result; but he could not fail, I think, to conclude that Shakespeare's characters are seldom thinking of their bodies when they say "I" or "me." And in this respect they appear to be representative of mankind in general.

As already suggested, instinctive self-feeling is doubtless connected in evolution with its important function in stimulating and unifying the special activities of individuals. It appears to be associated chiefly with ideas of the exercise of power, of being a cause, ideas that emphasize the antithesis between the mind and the rest of the world. The first definite thoughts that a child associates with self-feeling are probably those of his earliest endeavors to control visible objects— his limbs, his playthings, his bottle, and the like. Then he attempts to control the actions of the persons about him, and so his circle of power and of self-feeling widens without interruption to the most complex objects of mature ambition. Although he does not say "I" or "my" during the first year or two, yet he expresses so clearly by his actions the feeling that adults associate with these words that we cannot deny him a self even in the first weeks.

The correlation of self-feeling with purposeful activity is easily seen by observing the course of any productive enterprise. If a boy sets about making a boat, and has any success, his interest in the matter waxes, he gloats over it, the keel and stem are dear to his heart, and its ribs are more to him than those of his own frame. He is eager to call in his friends and acquaintances, saying to them, "See what I am doing! Is it not remarkable?" feeling elated when it is praised, and resentful or humiliated when fault is found with it. But so soon as he finishes it and turns to something else, his self-feeling begins to fade away from it, and in a few weeks at most he will have become comparatively indifferent. We all know that much the same course of feeling accompanies the achievements of adults. It is impossible to produce a picture, a poem, an essay, a difficult bit of masonry, or any other work of art or craft, without having self-feeling regarding it, amounting usually to considerable excitement and desire for some sort of appreciation; but this rapidly diminishes with the activity itself, and often lapses into indifference after it ceases.

It may perhaps be objected that the sense of self, instead of being limited to times of activity and definite purpose, is often most conspicuous when the mind is unoccupied or undecided, and that the idle and ineffectual are commonly the most sensitive in their self-esteem. This, however, may be regarded as an instance of the principle that all instincts are likely to assume troublesome forms when denied wholesome expression. The need to exert power, when thwarted in the open fields of life, is the more likely to assert itself in trifles.

The social self is simply any idea, or system of ideas, drawn from the communicative life, that the mind cherishes as its own. Self-feeling has its chief scope *within* the general life, not outside of it; the special endeavor or tendency of which it is the emotional aspect finds its principal field of exercise in a world of personal forces, reflected in the mind by a world of personal impressions.

As connected with the thought of other persons the self idea is always a consciousness of the peculiar or differentiated aspect of one's life, because that is the aspect that has to be sustained by purpose and endeavor, and its more aggressive forms tend to attach themselves to whatever one finds to be at once congenial to one's own tendencies and at variance with those of others with whom one is in mental contact. It is here that they are most needed to serve their function of stimulating characteristic activity, of fostering those personal variations which the general plan of life seems to require. Heaven, says Shakespeare, doth divide

> "The state of man in divers functions,
> Setting endeavor in continual motion,"

179

and self-feeling is one of the means by which this diversity is achieved.

Agreeably to this view we find that the aggressive self manifests itself most conspicuously in an appropriativeness of objects of common desire, corresponding to the individual's need of power over such objects to secure his own peculiar development, and to the danger of opposition from others who also need them. And this extends from material objects to lay hold, in the same spirit, of the attentions and affections of other people, of all sorts of plans and ambitions, including the noblest special purposes the mind can entertain, and indeed of any conceivable idea which may come to seem a part of one's life and in need of assertion against some one else. The attempt to limit the word self and its derivatives to the lower aims of personality is quite arbitrary; at variance with common sense as expressed by the emphatic use of "I" in connection with the sense of duty and other high motives, and unphilosophical as ignoring the function of the self as the organ of specialized endeavor of higher as well as lower kinds.

That the "I" of common speech has a meaning which includes some sort of reference to other persons is involved in the very fact that the word and the ideas it stands for are phenomena of language and the communicative life. It is doubtful whether it is possible to use language at all without thinking more or less distinctly of some one else, and certainly the things to which we give names and which have a large place in reflective thought are almost always those

180

which are impressed upon us by our contact with other people. Where there is no communication there can be no nomenclature and no developed thought. What we call "me," "mine," or "myself" is, then, not something separate from the general life, but the most interesting part of it, a part whose interest arises from the very fact that it is both general and individual. That is, we care for it just because it is that phase of the mind that is living and striving in the common life, trying to impress itself upon the minds of others. "I" is a militant social tendency, working to hold and enlarge its place in the general current of tendencies. So far as it can it waxes, as all life does. To think of it as apart from society is a palpable absurdity of which no one could be guilty who really *saw* it as a fact of life.

> "Der Mensch erkennt sich nur im Menschen, nur
> Das Leben lehret jedem was er sei." *

If a thing has no relation to others of which one is conscious he is unlikely to think of it at all, and if he does think of it he cannot, it seems to me, regard it as emphatically *his*. The appropriative sense is always the shadow, as it were, of the common life, and when we have it we have a sense of the latter in connection with it. Thus, if we think of a secluded part of the woods as "ours," it is because we think, also, that others do not go there. As regards the body I doubt if we have a vivid my-feeling about any

* "Only in man does man know himself; life alone teaches each one what he is."—Goethe, Tasso, act 2, sc. 3.

part of it which is not thought of, however vaguely, as having some actual or possible reference to some one else. Intense self-consciousness regarding it arises along with instincts or experiences which connect it with the thought of others. Internal organs, like the liver, are not thought of as peculiarly ours unless we are trying to communicate something regarding them, as, for instance, when they are giving us trouble and we are trying to get sympathy.

"I," then, is not all of the mind, but a peculiarly central, vigorous, and well-knit portion of it, not separate from the rest but gradually merging into it, and yet having a certain practical distinctness, so that a man generally shows clearly enough by his language and behavior what his "I" is as distinguished from thoughts he does not appropriate. It may be thought of, as already suggested, under the analogy of a central colored area on a lighted wall. It might also, and perhaps more justly, be compared to the nucleus of a living cell, not altogether separate from the surrounding matter, out of which indeed it is formed, but more active and definitely organized.

The reference to other persons involved in the sense of self may be distinct and particular, as when a boy is ashamed to have his mother catch him at something she has forbidden, or it may be vague and general, as when one is ashamed to do something which only his conscience, expressing his sense of social responsibility, detects and disapproves; but it is always there. There is no sense of "I," as in pride or shame, without its correlative sense of you, or he, or they.

182

Even the miser gloating over his hidden gold can feel the "mine" only as he is aware of the world of men over whom he has secret power; and the case is very similar with all kinds of hid treasure. Many painters, sculptors, and writers have loved to withhold their work from the world, fondling it in seclusion until they were quite done with it; but the delight in this, as in all secrets, depends upon a sense of the value of what is concealed.

I remarked above that we think of the body as "I" when it comes to have social function or significance, as when we say "I am looking well to-day," or "I am taller than you are." We bring it into the social world, for the time being, and for that reason put our self-consciousness into it. Now it is curious, though natural, that in precisely the same way we may call any inanimate object "I" with which we are identifying our will and purpose. This is notable in games, like golf or croquet, where the ball is the embodiment of the player's fortunes. You will hear a man say, "I am in the long grass down by the third tee," or "I am in position for the middle arch." So a boy flying a kite will say "I am higher than you," or one shooting at a mark will declare that he is just below the bullseye.

In a very large and interesting class of cases the social reference takes the form of a somewhat definite imagination of how one's self—that is any idea he appropriates—appears in a particular mind, and the kind of self-feeling one has is determined by the attitude toward this attributed to that other mind. A social self of this sort might be called the reflected or looking-glass self:

> "Each to each a looking-glass
> Reflects the other that doth pass."

As we see our face, figure, and dress in the glass, and are interested in them because they are ours, and pleased or otherwise with them according as they do or do not answer to what we should like them to be; so in imagination we perceive in another's mind some thought of our appearance, manners, aims, deeds, character, friends, and so on, and are variously affected by it.

A self-idea of this sort seems to have three principal elements: the imagination of our appearance to the other person; the imagination of his judgment of that appearance, and some sort of self-feeling, such as pride or mortification. The comparision with a looking-glass hardly suggests the second element, the imagined judgment, which is quite essential. The thing that moves us to pride or shame is not the mere mechanical reflection of ourselves, but an imputed sentiment, the imagined effect of this reflection upon another's mind. This is evident from the fact that the character and weight of that other, in whose mind we see ourselves, makes all the difference with our feeling. We are ashamed to seem evasive in the presence of a straightforward man, cowardly in the presence of a brave one, gross in the eyes of a refined one, and so on. We always imagine, and in imagining

184

share, the judgments of the other mind. A man will boast to one person of an action—say some sharp transaction in trade—which he would be ashamed to own to another.

It should be evident that the ideas that are associated with self-feeling and form the intellectual content of the self cannot be covered by any simple description, as by saying that the body has such a part in it, friends such a part, plans so much, etc., but will vary indefinitely with particular temperaments and environments. The tendency of the self, like every aspect of personality, is expressive of far-reaching hereditary and social factors, and is not to be understood or predicted except in connection with the general life. Although special, it is in no way separate—speciality and separateness are not only different but contradictory, since the former implies connection with a whole. The object of self-feeling is affected by the general course of history, by the particular development of nations, classes, and professions, and other conditions of this sort.

The truth of this is perhaps most decisively shown in the fact that even those ideas that are most generally associated or colored with the "my" feeling, such as one's idea of his visible person, of his name, his family, his intimate friends, his property, and so on, are not universally so associated, but may be separated from the self by peculiar social conditions. Thus the ascetics, who have played so large a part in the history of Christianity and of other religions and

philosophies, endeavored not without success to divorce their appropriative thought from all material
surroundings, and especially from their physical persons, which they sought to look upon as accidental
and degrading circumstances of the soul's earthly
sojourn. In thus estranging themselves from their
bodies, from property and comfort, from domestic
affections—whether of wife or child, mother, brother
or sister—and from other common objects of ambition, they certainly gave a singular direction to self-
feeling, but they did not destroy it: there can be no
doubt that the instinct, which seems imperishable
so long as mental vigor endures, found other ideas to
which to attach itself; and the strange and uncouth
forms which ambition took in those centuries when
the solitary, filthy, idle, and sense-tormenting an-
chorite was a widely accepted ideal of human life,
are a matter of instructive study and reflection. Even
in the highest exponents of the ascetic ideal, like St.
Jerome, it is easy to see that the discipline, far from
effacing the self, only concentrated its energy in lofty
and unusual channels. The self-idea may be that of
some great moral reform, of a religious creed, of the
destiny of one's soul after death, or even a cherished
conception of the deity. Thus devout writers, like
George Herbert and Thomas à Kempis, often address
my God, not at all conventionally as I conceive the
matter, but with an intimate sense of appropriation.
And it has been observed that the demand for the continued and separate existence of the individual soul
after death is an expression of self-feeling, as by J. A.

Symonds, who thinks that it is connected with the intense egotism and personality of the European races, and asserts that the millions of Buddhism shrink from it with horror.*

Habit and familiarity are not of themselves sufficient to cause an idea to be appropriated into the self. Many habits and familiar objects that have been forced upon us by circumstances rather than chosen for their congeniality remain external and possibly repulsive to the self; and, on the other hand, a novel but very congenial element in experience, like the idea of a new toy, or, if you please, Romeo's idea of Juliet, is often appropriated almost immediately, and becomes, for the time at least, the very heart of the self. Habit has the same fixing and consolidating action in the growth of the self that it has elsewhere, but is not its distinctive characteristic.

As suggested in the previous chapter, self-feeling may be regarded as in a sense the antithesis, or better perhaps, the complement, of that disinterested and contemplative love that tends to obliterate the sense of a divergent individuality. Love of this sort has no sense of bounds, but is what we feel when we are expanding and assimilating new and indeterminate experience, while self-feeling accompanies the appropriating, delimiting, and defending of a certain part of experience; the one impels us to receive life, the other to individuate it. The self, from this point

* John Addington Symonds, by H. F. Brown, vol. ii, p. 120.

of view, might be regarded as a sort of citadel of the mind, fortified without and containing selected treasures within, while love is an undivided share in the rest of the universe. In a healthy mind each contributes to the growth of the other: what we love intensely or for a long time we are likely to bring within the citadel, and to assert as part of ourself. On the other hand, it is only on the basis of a substantial self that a person is capable of progressive sympathy or love.

The sickness of either is to lack the support of the other. There is no health in a mind except as it keeps expanding, taking in fresh life, feeling love and enthusiasm; and so long as it does this its self-feeling is likely to be modest and generous; since these sentiments accompany that sense of the large and the superior which love implies. But if love closes, the self contracts and hardens: the mind having nothing else to occupy its attention and give it that change and renewal it requires, busies itself more and more with self-feeling, which takes on narrow and disgusting forms, like avarice, arrogance, and fatuity. It is necessary that we should have self-feeling about a matter during its conception and execution; but when it is accomplished or has failed the self ought to break loose and escape, renewing its skin like the snake, as Thoreau says. No matter what a man does, he is not fully sane or human unless there is a spirit of freedom in him, a soul unconfined by purpose and larger than the practicable world. And this is really what those mean who inculcate the suppression of the self; they mean that its rigidity must be broken up by growth and renewal, that it must be more or less decisively "born again." A healthy self must be both vigorous and plastic, a nucleus of solid, well-knit private purpose and feeling, guided and nourished by sympathy.

The view that "self" and the pronouns of the first person are names which the race has learned to apply to an instinctive attitude of mind, and which each child in turn learns to apply in a similar way, was impressed upon me by observing my child M. at the time when she was learning to use these pronouns. When she was two years and two weeks old I was surprised to discover that she had a clear notion of the first and second persons when used possessively. When asked, "Where is your nose?" she would put her hand upon it and say "my." She also understood that when some one else said "my" and touched an object, it meant something opposite to what was meant when she touched the same object and used the same word. Now, any one who will exercise his imagination upon the question how this matter must appear to a mind having no means of knowing anything about "I" and "my" except what it learns by hearing them used, will see that it should be very puzzling. Unlike other words, the personal pronouns have, apparently, no uniform meaning, but convey different and even opposite ideas when employed by different persons. It seems remarkable that children should master the problem before they arrive at considerable power of abstract reasoning. How should a little girl of two, not particularly reflective, have discovered that "my" was not the sign of a definite object like other words, but meant something different with each person who used it? And, still more surprising, how should she have achieved the correct use of it with reference to herself which, it would seem, *could not be copied from any one else,* simply because no one else used it to describe what belonged to her? The meaning of words is learned by associating them with other phenomena. But how is it possible to learn the meaning of one which, as used by others, is never associated with the same phenomenon as when properly used by one's self? Watching her use of the first person, I was at once struck with the fact that she employed it almost wholly in a possessive sense, and that, too, when in an aggressive, self-assertive mood. It was extremely common to see R. tugging at one end of a plaything and M. at the other, screaming, "My, my." "Me" was sometimes nearly equivalent to "my," and was also employed to call attention to herself when she wanted something done for her. Another common use of "my" was to demand something she did not have at all. Thus if R. had something the like of which she wanted, say a cart, she would exclaim, "Where's *my* cart?"

It seemed to me that she might have learned the use of these pronouns about as follows. The self-feeling had always been there. From the first week she had wanted things and cried and fought for them. She had also become familiar by observation and opposition with similar appropriative activities on the part of R. Thus she not only had the feeling herself, but by associating it with its visible expression had probably divined it, sympathized with it, resented it, in others. Grasping, tugging, and screaming would be associated with the feeling in her own case and would recall the feeling when observed in others. They would constitute a language, precedent to the use of first-personal pronouns, to express the self-idea. All was ready, then, for the word to name this experience. She now observed that R., when contentiously appropriating something, frequently exclaimed, *"my,"* *"mine,"* "give it to *me*," "*I* want it," and the like. Nothing more natural, then, than that she should adopt these words as names for a frequent and vivid experience with which she was already familiar in her own case and had learned to attribute to others. Accordingly it appeared to me, as I recorded in my notes at the time, that "'my' and 'mine' are simply names for concrete images of appropriativeness," embracing both the appropriative feeling and its manifestation. If this is true the child does not at first work out the I-and-you idea in an abstract form. The first-personal pronoun is a sign of a concrete thing after all, but that thing is not primarily the child's body, or his muscular sensations as such, but the phenomenon of aggressive appropriation, practised by himself, witnessed in others, and incited and interpreted by a hereditary instinct. This seems to get over the difficulty above mentioned, namely, the seeming lack of a common content between the meaning of "my"

191

when used by another and when used by one's self. This common content is found in the appropriative feeling and the visible and audible signs of that feeling. An element of difference and strife comes in, of course, in the opposite actions or purposes which the "my" of another and one's own "my" are likely to stand for. When another person says "mine" regarding something which I claim, I sympathize with him enough to understand what he means, but it is a hostile sympathy, overpowered by another and more vivid "mine" connected with the idea of drawing the object my way.

In other words, the meaning of "I" and "mine" is learned in the same way that the meanings of hope, regret, chagrin, disgust, and thousands of other words of emotion and sentiment are learned: that is, by having the feeling, imputing it to others in connection with some kind of expression, and hearing the word along with it. As to its communication and growth the self-idea is in no way peculiar that I see, but essentially like other ideas. In its more complex forms, such as are expressed by "I" in conversation and literature, it is a social sentiment, or type of sentiments, defined and developed by intercourse, in the manner suggested in a previous chapter.*

R., though a more reflective child than M., was much slower in understanding these pronouns, and in his thirty-fifth month had not yet straightened them out, sometimes calling his father "me." I imagine

* Compare my "Study of the Early Use of Self-Words by a Child," in the Psychological Review, vol. 15, p. 339.

that this was partly because he was placid and uncontentious in his earliest years, manifesting little social self-feeling, but chiefly occupied with impersonal experiment and reflection; and partly because he saw little of other children by antithesis to whom his self could be awakened. M., on the other hand, coming later, had R.'s opposition on which to whet her naturally keen appropriativeness. And her society had a marked effect in developing self-feeling in R., who found self-assertion necessary to preserve his playthings, or anything else capable of appropriation. He learned the use of "my," however, when he was about three years old, before M. was born. He doubtless acquired it in his dealings with his parents. Thus he would perhaps notice his mother claiming the scissors as *mine* and seizing upon them, and would be moved sympathetically to claim something in the same way—connecting the word with the act and the feeling rather than the object. But as I had not the problem clearly in mind at that time I made no satisfactory observations.

I imagine, then, that as a rule the child associates "I" and "me" at first only with those ideas regarding which his appropriative feeling is aroused and defined by opposition. He appropriates his nose, eye, or foot in very much the same way as a plaything—by antithesis to other noses, eyes, and feet, which he cannot control. It is not uncommon to tease little children by proposing to take away one of these organs, and they behave precisely as if the "mine" threatened were a separable object—which it might be for all they know. And, as I have suggested, even in adult life, "I," "me," and "mine" are applied with a strong sense of their meaning only to things distinguished as peculiar to us by some sort of opposition or contrast. They always imply social life and relation to other persons. That which is most distinctively mine is very private, it is true, but it is that part of the private which I am cherishing in antithesis to the rest of the world, not the separate but the special. The aggressive self is essentially a militant phase of the mind, having for its apparent function the energizing of peculiar activities, and, although the militancy may not go on in an obvious, external manner, it always exists as a mental attitude.

In some of the best-known discussions of the development of the sense of self in children the chief emphasis has been placed upon the speculative or quasi-metaphysical ideas concerning "I" which children sometimes formulate as a result either of questions from their elders, or of the independent development of a speculative instinct. The most obvious result of these inquiries is to show that a child, when he reflects upon the self in this manner, usually locates "I" in the body. Interesting and important as this juvenile metaphysics is, as one phase of mental development, it should certainly not be taken as an adequate expression of the childish sense of self, and probably President G. Stanley Hall, who has collected valuable material of this kind, does not so take it.*

* Compare Some Aspects of the Early Sense of Self, American Journal of Psychology, vol. 9, p. 351.

This analysis of the "I," asking one's self just where it is located, whether particular limbs are embraced in it, and the like, is somewhat remote from the ordinary, naïve use of the word, with children as with grown people. In my own children I only once observed anything of this sort, and that was in the case of R., when he was struggling to achieve the correct use of his pronouns; and a futile, and as I now think mistaken, attempt was made to help him by pointing out the association of the word with his body. On the other hand, every child who has learned to talk uses "I," "me," "mine," and the like hundreds of times a day, with great emphasis, in the simple, naïve way that the race has used them for thousands of years. In this usage they refer to claims upon playthings, to assertions of one's peculiar will or purpose, as "*I* don't want to do it that way," "*I* am going to draw a kitty," and so on, rarely to any part of the body. And when a part of the body is meant it is usually by way of claiming approval for it, as "Don't I look nice?" so that the object of chief interest is after all another person's attitude. The speculative "I," though a true "I," is not the "I" of common speech and workaday usefulness, but almost as remote from ordinary thought as the ego of metaphysicians, of which, indeed, it is an immature example.

That children, when in this philosophizing state of mind, usually refer "I" to the physical body, is easily explained by the fact that their materialism, natural to all crude speculation, needs to locate the self somewhere, and the body, the one tangible thing over which

195

they have continuous power, seems the most available home for it.

The process by which self-feeling of the looking-glass sort develops in children may be followed without much difficulty. Studying the movements of others as closely as they do they soon see a connection between their own acts and changes in those movements; that is, they perceive their own influence or power over persons. The child appropriates the visible actions of his parent or nurse, over which he finds he has some control, in quite the same way as he appropriates one of his own members or a plaything, and he will try to do things with this new possession, just as he will with his hand or his rattle. A girl six months old will attempt in the most evident and deliberate manner to attract attention to herself, to set going by her actions some of those movements of other persons that she has appropriated. She has tasted the joy of being a cause, of exerting social power, and wishes more of it. She will tug at her mother's skirts, wriggle, gurgle, stretch out her arms, etc., all the time watching for the hoped-for effect. These performances often give the child, even at this age, an appearance of what is called affectation, that is, she seems to be unduly preoccupied with what other people think of her. Affectation, at any age, exists when the passion to influence others seems to overbalance the established character and give it an obvious twist or pose. It is instructive to find that even Darwin was, in his childhood, capable of departing from truth for the sake of making an impression. "For instance," he says in his autobiography, "I once gathered much valuable fruit from my father's trees and hid it in the shrubbery, and then ran in breathless haste to spread the news that I had discovered a hoard of stolen fruit." *

The young performer soon learns to be different things to different people, showing that he begins to apprehend personality and to foresee its operation. If the mother or nurse is more tender than just she will almost certainly be "worked" by systematic weeping. It is a matter of common observation that children often behave worse with their mother than with other and less sympathetic people. Of the new persons that a child sees it is evident that some make a strong impression and awaken a desire to interest and please them, while others are indifferent or repugnant. Sometimes the reason can be perceived or guessed, sometimes not; but the fact of selective interest, admiration, prestige, is obvious before the end of the second year. By that time a child already cares much for the reflection of himself upon one personality and little for that upon another. Moreover, he soon claims intimate and tractable persons as *mine*, classes them among his other possessions, and maintains his ownership against all comers. M., at three years of age, vigorously resented R.'s claim upon their mother. The latter was *"my* mamma," whenever the point was raised.

Strong joy and grief depend upon the treatment

* Life and Letters of Charles Darwin, by F. Darwin, p. 27.

this rudimentary social self receives. In the case of M. I noticed as early as the fourth month a "hurt" way of crying which seemed to indicate a sense of personal slight. It was quite different from the cry of pain or that of anger, but seemed about the same as the cry of fright. The slightest tone of reproof would produce it. On the other hand, if people took notice and laughed and encouraged, she was hilarious. At about fifteen months old she had become "a perfect little actress," seeming to live largely in imaginations of her effect upon other people. She constantly and obviously laid traps for attention, and looked abashed or wept at any signs of disapproval or indifference. At times it would seem as if she could not get over these repulses, but would cry long in a grieved way, refusing to be comforted. If she hit upon any little trick that made people laugh she would be sure to repeat it, laughing loudly and affectedly in imitation. She had quite a repertory of these small performances, which she would display to a sympathetic audience, or even try upon strangers. I have seen her at sixteen months, when R. refused to give her the scissors, sit down and make-believe cry, putting up her under lip and snuffling, meanwhile looking up now and then to see what effect she was producing.*

In such phenomena we have plainly enough, it seems to me, the germ of personal ambition of every sort. Imagination co-operating with instinctive self-

* This sort of thing is very familiar to observers of children. See, for instance, Miss Shinn's Notes on the Development of a Child, p. 153.

feeling has already created a social "I," and this has become a principal object of interest and endeavor.

Progress from this point is chiefly in the way of a greater definiteness, fulness, and inwardness in the imagination of the other's state of mind. A little child thinks of and tries to elicit certain visible or audible phenomena, and does not go back of them; but what a grown-up person desires to produce in others is an internal, invisible condition which his own richer experience enables him to imagine, and of which expression is only the sign. Even adults, however, make no separation between what other people think and the visible expression of that thought. They imagine the whole thing at once, and their idea differs from that of a child chiefly in the comparative richness and complexity of the elements that accompany and interpret the visible or audible sign. There is also a progress from the naïve to the subtle in socially self-assertive action. A child obviously and simply, at first, does things for effect. Later there is an endeavor to suppress the appearance of doing so; affection, indifference, contempt, etc., are simulated to hide the real wish to affect the self-image. It is perceived that an obvious seeking after good opinion is weak and disagreeable.

I doubt whether there are any regular stages in the development of social self-feeling and expression common to the majority of children. The sentiments of self develop by imperceptible gradations out of the crude appropriative instinct of new-born babes, and their manifestations vary indefinitely in different cases.

Many children show "self-consciousness" conspicuously from the first half-year; others have little appearance of it at any age. Still others pass through periods of affectation whose length and time of occurrence would probably be found to be exceedingly various. In childhood, as at all times of life, absorption in some idea other than that of the social self tends to drive "self-consciousness" out.

Nearly every one, however, whose turn of mind is at all imaginative goes through a season of passionate self-feeling during adolescence, when, according to current belief, the social impulses are stimulated in connection with the rapid development of the functions of sex. This is a time of hero-worship, of high resolve, of impassioned revery, of vague but fierce ambition, of strenuous imitation that seems affected, of *gêne* in the presence of the other sex or of superior persons, and so on.

Many autobiographies describe the social self-feeling of youth which, in the case of strenuous, susceptible natures, prevented by weak health or uncongenial surroundings from gaining the sort of success proper to that age, often attains extreme intensity. This is quite generally the case with the youth of men of genius, whose exceptional endowment and tendencies usually isolate them more or less from the ordinary life about them. In the autobiography of John Addington Symonds we have an account of the feelings of an ambitious boy suffering from ill-health, plainness of feature—peculiarly mortifying to his strong æsthetic instincts—and mental backwardness. "I almost resented the attentions paid me as my father's son, . . . I regarded them as acts of charitable condescension. Thus I passed into an attitude of haughty shyness which had nothing respectable in it except a sort of self-reliant, world-defiant pride, a resolution to effectuate myself, and to win what I wanted by my exertions. . . . I vowed to raise myself somehow or other to eminence of some sort. . . . I felt no desire for wealth, no mere wish to cut a figure in society. But I thirsted with intolerable thirst for eminence, for recognition as a personality.* . . . The main thing which sustained me was a sense of self—imperious, antagonistic, unmalleable.† . . . My external self in these many ways was being perpetually snubbed, and crushed, and mortified. Yet the inner self hardened after a dumb, blind fashion. I kept repeating, 'Wait, wait. I will, I shall, I must.'"‡ At Oxford he overhears a conversation in which his abilities are depreciated and it is predicted that he will not get his "first." "The sting of it remained in me; and though I cared little enough for first classes, I then and there resolved that I would win the best first of my year. This kind of grit in me has to be notified. Nothing aroused it so much as a seeming slight, exciting my rebellious manhood." § Again he exclaims, "I look round me and find nothing in which I excel." ‖ . . . "I fret because I do not realize am-

* John Addington Symonds, by H. F. Brown, vol. i, p. 63.
† P. 70.   ‡ P. 74.
§ P. 120.   ‖ P. 125.

bition, because I have no active work, and cannot win a position of importance like other men." *

This sort of thing is familiar in literature, and very likely in our own experience. It seems worth while to recall it and to point out that this primal need of self-effectuation, to adopt Mr. Symonds's phrase, is the essence of ambition, and always has for its object the production of some effect upon the minds of other people. We feel in the quotations above the indomitable surging up of the individualizing, militant force of which self-feeling seems to be the organ.

Sex-difference in the development of the social self is apparent from the first. Girls have, as a rule, a more impressible social sensibility; they care more obviously for the social image, study it, reflect upon it more, and so have even during the first year an appearance of subtlety, *finesse*, often of affectation, in which boys are comparatively lacking. Boys are more taken up with muscular activity for its own sake and with construction, their imaginations are occupied somewhat less with persons and more with things. In a girl *das ewig Weibliche*, not easy to describe but quite unmistakable, appears as soon as she begins to take notice of people, and one phase of it is certainly an ego less simple and stable, a stronger impulse to go over to the other person's point of view and to stake joy and grief on the image in his mind. There can be no doubt that women are as a rule more dependent upon immediate personal support and cor-

* P. 348.

roboration than are men. The thought of the woman
needs to fix itself upon some person in whose mind
she can find a stable and compelling image of herself
by which to live. If such an image is found, either in
a visible or an ideal person, the power of devotion to
it becomes a source of strength. But it is a sort of
strength dependent upon this personal complement,
without which the womanly character is somewhat
apt to become a derelict and drifting vessel. Men,
being built more for aggression, have, relatively, a
greater power of standing alone. But no one can
really stand alone, and the appearance of it is due
simply to a greater momentum and continuity of
character which stores up the past and resists immediate influences. Directly or indirectly the imagination of how we appear to others is a controlling force
in all normal minds.

The vague but potent phases of the self associated
with the instinct of sex may be regarded, like other
phases, as expressive of a need to exert power and as
having reference to personal function. The youth, I
take it, is bashful precisely because he is conscious of
the vague stirring of an aggressive instinct which he
does not know how either to effectuate or to ignore.
And it is perhaps much the same with the other sex:
the bashful are always aggressive at heart; they are
conscious of an interest in the other person, of a need
to be something to him. And the more developed
sexual passion, in both sexes, is very largely an emotion of power, domination, or appropriation. There
is no state of feeling that says "mine, mine," more

fiercely. The need to be appropriated or dominated which, in women at least, is equally powerful, is of the same nature at bottom, having for its object the attracting to itself of a masterful passion. "The desire of the man is for the woman, but the desire of the woman is for the desire of the man." *

Although boys have generally a less impressionable social self than girls, there is great difference among them in this regard. Some of them have a marked tendency to *finesse* and posing, while others have almost none. The latter have a less vivid personal imagination; they are unaffected chiefly, perhaps, because they have no vivid idea of how they seem to others, and so are not moved to seem rather than to be; they are unresentful of slights because they do not feel them, not ashamed or jealous or vain or proud or remorseful, because all these imply imagination of another's mind. I have known children who showed no tendency whatever to lie; in fact, could not understand the nature or object of lying or of any sort of concealment, as in such games as hide-and-coop. This excessively simple way of looking at things may come from unusual absorption in the observation and analysis of the impersonal, as appeared to be the case with R., whose interest in other facts and their relations so much preponderated over his interest in personal attitudes that there was no temptation to sacrifice the former to the latter. A child of this sort gives the impression of being non-moral; he neither sins nor

* Attributed to Mme. de Staël.

repents, and has not the knowledge of good and evil. We eat of the tree of this knowledge when we begin to imagine the minds of others, and so become aware of that conflict of personal impulses which conscience aims to allay.

Simplicity is a pleasant thing in children, or at any age, but it is not necessarily admirable, nor is affectation altogether a thing of evil. To be normal, to be at home in the world, with a prospect of power, usefulness, or success, the person must have that imaginative insight into other minds that underlies tact and *savoir-faire,* morality and beneficence. This insight involves sophistication, some understanding and sharing of the clandestine impulses of human nature. A simplicity that is merely the lack of this insight indicates a sort of defect. There is, however, another kind of simplicity, belonging to a character that is subtle and sensitive, but has sufficient force and mental clearness to keep in strict order the many impulses to which it is open, and so preserve its directness and unity. One may be simple like Simple Simon, or in the sense that Emerson meant when he said, "To be simple is to be great." Affectation, vanity, and the like, indicate the lack of proper assimilation of the influences arising from our sense of what others think of us. Instead of these influences working upon the individual gradually and without disturbing his equilibrium, they overbear him so that he appears to be not himself, posing, out of function, and hence silly, weak, contemptible. The affected smile, the "foolish face of praise" is a type of all affectation, an external, put-on thing, a weak and fatuous petition for approval. Whenever one is growing rapidly, learning eagerly, preoccupied with strange ideals, he is in danger of this loss of equilibrium; and so we notice it in sensitive children, especially girls, in young people between fourteen and twenty, and at all ages in persons of unstable individuality.

This disturbance of our equilibrium by the outgoing of the imagination toward another person's point of view means that we are undergoing his influence. In the presence of one whom we feel to be of importance there is a tendency to enter into and adopt, by sympathy, his judgment of ourself, to put a new value on ideas and purposes, to recast life in his image. With a very sensitive person this tendency is often evident to others in ordinary conversation and in trivial matters. By force of an impulse springing directly from the delicacy of his perceptions he is continually imagining how he appears to his interlocutor, and accepting the image, for the moment, as himself. If the other appears to think him well-informed on some recondite matter, he is likely to assume a learned expression; if thought judicious he looks as if he were, if accused of dishonesty he appears guilty, and so on. In short, a sensitive man, in the presence of an impressive personality, tends to become, for the time, his interpretation of what the other thinks he is. It is only the heavy-minded who will not feel this to be true, in some degree, of themselves. Of course it is usually a temporary and somewhat superficial phenomenon; but it is typical of all ascendancy, and helps us to understand how persons have power over us through some hold upon our imaginations, and how our personality grows and takes form by divining the appearance of our present self to other minds.

So long as a character is open and capable of growth it retains a corresponding impressibility, which is not weakness unless it swamps the assimilating and organizing faculty. I know men whose careers are a proof of stable and aggressive character who have an almost feminine sensitiveness regarding their seeming to others. Indeed, if one sees a man whose attitude toward others is always assertive, never receptive, he may be confident that man will never go far, because he will never learn much. In character, as in every phase of life, health requires a just union of stability with plasticity.

There is a vague excitement of the social self more general than any particular emotion or sentiment. Thus the mere presence of people, a "sense of other persons," as Professor Baldwin says, and an awareness of their observation, often causes a vague discomfort, doubt, and tension. One feels that there is a social image of himself lurking about, and not knowing what it is he is obscurely alarmed. Many people, perhaps most, feel more or less agitation and embarrassment under the observation of strangers, and for some even sitting in the same room with unfamiliar or uncongenial people is harassing and exhausting. It is well known, for instance, that a visit from a stranger would often cost Darwin his night's sleep, and many similar examples could be collected from the records of men of letters. At this point, however, it is evident that we approach the borders of mental pathology.

Possibly some will think that I exaggerate the importance of social self-feeling by taking persons and periods of life that are abnormally sensitive. But I believe that with all normal and human people it remains, in one form or another, the mainspring of endeavor and a chief interest of the imagination throughout life. As is the case with other feelings, we do not think much of it so long as it is moderately and regularly gratified. Many people of balanced mind and congenial activity scarcely know that they care what others think of them, and will deny, perhaps with indignation, that such care is an important factor in what they are and do. But this is illusion. If failure or disgrace arrives, if one suddenly finds that the faces of men show coldness or contempt instead of the kindliness and deference that he is used to, he will perceive from the shock, the fear, the sense of being outcast and helpless, that he was living in the minds of others without knowing it, just as we daily walk the solid ground without thinking how it bears us up. This fact is so familiar in literature, especially in modern novels, that it ought to be obvious enough. The works of George Eliot are particularly strong in the exposition of it. In most of her novels there is some character like Mr. Bulstrode in "Middlemarch" or Mr. Jermyn in "Felix Holt," whose respectable and long-

208

established social image of himself is shattered by the coming to light of hidden truth.

It is true, however, that the attempt to describe the social self and to analyze the mental processes that enter into it almost unavoidably makes it appear more reflective and "self-conscious" than it usually is. Thus while some readers will be able to discover in themselves a quite definite and deliberate contemplation of the reflected self, others will perhaps find nothing but a sympathetic impulse, so simple that it can hardly be made the object of distinct thought. Many people whose behavior shows that their idea of themselves is largely caught from the persons they are with, are yet quite innocent of any intentional posing; it is a matter of subconscious impulse or mere suggestion. The self of very sensitive but non-reflective minds is of this character.

The group self or "we" is simply an "I" which includes other persons. One identifies himself with a group and speaks of the common will, opinion, service, or the like in terms of "we" and "us." The sense of it is stimulated by co-operation within and opposition without. A family that has had to struggle with economic difficulties usually develops solidarity—"We paid off the mortgage," "We sent the boys to college," and the like. A student identifies himself with his class or his university when it is performing a social function of some kind, especially when it is contending in games with other classes or institutions. "We won the tug of war," he says, or "We beat Wisconsin at football." Those of us who remained at home during the Great War nevertheless tell how "we" entered the war in 1917, how "we" fought decisively in the Argonne, and so on.

It is notable that the national self, indeed any group self, can be felt only in relation to a larger society, just as the individual self is felt only in relation to other individuals. We could have no patriotism unless we were aware of other nations, and the effect of a definitely organized society of nations, in whose activities we all took a generous interest, would be, not to diminish patriotism, as some have unintelligently asserted, but to raise its character, to make it more vivid, continuous, varied, and sympathetic. It would be like the self-consciousness of an intelligent individual in constant and friendly intercourse with others, as contrasted with the brutal self-assertion of one who knows his fellows only as objects of suspicion and hostility. The patriotism of the past has been of the latter kind, and we have hardly considered its higher possibilities. The national "we" can and should be a self of real honor, service, and humane aspiration.

CHAPTER VI

THE SOCIAL SELF—2. VARIOUS PHASES OF "I"

EGOTISM AND SELFISHNESS—THE USE OF "I" IN LITERATURE
AND CONVERSATION—INTENSE SELF-FEELING NECESSARY TO
PRODUCTIVITY—OTHER PHASES OF THE SOCIAL SELF—PRIDE
versus VANITY—SELF-RESPECT, HONOR, SELF-REVERENCE—
HUMILITY—MALADIES OF THE SOCIAL SELF—WITHDRAWAL—
SELF-TRANSFORMATION—PHASES OF THE SELF CAUSED BY IN-
CONGRUITY BETWEEN THE PERSON AND HIS SURROUNDINGS—
THE SELF IN SOCIAL PROBLEMS

IF self and the self-seeking that springs from it are
healthy and respectable traits of human nature, then
what are those things which we call egotism and selfishness,* and which are so commonly regarded as
objectionable? The answer to this appears to be
that it is not self-assertion as such that we stigmatize
by these names, but the assertion of a kind or phase
of self that is obnoxious to us. So long as we agree
with a man's thoughts and aims we do not think of
him as selfish or egotistical, however urgently he may
assert them; but so soon as we cease to agree, while
he continues persistent and perhaps intrusive, we are
likely to say hard things about him. It is at bottom
a matter of moral judgment, not to be comprised in
any simple definition, but to be determined by conscience after the whole situation is taken into account.

* I do not attempt to distinguish between these words, though
there is a difference, ill defined however, in their meanings. As
ordinarily used both designate a phase of self-assertion regarded
as censurable, and this is all I mean by either.

In this regard it is essentially one with the more general question of misconduct or personal badness. There is no distinct line between the behavior which we mildly censure as selfish and that which we call wicked or criminal; it is only a matter of degree.

It is quite apparent that mere self-assertion is not looked upon as selfishness. There is nothing more respected—and even liked—than a persistent and successful pursuit of one's peculiar aims, so long as this is done within the accepted limits of fairness and consideration for others. Thus one who has acquired ten millions must have expressed his appropriative instinct with much energy and constancy, but reasonable people do not conclude that he is selfish unless it appears that he has ignored social sentiments by which he should have been guided. If he has been dishonest, mean, hard, or the like, they will condemn him.

The men we admire most, including those we look upon as peculiarly good, are invariably men of notable self-assertion. Thus Martin Luther, to take a conspicuous instance, was a man of the most intense self-feeling, resentful of opposition, dogmatic, with "an absolute confidence in the infallibility, practically speaking, of his own judgment." This is a trait belonging to nearly all great leaders, and a main cause of their success. That which distinguishes Luther from the vulgarly ambitious and aggressive people we know is not the quality of his self-feeling, but the fact that it was identified in his imagination and endeavors with sentiments and purposes that we look

212

upon as noble, progressive, or right. No one could be more ambitious than he was, or more determined to secure the social aggrandizement of his self; but in his case the self for which he was ambitious and resentful consisted largely of certain convictions regarding justification by faith, the sacrilege of the sale of indulgences, and, more generally, of an enfranchising spirit and mode of thought fit to awaken and lead the aspiration of the time.

It is evident enough that in this respect Luther is typical of aggressive reformers in our own and every other time. Does not every efficient clergyman, philanthropist, or teacher become such by identifying some worthy object with a vigorous self-feeling? Is it ever really possible to separate the feeling for the cause from the feeling that it is *my* cause? I doubt whether it is. Some of the greatest and purest founders and propagators of religion have been among the greatest egotists in the sense that they openly identified the idea of good with the idea of self, and spoke of the two interchangeably. And I cannot think of any strong man I have known, however good, who does not seem to me to have had intense self-feeling about his cherished affair; though if his affair was a large and helpful one no one would call him selfish.

Since the judgment that a man is or is not selfish is a question of sympathies, it naturally follows that people easily disagree regarding it, their views depending much upon their temperaments and habits of thought. There are probably few energetic persons who do not make an impression of egotism upon some

213

of their acquaintances; and, on the other hand, how many there are whose selfishness seems obvious to most people, but is not apparent to their wives, sisters, and mothers. In so far as our self is identified with that of another it is, of course, unlikely that the aims of the latter should be obnoxious to us.

If we should question many persons as to why they thought this or that man selfish, a common answer would probably be, "He does not consider other people." What this means is that he is inappreciative of the social situation as we see it; that the situation does not awaken in him the same personal sentiments that it does in us, and so his action wounds those sentiments. Thus the commonest and most obvious form of selfishness is perhaps the failure to subordinate sensual impulses to social feeling, and this, of course, results from the apathy of the imaginative impulses that ought to effect this subordination. It would usually be impossible for a man to help himself to the best pieces on the platter if he conceived the disgust and resentment which he excites. And, though this is a very gross and palpable sort of selfishness, it is analogous in nature to the finer kinds. A fine-grained, subtle Egoist, such as is portrayed in George Meredith's novel of that name, or such as Isabel's husband in Henry James's "Portrait of a Lady," has delicate perceptions in certain directions, but along with these there is some essential narrowness or vulgarity of imagination which prevents him from grasping what we feel to be the true social situation, and having the sentiments that should respond to it. The æsthetic

214

refinement of Osmond which so impresses Isabel before her marriage turns out to be compatible with a general smallness of mind. He is "not a good fellow," as Ralph remarks, and incapable of comprehending her or her friends.

A lack of tact in face-to-face intercourse very commonly gives an impression of egotism, even when it is a superficial trait not really expressive of an unsympathetic character. Thus there are persons who in the simplest conversation do not seem to forget themselves, and enter frankly and disinterestedly into the subject, but are felt to be always preoccupied with the thought of the impression they are making, imagining praise or depreciation, and usually posing a little to avoid the one or gain the other. Such people are uneasy, and make others so; no relaxation is possible in their company, because they never come altogether out into open and common ground, but are always keeping back something. It is not so much that they have self-feeling as that it is clandestine and furtive, giving one a sense of insecurity. Sometimes they are aware of this lack of frankness, and try to offset it by reckless confessions, but this only shows their self-consciousness in another and hardly more agreeable aspect. Perhaps the only cure for this sort of egotism is to cherish very high and difficult ambitions, and so drain off the superabundance of self-feeling from these petty channels. People who are doing really important things usually appear simple and unaffected in conversation, largely because their selves are healthfully employed elsewhere.

One who has tact always sees far enough into the state of mind of the person with whom he is conversing to adapt himself to it and to seem, at least, sympathetic; he is sure to feel the situation. But if you tread upon the other person's toes, talk about yourself when he is not interested in that subject, and, in general, show yourself out of touch with his mind, he very naturally finds you disagreeable. And behavior analogous to this in the more enduring relations of life gives rise to a similar judgment.

So far as there is any agreement in judgments regarding selfishness it arises from common standards of right, fairness, and courtesy which all thoughtful minds work out from their experience, and which represent what the general good requires. The selfish man is one in whose self, or in whose style of asserting it, is something that falls below these standards. He is a transgressor of fair play and the rules of the game, an outlaw with whom no one ought to sympathize, but against whom all should unite for the general good.

It is the unhealthy or egotistical self that is usually meant by the word self when used in moral discussions; it is this that people need to get away from, both for their own good and that of the community. When we speak of getting out of one's "self" we commonly mean *any line of thought with which one tends to be unduly preoccupied;* so that to escape from it is indeed a kind of salvation.

There is perhaps no sort of self more subject to dangerous egotism than that which deludes itself with the notion that it is not a self at all, but something

216

else. It is well to beware of persons who believe that the cause, the mission, the philanthropy, the hero, or whatever it may be that they strive for, is outside of themselves, so that they feel a certain irresponsibility, and are likely to do things which they would recognize as wrong if done in behalf of an acknowledged self. Just as the Spanish armies in the Netherlands held that their indulgence in murder, torture, and brutal lust was sanctified by the supposed holy character of their mission, so in our own time the name of religion, science, patriotism, or charity sometimes enables people to indulge comfortably in browbeating, intrusion, slander, dishonesty, and the like. *Every cherished idea is a self:* and, though it appear to the individual, or to a class, or to a whole nation, worthy to swallow up all other selves, it is subject to the same need of discipline under rules of justice and decency as any other. It is healthy for every one to understand that he is, and will remain, a self-seeker, and that if he gets out of one self he is sure to form another which may stand in equal need of control.

Selfishness as a mental trait is always some sort of narrowness, littleness, or defect; an inadequacy of imagination. The perfectly balanced and vigorous mind can hardly be selfish, because it cannot be oblivious to any important social situation, either in immediate intercourse or in more permanent relations; it must always tend to be sympathetic, fair, and just, because it possesses that breadth and unity of view of which these qualities are the natural expression. To lack them is to be not altogether social and human,

217

and may be regarded as the beginning of degeneracy. Egotism is then not something additional to ordinary human nature, as the common way of speaking suggests, but rather a lack. The egotist is not more than a man, but less than a man; and as regards personal power he is as a rule the weaker for his egotism. The very fact that he has a bad name shows that the world is against him, and that he is contending against odds. The success of selfishness attracts attention and exaggeration because it is hateful to us; but the really strong generally work within the prevalent standards of justice and courtesy, and so escape condemnation.

There is infinite variety in egotism; but an important division may be based on the greater or less stability of the egotists' characters. According to this we may divide them into those of the unstable type and those of the rigid type Extreme instability is always selfish; the very weak cannot be otherwise, because they lack both the deep sympathy that enables people to penetrate the lives of others, and the consistency and self-control necessary to make sympathy effective if they had it. Their superficial and fleeting impulses are as likely to work harm as good and cannot be trusted to bring forth any sound fruit. If they are amiable at times they are sure to be harsh, cold, or violent at other times; there is no justice, no solid good or worth in them The sort of people I have in mind are, for instance, such as in times of affliction go about weeping and wringing their hands to the neglect of their duty to aid and comfort the survivors, possibly taking credit for the tenderness of their hearts.

The other sort of egotism, not sharply distinguished from this in all cases, belongs to people who have stability of mind and conduct, but still without breadth and richness of sympathy, so that their aims and sentiments are inadequate to the life around them—narrow, hard, mean, self-satisfied, or sensual. This I would call the rigid type of egotism because the essence of it is an arrest of sympathetic development and an ossification as it were of what should be a plastic and growing part of thought. Something of this sort is perhaps what is most commonly meant by the word, and every one can think of harsh, gross, grasping, cunning, or self-complacent traits to which he would apply it. The self, to be healthy or to be tolerable to other selves, must be ever moving on, breaking loose from lower habits, walking hand-in-hand with sympathy and aspiration. If it stops too long anywhere it becomes stagnant and diseased, odious to other minds and harmful to the mind it inhabits. The men that satisfy the imagination are chastened men; large, human, inclusive, feeling the breadth of the world. It is impossible to think of Shakespeare as arrogant, vain, or sensual; and if some, like Dante, had an exigent ego, they succeeded in transforming it into higher and higher forms.

Selfishness of the stable or rigid sort is as a rule more bitterly resented than the more fickle variety, chiefly, no doubt, because, having more continuity and purpose, it is more formidable.

219

One who accepts the idea of self, and of personality in general, already set forth, will agree that what is ordinarily called egotism cannot properly be regarded as the opposite of "altruism," or of any word implying the self-and-other classification of impulses. No clear or useful idea of selfishness can be reached on the basis of this classification, which, as previously stated, seems to me fictitious. It misrepresents the mental situation, and so tends to confuse thought. The mind has not, in fact, two sets of motives to choose from, the self-motives and the other-motives, the latter of which stand for the higher course, but has the far more difficult task of achieving a higher life by gradually discriminating and organizing a great variety of motives not easily divisible into moral groups. The proper antithesis of selfishness is right, justice, breadth, magnanimity, or something of that sort; something opposite to the narrowness of feeling and action in which selfishness essentially consists. It is a matter of more or less symmetry and stature, like the contrast between a gnarled and stunted tree and one of ample growth.

The ideas denoted by such phrases as *my* friend, *my* country, *my* duty, and so on, are just the ones that stand for broad or "unselfish" impulses, and yet they are self-ideas as shown by the first-personal pronoun. In the expression *"my duty"* we have in six letters a refutation of that way of thinking which makes right the opposite of self. That it stands for the right all will admit; and yet no one can pronounce it meaningly without perceiving that it is charged with intense self-feeling.

It is always vain to try to separate the outer aspect of a motive, the other people, the cause or the like, which we think of as external, from the private or self aspect, which we think of as internal. The apparent separation is purely illusive. It is surely a very simple truth that what makes us act in an unselfish or devoted manner is always some sort of sentiment in our own minds, and if we cherish this sentiment intimately it is a part of ourselves. We develop the inner life by outwardly directed thought and action, relating mostly to other persons, to causes, and the like. Is there no difference, then, it may be asked, between doing a kind act to please some one else and doing it to please one's self? I should say regarding this that while it is obvious, if one thinks of it, that pleasing another can exist for me only as a pleasant feeling in my own mind, which is the motive of my action, there is a difference in the meaning of these expressions as commonly used. Pleasing one's self ordinarily means that we act from some comparatively narrow sentiment not involving penetrating sympathy. Thus, if one gives Christmas presents to make a good impression or from a sense of propriety, he might be said to do it to please himself, while if he really imagined the pleasure the gift would bring to the recipient he would do it to please the latter. But it is clear enough that his own pleasure might be quite as great in the second case. Again, sometimes we do things "to please others" which we declare are painful to ourselves. But this, of course, means merely that there are conflicting impulses in our own minds, some of which are sacrificed to others. The satisfac-

221

tion, or whatever you choose to call it, that one gets when he prefers his duty to some other course is just as much his own as any pleasure he renounces. No self-sacrifice is admirable that is not the choice of a higher or larger aspect of the self over a lower or partial aspect. If a man's act is really self-sacrifice, that is, not properly *his own*, he would better not do it.

Some opponent of Darwin attempted to convict him of egotism by counting the number of times that the pronoun "I" appears upon the first few pages of the "Origin of Species." He was able to find a great many, and to cause Darwin, who was as modest a man as ever lived, to feel abashed at the showing; but it is doubtful if he convinced any reader of the book of the truth of the assertion. In fact, although the dictionary defines egotism as "the habit or practice of thinking and talking much of one's self," the use of the first-personal pronoun is hardly the essence of the matter. This use is always in some degree a self-assertion, but it has a disagreeable or egotistical effect only in so far as the self asserted is repellent to us. Even Montaigne, who says "I" on every other line, and whose avowed purpose is to display himself at large and in all possible detail, does not, it seems to me, really make an impression of egotism upon the congenial reader, because he contrives to make his self so interesting in every aspect that the more we are reminded of it the better we are pleased; and there is good sense in his doctrine that "not to speak roundly of a man's self implies some lack of courage; a firm

222

and lofty judgment, and that judges soundly and surely, makes use of his own example upon all occasions, as well as those of others." A person will not displease sensible people by saying "I" so long as the self thus asserted stands for something, is a pertinent, significant "I," and not merely a random self-intrusion. We are not displeased to see an athlete roll up his sleeves and show his muscles, although if a man of only ordinary development did so it would seem an impertinence; nor do we think less of Rembrandt for painting his own portrait every few months. The "I" should be functional, and so long as a man is functioning acceptably there can be no objection to his using it.

Indeed, it is a common remark that the most delightful companions, or authors of books, are often the most egotistical in the sense that they are always talking about themselves. The reason for this is that if the "I" is interesting and agreeable we adopt it for the time being and make it our own. Then, being on the inside as it were, it is our own self that is so expansive and happy. We adopt Montaigne, or Lamb, or Thackeray, or Stevenson, or Whitman, or Thoreau, and think of their words as our words. Thus even extravagant self-assertion, if the reader can only be led to enter into it, may be congenial. There may be quite as much egotism in the suppression of "I" as in the use of it, and a forced and obvious avoidance of this pronoun often gives a disagreeable feeling of the writer's self-consciousness. In short, egotism is a matter of character, not of forms of language, and if we are egotists the fact will out in spite of any conventional rules of decorum that we may follow.

It is possible to maintain that "I" is a more modest pronoun than "one," by which some writers seem to wish to displace it. If a man says "I think," he speaks only for himself, while if he says "one thinks," he insinuates that the opinion advanced is a general or normal view. To say "one does not like this picture," is a more deadly attack upon it than to say "I do not like it."

It would seem also that more freedom of self-expression is appropriate to a book than to ordinary intercourse, because people are not obliged to read books, and the author has a right to assume that his readers are, in a general way, sympathetic with that phase of his personality that he is trying to express. If we do not sympathize why do we continue to read? We may, however, find fault with him if he departs from that which it is the proper function of the book to assert, and intrudes a weak and irrelevant "I" in which he has no reason to suppose us interested. I presume we can all think of books that might apparently be improved by going through them and striking out passages in which the author has incontinently expressed an aspect of himself that has no proper place in the work.

In every higher kind of production a person needs to understand and believe in himself—the more thoroughly the better. It is precisely that in him which

224

he feels to be worthy and at the same time peculiar—the characteristic—that it is his duty to produce, communicate, and realize; and he cannot possess this, cannot differentiate it, cleanse it from impurities, consolidate and organize it, except through prolonged and interested self-contemplation. Only this can enable him to free himself from the imitative on the one hand and the whimsical on the other, and to stand forth without shame or arrogance for what he truly is. Consequently every productive mind must have intense self-feeling; it must delight to contemplate the characteristic, to gloat over it if you please, and in this way learn to define, arrange, and express it. If one will take up a work of literary art like, say, the Sentimental Journey, he will see that a main source of the charm of it is in the writer's assured and contented familiarity with himself. A man who writes like that has delighted to brood over his thoughts, jealously excluding everything not wholly congenial to him, and gradually working out an adequate expression. And the superiority, or at least the difference, in tone and manner of the earlier English literature as compared with that of the nineteenth century is apparently connected with a more assured and reposeful self-possession on the part of the older writers, made possible, no doubt, by a less urgent general life. The same fact of self-intensity goes with notable production in all sorts of literature, in every art, in statesmanship, philanthropy, religion; in all kinds of career.

Who does not feel at times what Goethe calls the

joy of dwelling in one's self, of surrounding himself with the fruits of his own mind, with things he has made, perhaps, books he has chosen, his familiar clothes and possessions of all sorts, with his wife, children, and old friends, and with his own thoughts, which some, like Robert Louis Stevenson, confess to a love of rereading in books, letters, or diaries? At times even conscientious people, perhaps, look kindly at their own faults, deficiencies, and mannerisms, precisely as they would on those of a familiar friend. Without self-love in some such sense as this any solid and genial growth of character and accomplishment is hardly possible. "Whatever any man has to effect must emanate from him like a second self; and how could this be possible were not his first self entirely pervaded by it?" Nor is it opposed to the love of others. "Indeed," says Mr. Stevenson, "he who loves himself, not in idle vanity, but with a plenitude of knowledge, is the best equipped of all to love his neighbors."

Self-love, Shakespeare says, is not so vile a sin as self-neglecting; and many serious varieties of the latter might be specified. There is, for instance, a culpable sort of self-dreading cowardice, not at all uncommon with sensitive people, which shrinks from developing and asserting a just "I" because of the stress of self-feeling—of vanity, uncertainty, and mortification—which is foreseen and shunned. If one is liable to these sentiments the proper course is to bear with them as with other disturbing conditions, rather than to allow them to stand in the way of what, after all, one is born to do. "Know your own bone," says Thoreau, "gnaw at it, bury it, unearth it, and gnaw it still." * "If I am not I, who will be?"

A tendency to secretiveness very often goes with this self-cherishing. Goethe was as amorous and jealous about his unpublished works, in some cases, as the master of a seraglio; fostering them for years, and sometimes not telling his closest friends of their existence. His Eugenie, "meine Liebling Eugenie," as he calls it, was vulgarized and ruined for him by his fatal mistake in publishing the first part before the whole was complete. It would not be difficult to show that the same cherishing of favorite and peculiar ideas is found also in painters, sculptors, and effective persons of every sort. As was suggested in an earlier chapter, this secretiveness has a social reference, and few works of art could be carried through if the artist was convinced they would have no value in the eyes of any one else. He hides his work that he may purify and perfect it, thus making it at once more wholly and delightfully his own and also more valuable to the world in the end. As soon as the painter exhibits his picture he loses it, in a sense; his system of ideas about it becomes more or less confused and disorganized by the inrush of impressions arising from a sense of what other people think of it; it is no longer the perfect and intimate thing which his thought cherished, but has become somewhat crude, vulgar, and disgusting, so that if he is sensitive he may wish never to look upon it again. This, I take it, is why

* Letters, p. 46.

Goethe could not finish Eugenie, and why Guignet, a French painter, of whom Hamerton speaks, used to alter or throw away a painting that any one by chance saw upon the easel. Likewise it was in order more perfectly to know and express himself—in his book called A Week on the Concord and Merrimack Rivers —that Thoreau retired to Walden Pond, and it was doubtless with the same view that Descartes quitted Paris and dwelt for eight years in Holland, concealing even his place of residence. The Self, like a child, is not likely to hold its own in the world unless it has had a mature prenatal development.

It may be said, perhaps, that these views contradict a well-known fact, namely, that we do our best work when we are not self-conscious, not thinking about effect, but filled with disinterested and impersonal passion. Such truth as there is in this idea is, however, in no way inconsistent with what has just been said. It is true that a certain abandonment and self-forgetting is often characteristic of high thought and noble action. But there would be no production, no high thought or noble action, if we relied entirely upon these impassioned moments without preparing ourselves to have them. It is only as we have self-consciousness that we can be aware of those special tendencies which we assert in production, or can learn how to express them, or even have the desire to do so. The moment of insight would be impossible without the persistent self-conscious endeavor that preceded it, nor has enthusiastic action any value without a similar discipline.

It is true, also, that in sensitive persons self-feeling often reaches a pitch of irritability that impedes production, or vulgarizes it through too great deference to opinion. But this is a matter of the control and discipline of particular aspects of the self rather than of its general tendency. When undisciplined this sort of feeling may be futile or harmful, just as fear, whose function is to cause us to avoid danger, may defeat its own aim through excessive and untimely operation, and anger may so excite us that we lose the power of inflicting injury.

If the people of our time and country are peculiarly selfish, as is sometimes alleged, it is certainly not because a too rigid or clearly differentiated type of self-consciousness is general among us. On the contrary, our most characteristic fault is perhaps a certain superficiality and vagueness of character and aims; and this seems to spring from a lack of collectedness and self-definition, which in turn is connected with the too eager mode of life common among us. I doubt, however, whether egotism, which is essentially a falling short of moral standards, can be said to be more prevalent in one age than another.

In Mr. Roget's Thesaurus may be found about six pages devoted to words denoting "Extrinsic personal affections, or personal affections derived from the opinions or feelings of others," an expression which seems to mean nearly the same as is here meant by social self-feeling of the reflected or looking-glass sort. Although the compiler fishes with a wide net

229

and brings in much that seems hardly to belong here, the number of words in common use indicating different varieties of this sort of feeling is surprising and suggestive. One cannot but think, What insight and what happy boldness of invention went to the devising of all these terms! What a psychologist is language, that thus labels and treasures up so many subtle aspects of the human mind!

We may profitably distinguish, as others have done, two general attitudes—the aggressive or self-assertive and the shrinking or humble. The first indicates that one thinks favorably of himself and tries to impose that favorable thought on others; the second, that he accepts and yields to a depreciating reflection of himself, and feels accordingly diminished and abased. Pride would, of course, be an example of the first way of feeling and acting, humility of the second.

But there are many phases of the aggressive self, and these, again, might be classified something as follows: first, in response to imagined approval we have pride, vanity, or self-respect; second, in response to imagined censure we have various sorts of resentment; and the humble self might be treated in a similar manner.

Pride and vanity are names which are commonly applied only to forms of self-approval that strike us as disagreeable or egotistical; but they may be used in a somewhat larger sense to indicate simply a more or less stable attitude of the social self toward the world in which it is reflected; the distinction being of the same sort as that between unstable and rigid egotism already suggested.

These differences in stability, which are of great importance in the study of social personality, are perhaps connected with the contrast between the more receptive and the more constructive types of mind. Although in the best minds reception and construction are harmoniously united, and although it may be shown that they are in a measure mutually dependent, so that neither can be perfect without the other, yet as a rule they are not symmetrically developed, and this lack of symmetry corresponds to divergences of personal character. Minds of one sort are, so to speak, endogenous or ingrowing in their natural bent, while those of another are exogenous or outgrowing; that is to say, those of the former kind have a relatively strong turn for working up old material, as compared with that for taking in new; cogitation is more pleasant to them than observation; they prefer the sweeping and garnishing of their house to the confusion of entertaining visitors; while of the other sort the opposite of this may be said. Now, the tendency of the endogenous or inward activities is to secure unity and stability of thought and character at the possible expense of openness and adaptability; because the energy goes chiefly into systematization, and in attaining this the mind is pretty sure to limit its new impressions to those that do not disturb too much that unity and system it loves so well. These traits are, of course, manifested in the person's relation to others. The friends he has "and their acceptance tried" he grapples to his soul with hooks of steel, but is likely to be unsympathetic and hard toward influences of a novel character. On the other hand, the exogenous or outgrowing mind, more active near the periphery than toward the centre, is open to all sorts of impressions, eagerly taking in new material, which is likely never to get much arrangement; caring less for the order of the house than that it should be full of guests, quickly responsive to personal influences, but lacking that depth and tenacity of sympathy that the other sort of mind shows with people congenial with itself.

Pride,* then, is the form social self-approval takes in the more rigid or self-sufficient sort of minds; the person who feels it is assured that he stands well with others whose opinion he cares for, and does not imagine any humiliating image of himself, but carries his mental and social stability to such a degree that it is likely to narrow his soul by warding off the enlivening pricks of doubt and shame. By no means independent of the world, it is, after all, distinctly a social sentiment, and gets its standards ultimately from social custom and opinion. But the proud man is not *immediately* dependent upon what others think; he has worked over his reflected self in his mind until it is a steadfast portion of his thought, an idea and conviction apart, in some measure, from its external origin. Hence this sentiment requires time for its development and flourishes in mature age rather than

* Compare Stanley, The Evolutionary Psychology of Feeling, p. 271 *et seq.*

232

in the open and growing period of youth. A man who is proud of his rank, his social position, his professional eminence, his benevolence, or his integrity, is in the habit of contemplating daily an agreeable and little changing image of himself as he believes he appears in the eyes of the world. This image is probably distorted, since pride deceives by a narrowing of the imagination, but it is stable, and because it is so, because he feels sure of it, he is not disturbed by any passing breath of blame. If he is aware of such a thing at all he dismisses it as a vagary of no importance, feeling the best judgment of the world to be securely in his favor. If he should ever lose this conviction, if some catastrophe should shatter the image, he would be a broken man, and, if far gone in years, would perhaps not raise his head again.

In a sense pride is strength; that is, it implies a stable and consistent character which can be counted on; it will do its work without watching, and be honorable in its dealings, according to its cherished standards; it has always a vigorous, though narrow, conscience. On the other hand, it stunts a man's growth by closing his mind to progressive influences, and so in the long run may be a source of weakness. Burke said, I believe, that no man ever had a point of pride that was not injurious to him; and perhaps this was what he meant. Pride also causes, as a rule, a deeper animosity on the part of others than vanity; it may be hated but hardly despised; yet many would rather live with it than with vanity, because, after all, one knows where to find it, and so can adapt himself to it.

233

The other is so whimsical that it is impossible to foresee what turn it will take next.

Language seldom distinguishes clearly between a way of feeling and its visible expression; and so the word vanity, which means primarily emptiness, indicates either a weak or hollow appearance of worth put on in the endeavor to impress others, or the state of feeling that goes with it. It is the form social self-approval naturally takes in a somewhat unstable mind, not sure of its image. The vain man, in his more confident moments, sees a delightful reflection of himself, but knowing that it is transient, he is afraid it will change. He has not fixed it, as the proud man has, by incorporation with a stable habit of thought, but, being immediately dependent for it upon others, is at their mercy and very vulnerable, living in the frailest of glass houses which may be shattered at any moment; and, in fact, this catastrophe happens so often that he gets somewhat used to it and soon recovers from it. While the image which the proud person contemplates is fairly consistent, and, though distorted, has a solid basis in his character, so that he will not accept praise for qualities he does not believe himself to possess; vanity has no stable idea of itself and will swallow any shining bait. The person will gloat now on one pleasing reflection of himself, now on another, trying to mimic each in its turn, and becoming, so far as he can, what any flatterer says he is, or what any approving person seems to think he is. It is characteristic of him to be so taken up with his own image in the other's mind that he is hypnotized by it, as it were, and sees it magnified, distorted, and out of its true relation to the other contents of that mind. He does not see, as so often happens, that he is being managed and made a fool of; he "gives himself away"—fatuity being of the essence of vanity. On the other hand, and for the same reason, a vain person is frequently tortured by groundless imaginings that some one has misunderstood him, slighted him, insulted him, or otherwise mistreated his social effigy.

Of course the immediate result of vanity is weakness, as that of pride is strength; but on a wider view there is something to be said for it. Goethe exclaims in Wilhelm Meister, "Would to heaven all men were vain! that is were vain with clear perception, with moderation, and in a proper sense: we should then, in the cultivated world, have happy times of it. Women, it is told us, are vain from the very cradle; yet does it not become them? do they not please us the more? How can a youth form himself if he is not vain? An empty, hollow nature will, by this means, at least contrive to give itself an outward show, and a proper man will soon train himself from the outside inwards." * That is to say, vanity, in moderation, may indicate an openness, a sensibility, a teachability, that is a good augury of growth. In youth, at least, it is much preferable to pride.

It is the obnoxious, or in some way conspicuous, manifestations of self-feeling that are likely to receive special names. Accordingly, there are many words

* Wilhelm Meister's Travels, chap. xii, Carlyle's Translation.

and phrases for different aspects of pride and vanity, while a moderate and balanced self-respect does not attract nomenclature. One who has this is more open and flexible in feeling and behavior than one who is proud; the image is not stereotyped, he is subject to humility; while at the same time he does not show the fluttering anxiety about his appearance that goes with vanity, but has stable ways of thinking about the image, as about other matters, and cannot be upset by passing phases of praise or blame. In fact, the healthy life of the self requires the same co-operation of continuity with change that marks normal development everywhere; there must be variability, openness, freedom, on a basis of organization: too rigid organization meaning fixity and death, and the lack of it weakness or anarchy. The self-respecting man values others' judgments and occupies his mind with them a great deal, but he keeps his head, he discriminates and selects, considers all suggestions with a view to his character, and will not submit to influences not in the line of his development. Because he conceives his self as a stable and continuing whole he always feels the need to *be*, and cannot be guilty of that separation between being and seeming that constitutes affectation. For instance, a self-respecting scholar, deferent to the standards set by the opinions of others, might wish to have read all the books on a certain subject, and feel somewhat ashamed not to have done so, but he could not affect to have read them when he had not. The pain of breaking the unity of his thought, of disfiguring his picture of himself as a sincere and

236

consistent man, would overbalance any gratification he might have in the imagined approval of his thoroughness. If he were vain he would possibly affect to have read the books; while if arrogant he might feel no compunctions for avowed ignorance of them.

Common sense approves a just mingling of deference and self-poise in the attitude of one man toward others: while the unyielding are certainly repellent, the too deferent are nearly as much so; they are tiresome and even disgusting, because they seem flimsy and unreal, and do not give that sense of contact with something substantial and interesting that we look for.

> "——you have missed
> The manhood that should yours resist,
> Its complement."

We like the manner of a person who appears interested in what we say and do, and not indifferent to our opinion, but has at the same time an evident reserve of stability and independence. It is much the same with a writer; we require of him a bold and determined statement of his own special view—that is what he is here for—and yet, with this, an air of hospitality, and an appreciation that he is after all only a small part of a large world.

With some, then, the self-image is an imitative sketch in the supposed style of the last person they have talked to; with others, it is a rigid, traditional thing, a lifeless repetition that has lost all relation to the forces that originally moulded it, like the Byzantine madonnas before the time of Cimabue; with

237

others again it is a true work of art in which individual tendencies and the influence of masters mingle in a harmonious whole; but all of us have it, unless we are so deficient in imagination as to be less than human. When we speak of a person as independent of opinion, or self-sufficient, we can only mean that, being of a constructive and stable character, he does not have to recur every day to the visible presence of his approvers, but can supply their places by imagination, can hold on to some influences and reject others, choose his leaders, individualize his conformity; and so work out a characteristic and fairly consistent career. The self must be built up by the aid of social suggestions, just as all higher thought is.

Honor is a finer kind of self-respect. It is used to mean either something one feels regarding himself, or something that other people think and feel regarding him, and so illustrates by the accepted use of language the fact that the private and social aspects of self are inseparable. One's honor, as he feels it, and his honor in the sense of honorable repute, as he conceives it to exist in the minds of others whose opinion he cares for, are two aspects of the same thing. No one can permanently maintain a standard of honor in his own mind if he does not conceive of some other mind or minds as sharing and corroborating this standard. If his immediate environment is degrading he may have resort to books or memory in order that his imagination may construct a better environment of nobler people to sustain his standard; but if he cannot do this it is sure to fall. Sentiments

238

of higher good or right, like other sentiments, find source and renewal in intercourse. On the other hand, we cannot separate the idea of honor from that of a sincere and stable private character. We cannot form a habit of thought about what is admirable, though it be derived from others, without creating a mental standard. A healthy mind cannot strive for outward honor without, in some measure, developing an inward conscience—training himself from the outside in, as Goethe says.

It is the result of physiological theories of ethics —certainly not intended by the authors of those theories—to make the impulses of an ideal self, like the sentiment of honor, seem far-fetched, extravagant, and irrational. They have to be justified by an elaborate course of reasoning which does not seem very convincing after all. No such impression, however, could result from the direct observation of social life. In point of fact, a man's honor, as he conceives it, is his self in its most immediate and potent reality, swaying his conduct without waiting upon any inquiry into its physiological antecedents. The preference of honor to life is not at all a romantic exception in human behavior, but something quite characteristic of man on a really human level. A despicable or degenerate person may save his body alive at the expense of honor, and so may almost any one in moments of panic or other kind of demoralization, but the typical man, in his place among his fellows and with his social sentiments about him, will not do so. We read in history of many peoples conquered because

239

they lacked discipline and strategy, or because their weapons were inferior, but we seldom read of any who were really cowardly in the sense that they would not face death in battle. And the readiness to face death commonly means that the sentiment of honor dominates the impulses of terror and pain. All over the ancient world the Roman legions encountered men who shunned death no more than themselves, but were not so skilful in inflicting it; and in Mexico and Peru the natives died by thousands in a desperate struggle against the Spanish arms. The earliest accounts we have of our own Germanic ancestors show a state of feeling and practice that made self-preservation, in a material sense, strictly subordinate to honor. "Death is better for every clansman than coward life," says Beowulf,* and there seems no doubt whatever that this was a general principle of action, so that cowardice was a rare phenomenon. In modern life we see the same subordination of sensation to sentiment among soldiers and in a hundred other careers involving bodily peril—not as a heroic exception but as the ordinary practice of plain men. We see it also in the general readiness to undergo all sorts of sensual pains and privations rather than cease to be respectable in the eyes of other people. It is well known, for instance, that among the poor thousands endure cold and partial starvation rather than lose their self-respect by begging. In short, it does not seem too favorable a view of mankind to say that under normal

* Quoted by Gummere, Germanic Origins, p. 266.

240

conditions their minds are ruled by the sentiment of Norfolk:

> "Mine honor is my life: both grow in one;
> Take honor from me and my life is done."

If we once grasp the fact that the self is primarily a social, ideal, or imaginative fact, and not a sensual fact, all this appears quite natural and not in need of special explanation.

In relation to the highest phases of individuality self-respect becomes self-reverence, in the sense of Tennyson, when he says:

> "Self-reverence, self-knowledge, self-control,
> These three alone lead life to sovereign power." *

or of Goethe when, in the first chapter of the second book of Wilhelm Meister's Wanderjahre, he names self-reverence—*Ehrfurcht vor sich selbst*—as the highest of the four reverences taught to youth in his ideal system of education.† Emerson uses self-reliance in a similar sense, in that memorable essay the note of which is "Trust thyself, every heart vibrates to that iron string," and throughout his works.

Self-reverence, as I understand the matter, means reverence for a higher or ideal self; a real "I," because it is based on what the individual actually is, as only he himself can know and appropriate it, but a better "I" of aspiration rather than attainment; it is simply the best he can make out of life.   Reverence

* Œnone.   † Travels, chap. x, in Carlyle's Translation.

241

for it implies, as Emerson urges, resistance to friends and counsellors and to any influence that the mind honestly rejects as inconsistent with itself; a man must feel that the final arbiter is within him and not outside of him in some master, living or dead, as conventional religion, for instance, necessarily teaches. Nevertheless this highest self is a social self, in that it is a product of constructive imagination working with the materials which social experience supplies. Our ideals of personal character are built up out of thoughts and sentiments developed by intercourse, and very largely by imagining how our selves would appear in the minds of persons we look up to. These are not necessarily living persons; any one that is at all real, that is imaginable, to us, becomes a possible occasion of social self-feeling; and idealizing and aspiring persons live largely in the imagined presence of masters and heroes to whom they refer their own life for comment and improvement. This is particularly true of youth, when ideals are forming; later the personal element in these ideals, having performed its function of suggesting and vivifying them, is likely to fade out of consciousness and leave only habits and principles whose social origin is forgotten.

Resentment, the attitude which an aggressive self takes in response to imagined depreciation, may be regarded as self-feeling with a coloring of anger; indeed, the relation between self-feeling and particular emotions like anger and fear is so close that the latter might be looked upon as simply specialized kinds of the former; it makes little difference whether we take this view or think of them as distinct, since such divisions must always be arbitrary. I shall say more of this sentiment in the next chapter.

If a person conceives his image as depreciated in the mind of another; and if, instead of maintaining an aggressive attitude and resenting that depreciation, he yields to it and accepts the image and the judgment upon it; then he feels and shows something in the way of humility. Here again we have a great variety of nomenclature, indicating different shades of humble feeling and behavior, such as shame, confusion, abasement, humiliation, mortification, meekness, bashfulness, diffidence, shyness, being out of countenance, abashed or crestfallen, contrition, compunction, remorse, and so on.

Humility, like self-approval, has forms that consist with a high type of character and are felt to be praiseworthy, and others that are felt to be base. There is a sort that goes with vanity and indicates instability, an excessive and indiscriminate yielding to another's view of one's self. We wish a man to be humble only before what, from his own characteristic point of view, is truly superior. His humility should imply self-respect; it should be that attitude of deference which a stable but growing character takes in the presence of whatever embodies its ideals. Every outreaching person has masters in whose imagined presence he drops resistance and becomes like clay in the hands of the potter, that they may make something better of him. He does this from a feeling that the master is more himself than he is; there is a receptive enthusiasm, a sense of new life that swallows up the old self and makes his ordinary personality appear tedious, base, and despicable. Humility of this sort goes with self-reverence, because a sense of the higher or ideal self plunges the present and commonplace self into humility. The man aims at "so high an ideal that he always feels his unworthiness in his own sight and that of others, though aware of his own desert by the ordinary standards of his community, country, or generation." * But a humility that is self-abandonment, a cringing before opinion alien to one's self, is felt to be mere cowardice and servility.

Books of the inner life praise and enjoin lowliness, contrition, repentance, self-abnegation; but it is apparent to all thoughtful readers that the sort of humility inculcated is quite consistent with the self-reverence of Goethe or the self-reliance of Emerson—comes, indeed, to much the same thing. The Imitatio Christi is the type of such teaching, yet it is a manly book, and the earlier part especially contains exhortations to self-trust worthy of Emerson. "Certa viriliter," the writer says, "consuetudo consuetudine vincitur. Si tu scis homines dimittere, ipsi bene te dimittent tua facta facere." † The yielding constantly enjoined is either to God—that is, to an ideal personality developed in one's own mind—or, if to men, it is a submission to external rule which is designed to

* Stanley, The Evolutionary Psychology of Feeling, p. 280.

† "Strive manfully; habit is subdued by habit. If you know how to dismiss men, they also will dismiss you, to do your own things."—De Imitatione Christi, book i, chap. xxi, par. 2.

leave the will free for what are regarded as its higher functions. The whole teaching tends to the aggrandizement of an ideal but intensely private self, worked out in solitary meditation—to insure which worldly ambition is to be renounced—and symbolized as God, conscience, or grace. The just criticism of the doctrine that Thomas stands for is not that it depreciates manhood and self-reliance, but that it calls these away from the worldly activities where they are so much needed, and exercises them in a region of abstract imagination. No healthy mind can cast out self-assertion and the idea of personal freedom, however the form of expression may seem to deny these things, and accordingly the Imitation, and still more the New Testament, are full of them. Where there is no self-feeling, no ambition of any sort, there is no efficacy or significance. To lose the sense of a separate, productive, resisting self, would be to melt and merge and cease to be.

Healthy, balanced minds, of only medium sensibility, in a congenial environment and occupied with wholesome activity, keep the middle road of self-respect and reasonable ambition. They may require no special effort, no conscious struggle with recalcitrant egotism, to avoid heart-burning, jealousy, arrogance, anxious running after approval, and other maladies of the social self. With enough self-feeling to stimulate and not enough to torment him, with a social circle appreciative but not flattering, with good health and moderate success, a man may go through life with very little use for the moral and religious weapons that have been wrought for the repression of a contumacious self. There are many, particularly in an active, hopeful, and materially prosperous time like this, who have little experience of inner conflict and no interest in the literature and doctrine that relate to it.

But nearly all persons of the finer, more sensitive sort find the social self at times a source of passion and pain. In so far as a man amounts to anything, stands for anything, is truly an individual, he has an ego about which his passions cluster, and to aggrandize which must be a principal aim with him. But the very fact that the self is the object of our schemes and endeavors makes it a centre of mental disturbance: its suggestions are of effort, responsibility, doubt, hope, and fear. Just as a man cannot enjoy the grass and trees in his own grounds with quite the peace and freedom that he can those abroad, because they remind him of improvements that he ought to make and the like; so any part of the self is, in its nature, likely to be suggestive of exertion rather than rest. Moreover, it would seem that self-feeling, though pleasant in normal duration and intensity, is disagreeable in excess, like any other sort of feeling. One reason why we get tired of ourselves is simply that we have exhausted our capacity for experiencing with pleasure a certain kind of emotion.

As we have seen, the self that is most importunate is a reflection, largely, from the minds of others. This phase of self is related to character very much as credit is related to the gold and other securities upon which it rests. It easily and willingly expands, in most of us, and is liable to sudden, irrational, and grievous collapses. We live on, cheerful, self-confident, conscious of helping make the world go round, until in some rude hour we learn that we do not stand so well as we thought we did, that the image of us is tarnished. Perhaps we do something, quite naturally, that we find the social order is set against, or perhaps it is the ordinary course of our life that is not so well regarded as we supposed. At any rate, we find with a chill of terror that the world is cold and strange, and that our self-esteem, self-confidence, and hope, being chiefly founded upon opinions attributed to others, go down in the crash. Our reason may tell us that we are no less worthy than we were before, but dread and doubt do not permit us to believe it. The sensitive mind will certainly suffer, because of the instability of opinion. *Cadet cum labili.* As social beings we live with our eyes upon our reflection, but have no assurance of the tranquillity of the waters in which we see it. In the days of witchcraft it used to be believed that if one person secretly made a waxen image of another and stuck pins into the image, its counterpart would suffer tortures, and that if the image was melted the person would die. This superstition is almost realized in the relation between the private self and its social reflection. They seem separate but are darkly united, and what is done to the one is done to the other.

If a person of energetic and fine-strung temperament is neither vain nor proud, and lives equably without suffering seriously from mortification, jealousy, and the like; it is because he has in some way learned to discipline and control his self-feeling, and thus to escape the pains to which it makes him liable. To effect some such escape has always been a present and urgent problem with sensitive minds, and the literature of the inner life is very largely a record of struggle with the inordinate passions of the social self. To the commoner and somewhat sluggish sorts of people these passions are, on the whole, agreeable and beneficent. Emulation, ambition, honor, even pride and vanity in moderation, belong to the higher and more imaginative parts of our thought; they awaken us from sensuality and inspire us with ideal and socially determined purposes. The doctrine that they are evil could have originated only with those who felt them so; that is, I take it, with unusually sensitive spirits, or those whom circumstances denied a normal and wholesome self-expression. To such the thought of self becomes painful, not because of any lack of self-feeling; but, quite the reverse, because, being too sensitive and tender, it becomes overwrought, so that this thought sets in vibration an emotional chord already strained and in need of rest. To such minds self-abnegation becomes an ideal, an ideal of rest, peace, and freedom, like green pastures and still waters. The prophets of the inner life, like Marcus Aurelius, St. Paul, St. Augustine, Thomas à Kempis, and Pascal, were men distinguished not by the lack of an aggressive self, but by a success in controlling and elevating it which makes them the examples of all who undergo a like struggle with it. If their ego had not been naturally importunate they would not have been forced to contend with it, and to develop the tactics of that contention for the edification of times to come.

The social self may be protected either in the negative way, by some sort of withdrawal from the suggestions that agitate and harass it, or in the positive way, by contending with them and learning to control and transform them, so that they are no longer painful; most teachers inculcating some sort of a combination of these two kinds of tactics.

Physical withdrawal from the presence of men has always been much in favor with those in search of a calmer, surer life. The passions to be regulated are sympathetic in origin, awakened by imagination of the minds of other persons with whom we come in contact. As Contarini Fleming remarks in Disraeli's novel, "So soon as I was among men I desired to influence them." To retire to the monastery, or the woods, or the sea, is to escape from the sharp suggestions that spur on ambition; and even to change from the associates and competitors of our active life into the company of strangers, or at least of those whose aims and ambitions are different from ours, has much the same effect. To get away from one's working environment is, in a sense, to get away from one's self; and this is often the chief advantage of travel and change. I can hardly agree with those who imagine that a special instinct of withdrawal is necessary

249

to explain the prominence of retirement in the ordinances of religion. People wish to retire from the world because they are weary, harassed, driven by it, so that they feel that they cannot recover their equanimity without getting away from it. To the impressible mind life is a theatre of alarms and contentions, even when a phlegmatic person can see no cause for agitation—and to such a mind peace often seems the one thing fair and desirable, so that the cloister or the forest, or the vessel on the lonesome sea, is the most grateful object of imagination. The imaginative self, which is, for most purposes, the real self, may be more battered, wounded, and strained by a striving, ambitious life than the material body could be in a more visible battle, and its wounds are usually more lasting and draw more deeply upon the vitality. Mortification, resentment, jealousy, the fear of disgrace and failure, sometimes even hope and elation, are exhausting passions; and it is after a severe experience of them that retirement seems most healing and desirable.

A subtler kind of withdrawal takes place in the imagination alone by curtailing ambition, by trimming down one's idea of himself to a measure that need not fear further diminution. How secure and restful it would be if one could be consistently and sincerely humble! There is no sweeter feeling than contrition, self-abnegation, after a course of alternate conceit and mortification. This also is an established part of the religious discipline of the mind. Thus we find the following in Thomas: "Son, now I will teach thee the way of peace and of true liberty. . . . Study to do another's will rather than thine own. Choose ever to have less rather than more. Seek ever the lower place and to be subject to all; ever wish and pray that the will of God may be perfectly done in thee and in all. Behold such a man enters the bounds of peace and calm." * In other words, lop off the aggressive social self altogether, renounce the ordinary objects of ambition, accustom yourself to an humble place in others' thoughts, and you will be at peace; because you will have nothing to lose, nothing to fear. No one at all acquainted with the moralists, pagan or Christian, will need to be more than reminded that this imaginative withdrawal of the self from strife and uncertainty has ever been inculcated as a means to happiness and edification. Many persons who are sensitive to the good opinion of others, and, by impulse, take great pleasure in it, shrink from indulging this pleasure because they know by experience that it puts them into others' power and introduces an element of weakness, unrest, and probable mortification. By recognizing a favorable opinion of yourself, and taking pleasure in it, you in a measure give yourself and your peace of mind into the keeping of another, of whose attitude you can never be certain. You have a new source of doubt and apprehension. One learns in time the wisdom of entering into such relations only with persons of whose sincerity, stability, and justice one is as sure as possible; and also of having nothing to do with approval of himself

* De Imitatione Christi, book iii, chap. xxiii, par. 1.

which he does not feel to have a secure basis in his character. And so regarding self-aggrandizement in the various forms implicitly condemned by Thomas's four rules of peace; if a man is of so eager a temperament that he does not need these motives to awaken him and call his faculties into normal action, he will be happier and possibly more useful to the world if he is able to subdue them by some sort of discipline. In this way, it seems to me, we may chiefly account for and justify the stringent self-suppression of Pascal and of many other fine spirits. "So jealous was he of any surprise of pleasure, of any thought of vanity or complacency in himself and his work, that he wore a girdle of iron next his skin, the sharp points of which he pressed closely when he thought himself in any danger. . . ." *

Of course the objection to withdrawal, physical or imaginative, is that it seems to be a refusal of social functions, a rejection of life, leading logically to other-worldism, to the idea that it is better to die than to live. According to this teaching, in its extreme form, the best thing that can happen to a man is to die and go to heaven; but if that is not permitted, then let the private, ambitious self, set to play the tunes of this world, die in him, and be replaced by humble and secluded meditation in preparation for the life to come. When this doctrine was taught and believed to such an extent that a great part of the finer spirits were led, during centuries, to isolate themselves in deserts and cloisters, or at least to renounce and depreciate the affections and duties of the family, the effect was no

* Tulloch's Pascal, p. 100.

doubt bad; but in our time there is little tendency to this extreme, and there is perhaps danger that the usefulness of partial or occasional withdrawal may be overlooked. Mr. Lecky thinks, for instance, that the complete suppression of the conventual system by Protestantism has been far from a benefit to women or the world, and that it is impossible to conceive of any institution more needed than one which should furnish a shelter for unprotected women and convert them into agents of charity. * The amount and kind of social stimulation that a man can bear without harm to his character and working power depends, roughly speaking, upon his sensitiveness, which determines the emotional disturbance, and upon the vigor of the controlling or co-ordinating functions, which measures his power to guide or quell emotion and make it subsidiary to healthy life. There has always been a class of persons, including a large proportion of those capable of the higher sorts of intellectual production, for whom the competitive struggles of ordinary life are overstimulating and destructive, and who therefore cannot serve the world well without apparently secluding themselves from it. It would seem, then, that withdrawal and asceticism are often too sweepingly condemned. A sound practical morality will consider these things in relation to various types of character and circumstance, and find, I believe, important functions for both.

But the most radical remedy for the mortifications and uncertainties of the social self is not the negative

* See his History of European Morals, vol. ii, p. 369.

one of merely secluding or diminishing the I, but the positive one of transforming it. The two are not easily distinguishable, and are usually phases of the same process. The self-instinct, though it cannot be suppressed while mental vigor remains, can be taught to associate itself more and more with ideas and aims of general and permanent worth, which can be thought of as higher than the more sensual, narrow, or temporary interests, and independent of them. It must always be borne in mind that the self is any idea or system of ideas with which is associated the peculiar appropriative attitude we call self-feeling. Anything whose depreciation makes me feel resentful is myself, whether it is my coat, my face, my brother, the book I have published, the scientific theory I accept, the philanthropic work to which I am devoted, my religious creed, or my country. The only question is, Am I identified with it in my thought, so that to touch it is to touch me? Thus in " Middlemarch " the true self of Mr. Casaubon, his most aggressive, persistent, and sensitive part, is his system of ideas relating to the unpublished "Key to All Mythologies." It is about this that he is proud, jealous, sore, and apprehensive. What he imagines that the Brasenose men will think of it is a large part of his social self, and he suffers hidden joy and torture according as he is hopeful or despondent of its triumphant publication. When he finds that his body must die his chief thought is how to keep this alive, and he attempts to impose its completion upon poor Dorothea, who is a pale shadow in his life compared with the Key, a mere instrument to minister to this fantastic ego. So if one, turning the leaves of history, could evoke the real selves of all the men of thought, what a strange procession they would be!—outlandish theories, unintelligible and forgotten creeds, hypotheses once despised but now long established, or *vice versa*—all conceived eagerly, jealously, devotedly, as the very heart of the self. There is no class more sensitive and none, not even the insane, in whom self-feeling attaches to such singular and remote conceptions. An astronomer may be indifferent when you depreciate his personal appearance, abuse his relatives, or question his pecuniary honesty; but if you doubt that there are artificial canals on Mars you cut him to the quick. And poets and artists of every sort have always and with good reason been regarded as a *genus irritabile*.

The ideas of self most commonly cherished, and the ambitions corresponding to these ideas, fail to appease the imagination of the idealist, for various reasons; chiefly, perhaps, for the following: first because they seem more or less at variance with the good of other persons, and so, to the imaginative and sympathetic mind, bring elements of inconsistency and wrong, which it cannot accept as consonant with its own needs; and second because their objects are at best temporary, so that even if thought of as achieved they fail to meet the need of the mind for a resting-place in some conception of permanent good or right. The transformation of narrow and temporary ambitions or ideals into something more fitted to satisfy the imagination in these respects, is an urgent need, a condition precedent to peace of mind, in many persons. The unquiet and discordant state of the unre-

255

generate is a commonplace, a thousand times repeated, of writings on the inner life. *"Superbus et avarus numquam quiescunt,"* they tell us, and to enable us to escape from such unrest is a chief aim of the discipline of self-feeling enjoined by ethical and religious teachers. "Self," "the natural man," and similar expressions indicate an aspect of the self thought of as lower —in part at least because of the insecure, inconsistent, and temporary character just indicated—which is to be so far as possible subjected and forgotten, while the feelings once attached to it find a less precarious object in ideas of justice and right, or in the conception of a personal deity, in whom all that is best of personality is to have secure existence and eternal success.

In this sense also we may understand the idea of freedom as it presented itself to Thomas à Kempis and similar minds. To forget "self" and live the larger life is to be free; free, that is, from the racking passions of the lower self, free to go onward into a self that is joyful, boundless, and without remorse. To gain this freedom the principal means is the control or mortification of sensual needs and worldly ambitions.

Thus the passion of self-aggrandizement is persistent but plastic; it will never disappear from a vigorous mind, but may become morally higher by attaching itself to a larger conception of what constitutes the self.

Wherever men find themselves out of joint with their social environment the fact will be reflected in some peculiarity of self-feeling. Thus it was in times when the general state of Europe was decadent and hopeless, or later when ceaseless wars and the common rule of violence prevailed, that finer spirits, for whose ambition the times offered no congenial career, so largely sought refuge in religious seclusion, and there built up among themselves a philosophy which compensated them by the vision of glory in another world for their insignificance in this. An institution so popular and enduring as monasticism and the system of belief that throve in connection with it must have answered to some deep need of human nature, and it would seem that, as regarded the more intellectual class, this need was largely that of creating a social self and system of selves which could thrive in the actual state of things. Their natures craved success, and, following a tendency always at work, though never more fantastic in its operation, they created an ideal or standard of success which they could achieve—very much as a farmer's boy with a weak body but an active brain sometimes goes into law, seeking and upholding an intellectual type of success. From this point of view—which is, of course, only one of many whence monasticism may be regarded— it appears as a wonderful exhibition of the power of human nature to effectuate itself in a co-operative manner in spite of the most untoward external circumstances.

If we have less flight from the world, corporeal or metaphysical, at the present day, it is doubtless in part because the times are more hospitable to the finer abilities, so that all sorts of men, within wide limits, find careers in which they may hope to gratify a reasonable ambition. But even now, where conditions are deranged and somewhat anarchical, so that many find themselves cut off from the outlook toward a congenial self-development, the wine of life turns bitter, and harrying resentments are generated which more or less disturb the stability of the social order. Each man must have his "I"; it is more necessary to him than bread; and if he does not find scope for it within the existing institutions he will be likely to make trouble.

Persons of great ambitions, or of peculiar aims of any sort, lie open to disorders of self-feeling, because they necessarily build up in their minds a self-image which no ordinary social environment can understand or corroborate, and which must be maintained by hardening themselves against immediate influences, enduring or repressing the pains of present depreciation, and cultivating in imagination the approval of some higher tribunal. If the man succeeds in becoming indifferent to the opinions of his neighbors he runs into another danger, that of a distorted and extravagant self of the pride sort, since by the very process of gaining independence and immunity from the stings of depreciation and misunderstanding, he has perhaps lost that wholesome deference to some social tribunal that a man cannot dispense with and remain quite sane. The image lacks verification and correction and becomes too much the reflection of an undisciplined self-feeling. It would seem that the megalomania or delusion of greatness which Lombroso, with more or less plausibility, ascribes to Victor Hugo and many other men of genius, is to be explained largely in this way.

Much the same may be said regarding the relation of self-feeling to mental disorder, and to abnormal personality of all sorts. It seems obvious, for instance, that the delusions of greatness and delusions of persecution so common in insanity are expressions of self-feeling escaped from normal limitation and control. The instinct which under proper regulation by reason and sympathy gives rise to just and sane ambition, in the absence of it swells to grotesque proportions; while the delusion of persecution appears to be a like extravagant development of that jealousy regarding what others are thinking of us which often reaches an almost insane point in irritable people whose sanity is not questioned.

The peculiar relations to other persons attending any marked personal deficiency or peculiarity are likely to aggravate, if not to produce, abnormal manifestations of self-feeling. Any such trait sufficiently noticeable to interrupt easy and familiar intercourse with others, and make people talk and think *about* a person or *to* him rather than *with* him, can hardly fail to have this effect. If he is naturally inclined to pride or irritability, these tendencies, which depend for correction upon the flow of sympathy, are likely to be increased. One who shows signs of mental aberration is, inevitably perhaps, but cruelly, shut off from familiar, thoughtless intercourse, partly excommunicated; his isolation is unwittingly proclaimed to him on every countenance by curiosity, indifference, aversion, or pity, and in so far as he is human enough to need free and equal communication and feel the lack of it, he suffers pain and loss of a kind and degree which others can only faintly imagine, and for the most part ignore. He finds himself apart, "not in it," and feels chilled, fearful, and suspicious. Thus "queerness" is no sooner perceived than it is multiplied by reflection from other minds. The same is true in some degree of dwarfs, deformed or disfigured persons, even the deaf and those suffering from the infirmities of old age. The chief misery of the decline of the faculties, and a main cause of the irritability that often goes with it, is evidently the isolation, the lack of customary appreciation and influence, which only the rarest tact and thoughtfulness on the part of others can alleviate.

An unhealthy self is at the heart of nearly all social discontent. That is, if classes of men find themselves leading a kind of life that does not fulfil the deep needs of human nature, they are certain to manifest their inner trouble by some sort of untoward behavior. It is true that the self has great adaptability. Hardship does not necessarily impair it; in fact strenuous occupation is one of its needs. But there are other needs, equally essential, whose gratification is often denied by the conditions of life. Leaving aside individual peculiarities, the additional needs shared by all of us may perhaps be summed up in three, self-expression, appreciation, and a reasonable security. No man can or ought to be content unless he has a chance to work out his personality, to form, strive for, and gratify reasonable ambitions. In connection with this, indeed really as a part of it, he needs fellowship and that appreciation by others which gives his self social corroboration and support. And, finally, he cannot take much satisfaction in life unless he feels that he is not at the mercy of chance or of others' wills, but has a fair prospect, if he strives steadily, of maintaining his position. No one can study sympathetically the actual state of men and women in our social order without being convinced that large numbers of them are denied some or all of these fundamentals of human living.

We find, for example, workmen who have no security in their work, but are hired and fired arbitrarily, or perhaps lose their occupation altogether for reasons having no apparent relation to their merit. Very commonly their work itself does not admit of that exercise of the will and growth in skill and power which keeps the sense of self alive and interested. And if there is nothing in the work itself, or in appreciation by his employer, to gratify the self-feeling of the worker, it may well be that resentment and occasional rebellion are the only way to preserve his self-respect. One of the great reasons for the popularity of strikes is that they give the suppressed self a sense of power. For once the human tool knows itself a man, able to stand up and speak a word or strike a blow. Many occupations, also, are of an irregular or nomadic character which makes it impossible for men and women to have that primary self-expression which we get from a family and a settled home.

The immigrant has for the most part been treated purely as a source of labor, with little or no regard to the fact that he is a human being, with a self like the rest of us. There is nothing less to our credit than our neglect of the foreigner and his children, unless it be the arrogance most of us betray when we set out to "americanize" him.

The negro question includes a similar situation. There is no understanding it without realizing the kind of self-feeling a race must have who, in a land where men are supposed to be equal, find themselves marked with indelible inferiority. And so with many other classes; with offenders against the law, for example, whom we often turn into hardened criminals by a treatment which destroys their self-respect— or rather convinces them that their only chance of self-respect is in defiance of authority. The treatment of children, in and out of school, involves similar questions, and so of domestic workers, married women, and other sorts of people more or less subject to the arbitrary will of others. In general only a resolute exercise of sympathetic imagination, informed by study of the facts, will give us a right point of view.*

* The modern study, aspiring to become a science, called Psychoanalysis, endeavors in a more or less systematic way to investigate the history and working of the self, with a view especially to understanding its maladies and finding a cure for them. There can be no doubt of the need for such a study, or of its

great practical use, even if it does not yield enough definite and settled results to establish it as a science. The human mind is indeed a cave swarming with strange forms of life, most of them unconscious and unilluminated. Unless we can understand something as to how the motives that issue from this obscurity are generated, we can hardly hope to foresee or control them. The literature of psychoanalysis is suggestive and stimulating, but the more general theories to be found in it are perhaps only provisional. A sociologist will note especially the tendency to work too directly from supposed instincts, without allowing for the transforming action of social institutions and processes.

CHAPTER VII

HOSTILITY

SIMPLE OR ANIMAL ANGER—SOCIAL ANGER—THE FUNCTION OF HOSTILITY—THE DOCTRINE OF NON-RESISTANCE—CONTROL AND TRANSFORMATION OF HOSTILITY BY REASON—HOSTILITY AS PLEASURE OR PAIN—THE IMPORTANCE OF ACCEPTED SOCIAL STANDARDS—FEAR

I GIVE a chapter to Hostility not only because it is an important phase of human nature, but because I wish to use it as a type of the development in social life of an instinctive emotion. The process of transformation here indicated goes on very similarly in the cases of fear, love, grief, and other emotions of which I shall not treat in detail.

Anger, like other emotions, seems to exist at birth as a simple, instinctive animal tendency, and to undergo differentiation and development parallel with the growth of imagination. Perez, speaking of children at about the age of two months, says, "they begin to push away objects that they do not like, and have real fits of passion, frowning, growing red in the face, trembling all over, and sometimes shedding tears." They also show anger at not getting the breast or bottle, or when washed or undressed, or when their toys are taken away. At about one year old "they will beat people, animals, and inanimate objects if they are angry with them," * throw things at offending persons, and the like.

I have observed phenomena similar to these, and no doubt all have who have seen anything of little children. If there are any writers who tend to regard the mind at birth as almost *tabula rasa* so far as special instincts are concerned, consisting of little more than a faculty of receiving and organizing impressions, it must be wholesome for them to associate with infants and notice how unmistakable are the signs of a distinct and often violent emotion, apparently identical with the anger or rage of adults. What grown-up persons feel seems to be different, not in its emotional essence, but in being modified by association with a much more complicated system of ideas.

This simple, animal sort of anger, excited immediately by something obnoxious to the senses, does not entirely disappear in adult life. Probably most persons who step upon a barrel-hoop or run their heads against a low doorway can discern a moment of instinctive anger toward the harming object. Even our more enduring forms of hostility seem often to partake of this direct, unintellectual character. Most people, but especially those of a sensitive, impressible nature, have antipathies to places, animals, persons, words—to all sorts of things in fact—which appear to spring directly out of the subconscious life, without any mediation of thought. Some think that an animal or instinctive antipathy to human beings of a different race is natural to all mankind. And among

* Perez, The First Three Years of Childhood, p. 66.

people of the same race there are undoubtedly persons whom other persons loathe without attributing to them any hostile state of mind, but with a merely animal repugnance. Even when the object of hostility is quite distinctly a mental or moral trait, we often seem to feel it in an external way, that is, we *see* it as behavior but do not really understand it as thought or sentiment. Thus duplicity is hateful whether we can see any motive for it or not, and gives a sense of slipperiness and insecurity so tangible that one naturally thinks of some wriggling animal. In like manner vacillation, fawning, excessive protestation or self-depreciation, and many other traits, may be obnoxious to us in a somewhat physical way without our imagining them as states of mind.

But for a social, imaginative being, whose main interests are in the region of communicative thought and sentiment, the chief field of anger, as of other emotions, is transferred to this region. Hostility ceases to be a simple emotion due to a simple stimulus, and breaks up into innumerable hostile sentiments associated with highly imaginative personal ideas. In this mentally higher form it may be regarded as hostile sympathy, or a hostile comment on sympathy. That is to say, we enter by sympathy or personal imagination into the state of mind of others, or think we do, and if the thoughts we find there are injurious to or uncongenial with the ideas we are already cherishing, we feel a movement of anger.

This is forcibly expressed in a brief but admirable

study of antipathy by Sophie Bryant. Though the antipathy she describes is of a peculiarly subtle kind, it is plain that the same sort of analysis may be applied to any form of imaginative hostility.

"A is drawn out toward B to feel what he feels. If the new feeling harmonizes, distinctly or obscurely, with the whole system of A's consciousness—or the part then identified with his will—there follows that joyful expansion of self beyond self which is sympathy. But if not—if the new feeling is out of keeping with the system of A's will—tends to upset the system, and brings discord into it—there follows the reaction of the whole against the hostile part which, transferred to its cause in B, pushes out B's state, as the antithesis of self, yet threatening self, and offensive." Antipathy, she says, "is full of horrid thrill." "The peculiar horror of the antipathy springs from the unwilling response to the state abhorred. We feel ourselves actually like the other person, selfishly vain, cruelly masterful, artfully affected, insincere, ungenial, and so on." . . . "There is some affinity between those who antipathize." * And with similar meaning Thoreau remarks that "you cannot receive a shock unless you have an electric affinity for that which shocks you," and that "He who receives an injury is to some extent an accomplice of the wrongdoer." †

Thus the cause of hostility is imaginative or sympathetic, an inimical idea attributed to another mind.

* Mind, new series, vol. iv., p. 365.
† A Week on the Concord and Merrimack Rivers, pp. 303, 328.

We cannot feel this way toward that which is totally unlike us, because the totally unlike is unimaginable, has no interest for us. This, like all social feeling, requires a union of likeness with difference.

It is clear that closer association and more knowledge of one another, offer no security against hostile feeling. Whether intimacy will improve our sentiment toward another man or not depends upon the true relation of his way of thinking and feeling to ours, which intimacy is likely to reveal. There are many persons with whom we get on very well at a certain distance, who would turn out intensely antipathetic if we had to live in the same house with them. Probably all of us have experienced in one form or another the disgust and irritation that may come from enforced intimacy with people we liked well enough as mere acquaintances, and with whom we can find no particular fault, except that they rub us the wrong way. Henry James, speaking of the aversion of the brothers Goncourt for Sainte-Beuve, remarks that it was "a plant watered by frequent intercourse and protected by punctual notes." * It is true that an active sense of justice may do much to overcome unreasonable antipathies; but there are so many urgent uses for our sense of justice that it is well not to fatigue it by excessive and unnecessary activity. Justice involves a strenuous and symmetrical exercise of the imagination and reason, which no one can keep up all the time; and those who display it most on important occasions ought to be free to indulge somewhat their whims and prejudices in familiar intercourse.

* See his essay on the Journal of the Brothers Goncourt.

Neither do refinement, culture, and taste have any necessary tendency to diminish hostility. They make a richer and finer sympathy possible, but at the same time multiply the possible occasions of antipathy. They are like a delicate sense of smell, which opens the way to as much disgust as appreciation. Instead of the most sensitive sympathy, the finest mental texture, being a safeguard against hostile passions, it is only too evident from a study of the lives of men of genius that these very traits make a sane and equable existence peculiarly difficult. Read, for instance, the confessions of Rousseau, and observe how a fine nature, full of genuine and eager social idealism, is subject to peculiar sufferings and errors through the sensibility and imagination such a nature must possess. The quicker the sympathy and ideality, the greater the suffering from neglect and failure, the greater also the difficulty of disciplining the multitude of intense impressions and maintaining a sane view of the whole. Hence the pessimism, the extravagant indignation against real or supposed wrong-doers, and not infrequently, as in Rousseau's case, the almost insane bitterness of jealousy and mistrust.

The commonest forms of imaginative hostility are grounded on social self-feeling, and come under the head of resentment. We impute to the other person an injurious thought regarding something which we cherish as a part of our self, and this awakens anger, which we name pique, animosity, umbrage, estrangement, soreness, bitterness, heart-burning, jealousy, indignation, and so on; in accordance with variations which these words suggest. They all rest upon a feeling that the other person harbors ideas injurious to us, so that the thought of him is an attack upon our self. Suppose, for instance, there is a person who has reason to believe that he has caught me in a lie. It makes little difference, perhaps, whether he really has or not; so long as I have any self-respect left, and believe that he entertains this depreciatory idea of me, I must resent the idea whenever, through my thinking of him, it enters my mind. Or suppose there is a man who has met me running in panic from the field of battle; would it not be hard not to hate him? These situations are perhaps unusual, but we all know persons to whom we attribute depreciation of our characters, our friends, our children, our workmanship, our cherished creed or philanthropy; and we do not like them.

The resentment of charity or pity is a good instance of hostile sympathy. If a man has self-respect, he feels insulted by the depreciating view of his manhood implied in commiserating him or offering him alms. Self-respect means that one's reflected self is up to the social standard: and the social standard requires that a man should not need pity or alms except under very unusual conditions. So the assumption that he does need them is an injury—whether he does or not— precisely as it is an insult to a woman to commiserate her ugliness and bad taste, and suggest that she wear a veil or employ some one to select her gowns. The curious may find interest in questions like this: whether a tramp can have self-respect unless he deceives the one who gives him aid, and so feels superior to him,

270

and not a mere dependent. In the same way we can easily see why criminals look down upon paupers.

The word indignation suggests a higher sort of imaginative hostility. It implies that the feeling is directed toward some attack upon a standard of right, and is not merely an impulse like jealousy or pique. A higher degree of rationalization is involved; there is some notion of a reasonable adjustment of personal claims, which the act or thought in question violates. We frequently perceive that the simpler forms of resentment have no rational basis, could not be justified in open court, but indignation always claims a general or social foundation. We feel indignant when we think that favoritism and not merit secures promotion, when the rich man gets a pass on the railroad, and so on.

It is thus possible rudely to classify hostilities under three heads, according to the degree of mental organization they involve; namely, as

1. Primary, immediate, or animal.

2. Social, sympathetic, imaginative, or personal, of a comparatively direct sort, that is, without reference to any standard of justice.

3. Rational or ethical; similar to the last but involving reference to a standard of justice and the sanction of conscience.

The function of hostility is, no doubt, to awaken a fighting energy, to contribute an emotional motive force to activities of self-preservation or aggrandizement.

In its immediate or animal form this is obvious enough. The wave of passion that possesses a fighting dog stimulates and concentrates his energy upon a few moments of struggle in which success or failure may be life or death; and the simple, violent anger of children and impulsive adults is evidently much the same thing. Vital force explodes in a flash of aggression; the mind has no room for anything but the fierce instinct. It is clear that hostility of this uncontrolled sort is proper to a very simple state of society and of warfare, and is likely to be a source of disturbance and weakness in that organized state which calls for corresponding organization in the individual mind.

There is a transition by imperceptible degrees from the blind anger that thinks of nothing to the imaginative anger that thinks of persons, and pursues the personal idea into all possible degrees of subtlety and variety. The passion itself, the way we feel when we are angry, does not seem to change much, except, perhaps, in intensity, the change being mostly in the idea that awakens it. It is as if anger were a strong and peculiar flavor which might be taken with the simplest food or the most elaborate, might be used alone, strong and plain, or in the most curious and recondite combinations with other flavors.

While it is evident enough that animal anger is one of those instincts that are readily explained as conducive to self-preservation, it is not, perhaps, so obvious that socialized anger has any such justification. I think, however, that, though very liable to be excessive and unmanageable, and tending continually to be economized as the race progresses, so that most forms of it are properly regarded as wrong, it nevertheless plays an indispensable part in life.

The mass of mankind are sluggish and need some resentment as a stimulant; this is its function on the higher plane of life as it is on the lower. Surround a man with soothing, flattering circumstances, and in nine cases out of ten he will fail to do anything worthy, but will lapse into some form of sensualism or dilettanteism. There is no tonic, to a nature substantial enough to bear it, like chagrin—"erquickender Verdruss," as Goethe says. Life without opposition is Capua. No matter what the part one is fitted to play in it, he can make progress in his path only by a vigorous assault upon the obstacles, and to be vigorous the assault must be supported by passion of some sort. With most of us the requisite intensity of passion is not forthcoming without an element of resentment; and common sense and careful observation will, I believe, confirm the opinion that few people who amount to much are without a good capacity for hostile feeling, upon which they draw freely when they need it. This would be more readily admitted if many people were not without the habit of penetrating observation, either of themselves or others, in such matters, and so are enabled to believe that anger, which is conventionally held to be wrong, has no place in the motives of moral persons.

I have in mind a man who is remarkable for a certain kind of aggressive, tenacious, and successful pursuit of the right. He does the things that every one else agrees ought to be done but does not do—especially things involving personal antagonism. While the other people deplore the corruption of politics, but have no stomach to amend it, he is the man to beard the corrupt official in his ward, or expose him in the courts or the public press—all at much pains and cost to himself and without prospect of honor or any other recompense. If one considers how he differs from other conscientious people of equal ability and opportunity, it appears to be largely in having more bile in him. He has a natural fund of animosity, and instead of spending it blindly and harmfully, he directs it upon that which is hateful to the general good, thus gratifying his native turn for resentment in a moral and fruitful way. Evidently if there were more men of this stamp it would be of benefit to the moral condition of the country. Contemporary conditions seem to tend somewhat to dissipate that righteous wrath against evil which, intelligently directed, is a main instrument of progress.

Thomas Huxley, to take a name known to all, was a man in whom there was much fruitful hostility. He did not seek controversy, but when the enemies of truth offered battle he felt no inclination to refuse; and he avowed—perhaps with a certain zest in contravening conventional teaching—that he loved his friends and hated his enemies.* His hatred was of a noble sort, and the reader of his Life and Letters can hardly doubt that he was a good as well as a

* See his Life and Letters, vol. ii, p. 192.

great man, or that his pugnacity helped him to be such. Indeed I do not think that science or letters could do without the spirit of opposition, although much energy is dissipated and much thought clouded by it. Even men like Darwin or Emerson, who seem to wish nothing more than to live at peace with every one, may be observed to develop their views with unusual fulness and vigor where they are most in opposition to authority. There is something analogous to political parties in all intellectual activity; opinion divides, more or less definitely, into opposing groups, and each side is stimulated by the opposition of the other to define, corroborate, and amend its views, with the purpose of justifying itself before the constituency to which it appeals. What we need is not that controversy should disappear, but that it should be carried on with sincere and absolute deference to the standard of truth.

A just resentment is not only a needful stimulus to aggressive righteousness, but has also a wholesome effect upon the mind of the person against whom it is directed, by awakening a feeling of the importance of the sentiments he has trangressed. On the higher planes of life an imaginative sense that there is resentment in the minds of other persons performs the same function that physical resistance does upon the lower.* It is an attack upon my mental self, and as a sympathetic and imaginative being I feel it more than I would a mere blow; it forces me to consider the

* Compare Professor Simon N. Patten's Theory of Social Forces, p. 135.

other's view, and either to accept it or to bear it down by the stronger claims of a different one. Thus it enters potently into our moral judgments.

> "Let such pure hate still underprop
> Our love that we may be
> Each other's conscience." *

I think that no one's character and aims can be respected unless he is perceived to be capable of some sort of resentment. We feel that if he is really in earnest about anything he should feel hostile emotion if it is attacked, and if he gives no sign of this, either at the moment of attack or later, he and what he represents become despised. No teacher, for instance, can maintain discipline unless his scholars feel that he will in some manner resent a breach of it.

Thus we seldom feel keenly that our acts are wrong until we perceive that they arouse some sort of resentment in others, and whatever selfish aggression we can practise without arousing resistance, we presently come to look upon as a matter of course. Judging the matter from my own consciousness and experience, I have no belief in the theory that non-resistance has, as a rule, a mollifying influence upon the aggressor. I do not wish people to turn me the other cheek when I smite them, because, in most cases, that has a bad effect upon me. I am soon used to submission and may come to think no more of the unresisting sufferer than I do of the sheep whose flesh I eat at dinner.

* Thoreau, A Week, etc., p. 304.

276

Neither, on the other hand, am I helped by extravagant and accusatory opposition; that is likely to put me into a state of unreasoning anger. But it is good for us that every one should maintain his rights, and the rights of others with whom he sympathizes, exhibiting a just and firm resentment against any attempt to tread upon them. A consciousness, based on experience, that the transgression of moral standards will arouse resentment in the minds of those whose opinion we respect, is a main force in the upholding of such standards.

But the doctrine of non-resistance, like all ideas that have appealed to good minds, has a truth wrapped up in it, notwithstanding what appears to be its flagrant absurdity. What the doctrine really means, as taught in the New Testament and by many individuals and societies in our own day, is perhaps no more than this, that we should discard the coarser weapons of resistance for the finer, and threaten a moral resentment instead of blows or lawsuits. It is quite true that we can best combat what we regard as evil in another person of ordinary sensibility by attacking the higher phases of his self rather than the lower. If a man appears to be about to do something brutal or dishonest, we may either encounter him on his present low plane of life by knocking him down or calling a policeman, or we may try to work upon his higher consciousness by giving him to understand that we feel sure a person of his self-respect and good repute will not degrade himself, but that if anything so improbable and untoward should occur, he must, of course, expect the disappointment and contempt of those who before thought well of him. In other words, we threaten, as courteously as possible, his social self. This method is often much more efficient than the other, is morally edifying instead of degrading, and is practised by men of address who make no claim to unusual virtue.

This seems to be what is meant by non-resistance; but the name is misleading. It *is* resistance, and directed at what is believed to be the enemy's weakest point. As a matter of strategy it is an attack upon his flank, aggression upon an unprotected part of his position. Its justification, in the long run, is in its success. If we do not succeed in making our way into the other man's mind and changing his point of view by substituting our own, the whole manœuvre falls flat, the injury is done, the ill-doer is confirmed in his courses, and you would better have knocked him down. It is good to appeal to the highest motives we can arouse, and to exercise a good deal of faith as to what can be aroused, but real non-resistance to what we believe to be wrong is mere pusillanimity. There is perhaps no important sect or teacher that really inculcates such a doctrine, the name non-resistance being given to attacks upon the higher self under the somewhat crude impression that resistance is not such unless it takes some obvious material form, and probably all teachers would be found to vary their tactics somewhat according to the sort of people with whom they are dealing. Although Christ taught the turning of the other cheek to the smiter, and that the coat should follow the cloak, it does not appear that he suggested to those who were desecrating the Temple that they should double their transactions, but, apparently regarding them as beyond the reach of moral suasion, he "went into the Temple, and began to cast out them that sold and bought in the Temple, and overthrew the tables of the money-changers and the seats of them that sold doves." It seems that he even used a scourge on this occasion. I cannot see much in the question regarding non-resistance beyond a vague use of terms and a difference of opinion as to what kind of resistance is most effective in certain cases.

It is easy and not uncommon to state too exclusively the pre-eminence of affection in human ideals. No one, I suppose, believes that the life of Fra Angelico's angels, such as we see them in his "Last Judgment," circling on the flowery sward of Paradise, would long content any normal human creature. If it appears beautiful and desirable at times, this is perhaps because our world is one in which the supply of amity and peace mostly falls short of the demand for them. Many of us have seen times of heat and thirst when it seemed as if a bit of shade and a draft of cold water would appease all earthly wants. But when we had the shade and the water we presently began to think about something else. So with these ideals of unbroken peace and affection. Even for those sensitive spirits that most cherish them, they would hardly suffice as a continuity. An indiscriminate and unvarying amity is, after all, disgusting.

Human ideals and human nature must develop together, and we cannot foresee what either may become; but for the present it would seem that an honest and reasonable idealism must look rather to the organization and control of all passions with reference to some conception of right, than to the expulsion of some passions by others. I doubt whether any healthy and productive love can exist which is not resentment on its obverse side. How can we rightly care for anything without in some way resenting attacks upon it?

Apparently, the higher function of hostility is to put down wrong; and to fulfil this function it must be rationally controlled with a view to ideals of justice. In so far as a man has a sound and active social imagination, he will feel the need of this control, and will tend with more or less energy, according to the vigor of his mind, to limit his resentment to that which his judgment tells him is really unjust or wrong. Imagination presents us with all sorts of conflicting views, which reason, whose essence is organization, tries to arrange and control in accordance with some unifying principle, some standard of equity: moral principles result from the mind's instinctive need to achieve unity of view. All special impulses, and hostile feeling among them, are brought to the bar of conscience and judged by such standards as the mind has worked out. If declared right or justifiable, resentment is indorsed and enforced by the will; we think of it as righteous and perhaps take credit with ourselves for it. But if it appears grounded on no broad

280

and unifying principle, our larger thought disowns it, and tends with such energy as it may have to ignore and suppress it. Thus we overlook accidental injury, we control or avoid mere antipathy, but we act upon indignation. The latter is enduring and powerful because consistent with cool thought; while impulsive, unreasoning anger, getting no reinforcement from such thought, has little lasting force.

Suppose, for illustration, one goes with a request to some person in authority, and meets a curt refusal. The first feeling is doubtless one of blind, unthinking anger at the rebuff. Immediately after that the mind busies itself more deeply with the matter, imagining motives, ascribing feelings, and the like; and anger takes a more bitter and personal form, it rankles where at first it only stung. But if one is a fairly reasonable man, accustomed to refer things to standards of right, one presently grows calmer and, continuing the imaginative process in a broader way, endeavors to put himself at the other person's point of view and see what justification, if any, there is for the latter's conduct. Possibly he is one subject to constant solicitation, with whom coldness and abruptness are necessary to the despatch of business—and so on. If the explanation seems insufficient, so that his rudeness still appears to be mere insolence, our resentment against him lasts, reappearing whenever we think of him, so that we are likely to thwart him somehow if we get a chance, and justify our action to ourselves and others on grounds of moral disapproval.

Or suppose one has to stand in line at the post-office, with a crowd of other people, waiting to get his mail. There are delay and discomfort to be borne; but these he will take with composure because he sees that they are a part of the necessary conditions of the situation, which all must submit to alike. Suppose, however, that while patiently waiting his turn he notices some one else, who has come in later, edging into the line ahead of him. Then he will certainly be angry. The delay threatened is only a matter of a few seconds; but here is a question of justice, a case for indignation, a chance for anger to come forth with the sanction of thought.

Another phase of the transformation of hostility by reason and imagination, is that it tends to become more discriminating or selective as regards its relation to the idea of the person against whom it is directed. In a sense the higher hostility is less personal than the lower; that is, in the sense that it is no longer aimed blindly at persons as wholes, but distinguishes in some measure between phases or tendencies of them that are obnoxious and others that are not. It is not the mere thought of X's countenance, or other symbol, that arouses resentment, but the thought of him as exhibiting insincerity, or arrogance, or whatever else it may be that we do not like; while we may preserve a liking for him as exhibiting other traits. Generally speaking, all persons have much in them which, if imagined, must appear amiable; so that if we feel only animosity toward a man it must be because we have apprehended him only in a partial aspect. An undisciplined anger, like any other un-

282

disciplined emotion, always tends to produce these partial and indiscriminate notions, because it overwhelms symmetrical thought and permits us to see only that which agrees with itself. But a more chastened sentiment allows a juster view, so that it becomes conceivable that we should love our enemies as well as antagonize the faults of our friends. A just parent or teacher will resent the insubordinate behavior of a child or pupil without letting go of affection, and the same principle holds good as regards criminals, and all proper objects of hostility. The attitude of society toward its delinquent members should be stern, yet sympathetic, like that of a father toward a disobedient child.

It is the tendency of modern life, by educating the imagination and rendering all sorts of people conceivable, to discredit the sweeping conclusions of impulsive thought—as, for instance, that all who commit violence or theft are hateful ill-doers, and nothing more—and to make us feel the fundamental likeness of human nature wherever found. Resentment against ill-doing should by no means disappear; but while continuing to suppress wrong by whatever means proves most efficacious, we shall perhaps see more and more clearly that the people who are guilty of it are very much like ourselves, and are acting from motives to which we also are subject.

It is often asserted or assumed that hostile feeling is in its very nature obnoxious and painful to the human mind, and persists in spite of us, as it were, because it is forced upon us by the competitive conditions of existence. This view seems to me hardly sound. I should rather say that the mental and social harmfulness of anger, in common experience, is due not so much to its peculiar character as hostile feeling, as to the fact that, like lust, it is so surcharged with instinctive energy as to be difficult to control and limit to its proper function; while, if not properly disciplined, it of course introduces disorder and pain into the mental life.

To a person in robust condition, with plenty of energy to spare, a thoroughgoing anger, far from being painful, is an expansive, I might say glorious, experience, *while the fit is on and has full control*. A man in a rage does not want to get out of it, but has a full sense of life which he impulsively seeks to continue by repelling suggestions tending to calm him. It is only when it has begun to pall upon him that he is really willing to be appeased. This may be seen by observing the behavior of impulsive children, and also of adults whose passions are undisciplined.

An enduring hatred may also be a source of satisfaction to some minds, though this I believe to be unusual in these days, and becoming more so. One who reads Hazlitt's powerful and sincere, though perhaps unhealthy, essay on the Pleasure of Hating, will see that the thing is possible. In most cases remorse and distress set in so soon as the fit of anger begins to abate, and its destructive incompatibility with the established order and harmony of the mind

284

begins to be felt. There is a conviction of sin, the pain of a shattered ideal, just as there is after yielding to any other unchastened passion. The cause of the pain seems to be not so much the peculiar character of the feeling as its exorbitant intensity.

Any simple and violent passion is likely to be felt as painful and wrong in its after-effects because it destroys that harmony or synthesis that reason and conscience strive to produce; and this effect is probably more and more felt as the race advances and mental life becomes more complex. The conditions of civilization require of us so extensive and continuous an expenditure of psychical force, that we no longer have the superabundance of emotional energy that makes a violent outlet agreeable. Habits and principles of self-control naturally arise along with the increasing need for economy and rational guidance of emotion; and whatever breaks through them causes exhaustion and remorse. Any gross passion comes to be felt as "the expense of spirit in a waste of shame." Spasms of violent feeling properly belong with a somewhat apathetic habit of life, whose accumulating energies they help to dissipate, and are as much out of place to-day as the hard-drinking habits of our Saxon ancestors.

The sort of men that most feel the need of hostility as a spur to exertion are, I imagine, those of superabundant vitality and somewhat sluggish temperament, like Goethe and Bismarck, both of whom declared that it was essential to them. There is also a great deal of old-fashioned personal hatred in remote and quiet places, like the mountains of North Carolina, and probably among all classes who do not much feel the stress of civilization. But to most of those who share fully in the life of the time, intense personal animosities are painful and destructive, and many fine spirits are ruined by failure to inhibit them.

The kind of man most characteristic of these times, I take it, does not allow himself to be drawn into the tangle of merely personal hatred, but, cultivating a tolerance for all sorts of men, he yet maintains a sober and determined antagonism toward all tendencies or purposes that conflict with his true self, with whatever he has most intimately appropriated and identified with his character. He is always courteous, cherishes as much as possible those kindly sentiments which are not only pleasant and soothing but do much to oil the machinery of his enterprises, and by wasting no energy on futile passion is enabled to think all the more clearly and act the more inflexibly when he finds antagonism necessary. A man of the world of the modern type is hardly ever dramatic in the style of Shakespeare's heroes. He usually expresses himself in the most economical manner possible, and if he has to threaten, for instance, knows how to do it by a movement of the lips, or the turn of a phrase in a polite note. If cruder and more violent tactics are necessary, to impress vulgar minds, he is very likely to depute this rough work to a subordinate. A foreman of track hands may have to be a loud-voiced, strong-armed, palpably aggressive person; but the president of the road is commonly quiet and mild-mannered.

The mind is greatly aided in the control of animosity by the existence of ready-made and socially accepted standards of right. Suffering from his own angry passions and from those of others, one looks out for some criterion, some rule of what is just and fair among persons, which he may hold himself and others to, and moderate antagonism by removing the sense of peculiar injury. Opposition itself, within certain limits, comes to be regarded as part of the reasonable order of things. In this view the function of moral standards is the same as that of courts of justice in grosser conflicts. All good citizens want the laws to be definite and vigorously enforced, in order to avoid the uncertainty, waste, and destruction of a lawless condition. In the same way right-minded people want definite moral standards, enforced by general opinion, in order to save the mental wear and tear of unguided feeling. It is a great relief to a person harassed by hostile emotion to find a point of view from which this emotion appears wrong or irrational, so that he can proceed definitely and with the sanction of his reason to put it down. The next best thing, perhaps, is to have the hostility definitely approved by reason, so that he may indulge it without further doubt. The unsettled condition is worst of all.

This control of hostility by a sense of common allegiance to rule is well illustrated by athletic games.

When properly conducted they proceed upon a definite understanding of what is fair, and no lasting anger is felt for any hurts inflicted, so long as this standard of fairness is maintained. It is the same in war: soldiers do not necessarily feel any anger at other soldiers who are trying to shoot them to death. That is thought of as within the rules of the game. As Admiral Cervera's chief of staff is reported to have said to Admiral Sampson, "You know there is nothing personal in this." But if the white flag is used treacherously, explosive bullets employed, or the moral standard otherwise transgressed, there is hard feeling. It is very much the same with the multiform conflicts of purpose in modern industrial life. It is not clear that competition as such, apart from the question of fairness or unfairness, has any tendency to increase hostility. Competition and the clash of purposes are inseparable from activity, and are felt to be so. Ill-feeling flourishes no more in an active, stirring state of society than in a stagnant state. The trouble with our industrial relations is not the mere extent of competition, but the partial lack of established laws, rules, and customs, to determine what is right and fair in it. This partical lack of standards is connected with the rapid changes in industry and industrial relations among men, with which the development of law and of moral criteria has by no means kept pace. Hence there arises great uncertainty as to what some persons and classes may rightly and fairly require of other persons and classes; and this uncertainty lets loose angry imaginations.

It will be evident that I do not look upon affection, or anger, or any other particular mode of feeling, as in itself good or bad, social or antisocial, progressive or retrogressive. It seems to me that the essentially good, social, or progressive thing, in this regard, is the organization and discipline of all emotions by the aid of reason, in harmony with a developing general life, which is summed up for us in conscience. That this development of the general life is such as to tend ultimately to do away with hostile feeling altogether, is not clear. The actively good people, the just men, reformers, and prophets, not excepting him who drove the money-changers from the Temple, have been and are, for the most part, people who feel the spur of resentment; and it is not evident that this can cease to be the case. The diversity of human minds and endeavors seems to be an essential part of the general plan of things, and shows no tendency to diminish. This diversity involves a conflict of ideas and purposes, which, in those who take it earnestly, is likely to occasion hostile feeling. This feeling should become less wayward, violent, bitter, or personal, in a narrow sense, and more disciplined, rational, discriminating, and quietly persistent. That it ought to disappear is certainly not apparent.

Something similar to what has been said of anger will hold true of any well-marked type of instinctive emotion. If we take fear, for instance, and try to recall our experience of it from early childhood on, it seems clear that, while the emotion itself may

289

change but little, the ideas, occasions, suggestions that excite it depend upon the state of our intellectual and social development, and so undergo great alteration. The feeling does not tend to disappear, but to become less violent and spasmodic, more and more social as regards the objects that excite it, and more and more subject, in the best minds, to the discipline of reason.

The fears of little children* are largely excited by immediate sensible experiences—darkness, solitude, sharp noises, and so on. Sensitive persons often remain throughout life subject to irrational fears of this sort, and it is well known that they play a conspicuous part in hysteria, insanity, and other weak or morbid conditions. But for the most part the healthy adult mind becomes accustomed and indifferent to these simple phenomena, and transfers its emotional sensibility to more complex interests. These interests are for the most part sympathetic, involving our social rather than our material self—our standing in the minds of other people, the well-being of those we care for, and so on. Yet these fears—fear of standing alone, of losing one's place in the flow of human action and sympathy, fear for the character and success of those near to us—have often the very quality of childish fear. A man cast out of his regular occupation and secure place in the system of the world feels a terror like that of the child in the dark; just as impulsive, perhaps just as purposeless and paralyz-

* Compare G. Stanley Hall's study of Fear in the American Journal of Psychology, vol. 8, p. 147.

ing. The main difference seems to be that the latter fear is stimulated by a complex idea, implying a socially imaginative habit of mind.

Social fear, of a sort perhaps somewhat morbid, is vividly depicted by Rousseau in the passage of his Confessions where he describes the feeling that led him falsely to accuse a maid-servant of a theft which he had himself committed. "When she appeared my heart was agonized, but the presence of so many people was more powerful than my compunction. I did not fear punishment, but I dreaded shame: I dreaded it more than death, more than the crime, more than all the world. I would have buried, hid myself in the centre of the earth: invincible shame bore down every other sentiment; shame alone caused all my impudence, and in proportion as I became criminal the fear of discovery rendered me intrepid. I felt no dread but that of being detected, of being publicly and to my face declared a thief, liar, and calumniator. . . ." *

So also we might distinguish, as in the case of anger, a higher form of social fear, one that is not narrowly personal, but relates to some socially derived ideal of good or right. For instance, in a soldier the terror of roaring guns and singing bullets would be a fear of the lowest or animal type. Dread of the disgrace to

* The terrors of our dreams are caused largely by social imaginations. Thus Stevenson, in one of his letters, speaks of "my usual dreams of social miseries and misunderstandings and all sorts of crucifixions of the spirit."—Letters of Robert Louis Stevenson, i, p. 79. Many of us know that dream of being in some public place without decent clothing.

follow running away would be a social fear, yet not of the highest sort, because the thing dreaded is not wrong but shame—a comparatively simple and non-rational idea. People often do what they know is wrong under the influence of such fear, as did Rousseau in the incident quoted above. But, supposing the soldier's highest ideal to be the success of his army and his country, a fear for that, overcoming all lower and cruder fears—selfish fears as they would ordinarily be called—would be moral or ethical.

CHAPTER VIII

EMULATION

CONFORMITY—NON-CONFORMITY—THE TWO VIEWED AS COMPLE-
MENTARY PHASES OF LIFE—RIVALRY—RIVALRY IN SOCIAL SER-
VICE—CONDITIONS UNDER WHICH EMULATION IN SERVICE MAY
PREVAIL—HERO-WORSHIP

IT will be convenient to distinguish three sorts of emulation—conformity, rivalry, and hero-worship.

Conformity may be defined as the endeavor to maintain a standard set by a group. It is a voluntary imitation of prevalent modes of action, distinguished from rivalry and other aggressive phases of emulation by being comparatively passive, aiming to keep up rather than to excel, and concerning itself for the most part with what is outward and formal. On the other hand, it is distinguished from involuntary imitation by being intentional instead of mechanical. Thus it is not conformity, for most of us, to speak the English language, because we have practically no choice in the matter, but we might choose to conform to particular pronunciations or turns of speech used by those with whom we wish to associate.

The ordinary motive to conformity is a sense, more or less vivid, of the pains and inconveniences of non-conformity. Most people find it painful to go to an evening company in any other than the customary dress; the source of the pain appearing to be a vague sense of the depreciatory curiosity which one imagines

293

that he will excite. His social self-feeling is hurt by an unfavorable view of himself that he attributes to others. This example is typical of the way the group coerces each of its members in all matters concerning which he has no strong and definite private purpose. The world constrains us without any definite intention to do so, merely through the impulse, common to all, to despise peculiarity for which no reason is perceived. "Nothing in the world more subtle," says George Eliot, speaking of the decay of higher aims in certain people, "than the process of their gradual change! In the beginning they inhaled it unknowingly; you and I may have sent some of our breath toward infecting them, when we uttered our conforming falsities or drew our silly conclusions: or perhaps it came with the vibrations from a woman's glance." "Solitude is fearsome and heavy-hearted," and non-conformity condemns us to it by causing *gêne*, if not dislike, in others, and so interrupting that relaxation and spontaneity of attitude that is required for the easy flow of sympathy and communication. Thus it is hard to be at ease with one who is conspicuously worse or better dressed than we are, or whose manners are notably different; no matter how little store our philosophy may set by such things. On the other hand, a likeness in small things that enables them to be forgotten gives people a *prima facie* at-homeness with each other highly favorable to sympathy; and so we all wish to have it with people we care for.

It would seem that the repression of non-conformity is a native impulse, and that tolerance always requires some moral exertion. We all cherish our habitual system of thought, and anything that breaks in upon it in a seemingly wanton manner, is annoying to us and likely to cause resentment. So our first tendency is to suppress the peculiar, and we learn to endure it it only when we must, either because it is shown to be reasonable or because it proves refractory to our opposition. The innovator is nearly as apt as any one else to put down innovation in others. Words denoting singularity usually carry some reproach with them; and it would perhaps be found that the more settled the social system is, the severer is the implied condemnation. In periods of disorganization and change, such as ours is in many respects, people are educated to comparative tolerance by unavoidable familiarity with conflicting views—as religious toleration, for instance, is the outcome of the continued spectacle of competing creeds.

Sir Henry Maine, in discussing the forces that controlled the legal decisions of a Roman prætor, remarks that he "was kept within the narrowest bounds by the prepossessions imbibed from early training and by the strong restraints of professional opinion, restraints of which the stringency can only be appreciated by those who have personally experienced them." * In the same way every profession, trade, or handicraft, every church, circle, fraternity, or clique, has its more or less definite standards, conformity to which it tends to impose on all its members. It is not at all essential that there should be any deliberate

* Maine, Ancient Law, p. 62.

295

purpose to set up these standards, or any special machinery for enforcing them. They spring up spontaneously, as it were, by an unconscious process of assimilation, and are enforced by the mere inertia of the minds constituting the group.

Thus every variant idea of conduct has to fight its way: as soon as any one attempts to do anything unexpected the world begins to cry, "Get in the rut! Get in the rut! Get in the rut!" and shoves, stares, coaxes, and sneers until he does so—or until he makes good his position, and so, by altering the standard in a measure, establishes a new basis of conformity. There are no people who are altogether non-conformers, or who are completely tolerant of non-conformity in others. Mr. Lowell, who wrote some of the most stirring lines in literature in defense of non-conformity, was himself conventional and an upholder of conventions in letters and social intercourse. Either to be exceptional or to appreciate the exceptional requires a considerable expenditure of energy, and no one can afford this in many directions. There are many persons who take pains to keep their minds open; and there are groups, countries, and periods which are comparatively favorable to open-mindedness and variation; but conformity is always the rule and non-conformity the exception.

Conformity is a sort of co-operation: one of its functions is to economize energy. The standards which it presses upon the individual are often elaborate and valuable products of cumulative thought and experience, and whatever imperfections they may have

they are, as a whole, an indispensable foundation
for life: it is inconceivable that any one should dispense with them. If I imitate the dress, the manners,
the household arrangements of other people, I save
so much mental energy for other purposes. It is best
that each should originate where he is specially fitted
to do so, and follow others where they are better
qualified to lead. It is said with truth that conformity is a drag upon genius; but it is equally true
and important that its general action upon human
nature is elevating. We get by it the selected and
systematized outcome of the past, and to be brought
up to its standards is a brief recapitulation of social
development: it sometimes levels down but more
generally levels up. It may be well for purposes of
incitement to goad our individuality by the abuse of
conformity; but statements made with this in view
lack accuracy. It is good for the young and aspiring
to read Emerson's praise of self-reliance, in order
that they may have courage to fight for their ideas;
but we may also sympathize with Goethe when he
says that "nothing more exposes us to madness than
distinguishing us from others, and nothing more contributes to maintaining our common sense than living
in the universal way with multitudes of men." *

There are two aspects of non-conformity: first, a
rebellious impulse or "contrary suggestion" leading
to an avoidance of accepted standards in a spirit of
opposition, without necessary reference to any other

* Wilhelm Meister's Apprenticeship, v, 16, Carlyle's Translation.

standards; and, second, an appeal from present and commonplace standards to those that are comparatively remote and unusual. These two usually work together. One is led to a mode of life different from that of the people about him, partly by intrinsic contrariness, and partly by fixing his imagination on the ideas and practices of other people whose mode of life he finds more congenial.

But the essence of non-conformity as a personal attitude consists in contrary suggestion or the spirit of opposition. People of natural energy take pleasure in that enhanced feeling of self that comes from consciously *not* doing that which is suggested or enjoined upon them by circumstances and by other persons. There is joy in the sense of self-assertion: it is sweet to do one's own things; and if others are against him one feels sure they *are* his own. To brave the disapproval of men is tonic; it is like climbing along a mountain path in the teeth of the wind; one feels himself as a cause, and knows the distinctive efficacy of his being. Thus self-feeling, which, if somewhat languid and on the defensive, causes us to avoid peculiarity, may, when in a more energetic condition, cause us to seek it; just as we rejoice at one time to brave the cold, and at another to cower over the fire, according to the vigor of our circulation.

This may easily be observed in vigorous children: each in his way will be found to attach himself to methods of doing things which he regards as peculiarly his own, and to delight in asserting these methods against opposition. It is also the basis of some of the deepest and most significant differences between races and individuals. Controlled by intellect and purpose this passion for differentiation becomes self-reliance, self-discipline, and immutable persistence in a private aim: qualities which more than any others make the greater power of superior persons and races. It is a source of enterprise, exploration, and endurance in all kinds of undertakings, and of fierce defense of private rights. How much of Anglo-Saxon history is rooted in the intrinsic cantankerousness of the race! It is largely this that makes the world-winning pioneer, who keeps pushing on because he wants a place all to himself, and hates to be bothered by other people over whom he has no control. On the frontier a common man defines himself better as a cause. He looks round at his clearing, his cabin, his growing crops, his wife, his children, his dogs, horses, and cattle, and says, *I did it: they are mine.* All that he sees recalls the glorious sense of things won by his own hand.

Who does not feel that it is a noble thing to stand alone, to steer due west into an unknown universe, like Columbus, or, like Nansen, ground the ship upon the ice-pack and drift for the North Pole? "Adhere to your own act," says Emerson, "and congratulate yourself if you have done something strange and extravagant, and broken the monotony of a decorous age." We like that epigram, *Victrix causa diis placuit, sed victa Catoni,* because we like the thought that a man stood out alone against the gods themselves, and set his back against the course of nature. The

"souls that stood alone,
While the men they agonized for hurled the contumelious
stone,"

are not to be thought of as victims of self-sacrifice.
Many of them rejoiced in just that isolation, and daring, and persistence; so that it was not self-sacrifice
but self-realization. Conflict is a necessity of the active soul, and if a social order could be created from
which it were absent, that order would perish as uncongenial to human nature. "To be a man is to be
a non-conformer."

I think that people go into all sorts of enterprises,
for instance into novel and unaccredited sorts of philanthropy, with a spirit of adventure not far removed
from the spirit that seeks the North Pole. It is neither
true nor wholesome to think of the "good" as ac-
tuated by motives radically different in kind from
those of ordinary human nature; and I imagine the
best of them are far from wishing to be thus thought
of. Undertakings of reform and philanthropy appeal
to the mind in a double aspect. There is, of course,
the desire to accomplish some worthy end, to effectuate some cherished sentiment which the world appears to ignore, to benefit the oppressed, to advance
human knowledge, or the like. But behind that is
the vague need of self-expression, of creation, of a
momentous experience, so that one may know that
one has really lived. And the finer imaginations are
likely to find this career of novelty and daring, not in
the somewhat outworn paths of war and exploration,
but in new and precarious kinds of social activity.

300

So one may sometimes meet in social settlements and charity-organization bureaus the very sort of people that led the Crusades into Palestine. I do not speak at random, but have several persons in mind who seem to me to be of this sort.

In its second aspect non-conformity may be regarded as a remoter conformity. The rebellion against social influence is only partial and apparent; and the one who seems to be out of step with the procession is really keeping time to another music. As Thoreau said, he hears a different drummer. If a boy refuses the occupation his parents and friends think best for him, and persists in working at something strange and fantastic, like art or science, it is sure to be the case that his most vivid life is not with those about him at all, but with the masters he has known through books, or perhaps seen and heard for a few moments. Environment, in the sense of social influence actually at work, is far from the definite and obvious thing it is often assumed to be. Our real environment consists of those images which are most present to our thoughts, and in the case of a vigorous, growing mind, these are likely to be something quite different from what is most present to the senses. The group to which we give allegiance, and to whose standards we try to conform, is determined by our own selective affinity, choosing among all the personal influences accessible to us; and so far as we select with any independence of our palpable companions, we have the appearance of non-conformity.

All non-conformity that is affirmative or constructive must act by this selection of remoter relations; opposition, by itself, being sterile, and meaning nothing beyond personal peculiarity. There is, therefore, no definite line between conformity and non-conformity; there is simply a more or less characteristic and unusual way of selecting and combining accessible influences. It is much the same question as that of invention *versus* imitation. As Professor Baldwin points out, there is no radical separation between these two aspects of human thought and action. There is no imitation that is absolutely mechanical and uninventive—a man cannot repeat an act without putting something of his idiosyncrasy into it—neither is there any invention that is not imitative in the sense that it is made up of elements suggested by observation and experience. What the mind does, in any case, is to reorganize and reproduce the suggested materials in accordance with its own structure and tendency; and we judge the result as imitative or inventive, original or commonplace, according as it does or does not strike us as a new and fruitful employment of the common material.*

A just view of the matter should embrace the whole of it at once, and see conformity and non-conformity

* In reading studies of a particular aspect of life, like M. Tarde's brilliant work, Les Lois de l'Imitation, it is well to remember that there are many such aspects, any of which, if expounded at length and in an interesting manner, might appear for the time to be of more importance than any other. I think that other phases of social activity, such, for instance, as communication, competition, differentiation, adaptation, idealization, have as good claims as imitation to be regarded as the social process, and that a book similar in character to M. Tarde's might, perhaps, be written upon any one of them. The truth is that the real process is a multiform thing of which these are

as normal and complementary phases of human activity. In their quieter moods men have a pleasure in social agreement and the easy flow of sympathy, which makes non-conformity uncomfortable. But when their energy is full and demanding an outlet through the instincts, it can only be appeased by something which gives the feeling of self-assertion. They are agitated by a "creative impatience," an outburst of the primal need to act; like the Norsemen, of whom Gibbon says: "Impatient of a bleak climate and narrow limits, they started from the banquet, sounded their horn, ascended their vessels, and explored every coast that promised either spoil or settlement." * In social intercourse this active spirit finds its expression largely in resisting the will of others; and the spirit of opposition and self-differentiation thus arising is the principal direct stimulus to non-conformity. This spirit, however, has no power of absolute creation, and is forced to seek for suggestions and materials in the minds of others; so that the independence is only relative to the more immediate and obvious environment, and never constitutes a real revolt from the social order.

glimpses. They are good so long as we recognize that they *are* glimpses and use them to help out our perception of that many-sided whole which life is; but if they become *doctrines* they are objectionable.

The Struggle for Existence is another of these glimpses of life which just now seems to many the dominating fact of the universe, chiefly because attention has been fixed upon it by copious and interesting exposition. As it has had many predecessors in this place of importance, so doubtless it will have many successors.

* Decline and Fall, vol. vii, p. 82; Milman-Smith edition.

Naturally non-conformity is characteristic of the more energetic states of the human mind. Men of great vigor are sure to be non-conformers in some important respect; youth glories in non-conformity, while age usually comes back to the general point of view. "Men are conservatives when they are least vigorous, or when they are most luxurious. They are conservatives after dinner, or before taking their rest; when they are sick or aged. In the morning, or when their intellect or their conscience has been aroused, when they hear music, or when they read poetry, they are radicals." *

The rational attitude of the individual toward the question of conformity or non-conformity in his own life, would seem to be: assert your individuality in matters which you deem important; conform in those you deem unimportant. To have a conspicuously individual way of doing everything is impossible to a sane person, and to attempt it would be to do one's self a gratuitous injury, by closing the channels of sympathy through which we partake of the life around us. We should save our strength for matters in regard to which persistent conviction impels us to insist upon our own way.

Society, like every living, advancing whole, requires a just union of stability and change, uniformity, and differentiation. Conformity is the phase of stability and uniformity, while non-conformity is the phase of differentiation and change. The latter cannot introduce anything wholly new, but it can and does effect

* Emerson, address on New England Reformers.

such a reorganization of existing material as constantly to transform and renew human life.

I mean by rivalry a competitive striving urged on by the desire to win. It resembles conformity in that the impelling idea is usually a sense of what other people are doing and thinking, and especially of what they are thinking of us: it differs from it chiefly in being more aggressive. Conformity aims to keep up with the procession, rivalry to get ahead of it. The former is moved by a sense of the pains and inconveniences of differing from other people, the latter by an eagerness to compel their admiration. Winning, to the social self, usually means conspicuous success in making some desired impression upon other minds, as in becoming distinguished for power, wealth, skill, culture, beneficence, or the like.

On the other hand, rivalry may be distinguished from finer sorts of emulation by being more simple, crude, and direct. It implies no very subtle mental activity, no elaborate or refined ideal. If a spirited horse hears another overtaking him from behind, he pricks up his ears, quickens his steps, and does his best to keep ahead. And human rivalry appears to have much of this instinctive element in it; to become aware of life and striving going on about us seems to act immediately upon the nerves, quickening an impulse to live and strive in like manner. An eager person will not hear or read of vivid action of any sort without feeling some impulse to get into it;

just as he cannot mingle in a hurrying, excited crowd without sharing in the excitement and hurry, whether he knows what it is all about or not. The genesis of ambition is often something as follows: one mingles with men, his self-feeling is vaguely aroused, and he wishes to be something to them. He sees, perhaps, that he cannot excel in just what they are doing, and so he takes refuge in his imagination, thinking what he *can* do which is admirable, and determining to do it. Thus he goes home nursing secret ambitions.

The motive of rivalry, then, is a strong sense that there is a race going on, and an impulsive eagerness to be in it. It is rather imitative than inventive; the idea being not so much to achieve an object for its own sake, because it is reflectively judged to be worthy, as to get what the rest are after. There is conformity in ideals combined with a thirst for personal distinction. It has little tendency toward innovation, notwithstanding the element of antagonism in it; but takes its color and character from the prevalent social life, accepting and pursuing the existing ideal of success, and whatever special quality it has depends upon the quality of that ideal. There is, for instance, nothing so gross or painful that it may not become an object of pursuit through emulation. Charles Booth, who has studied so minutely the slums of London, says that "among the poor, men drink on and on from a perverted pride," and among another class a similar sentiment leads women to inflict surprising deformities of the trunk upon themselves.

Professor William James suggests that rivalry does

nine-tenths of the world's work.* Certainly no motive is so generally powerful among active, efficient men of the ordinary type, the type that keeps the ball moving all over the world. Intellectual initiative, high and persistent idealism, are rare. The great majority of able men are ambitious, without having intrinsic traits that definitely direct their ambition to any particular object. They feel their way about among the careers which their time, their country, their early surroundings and training, make accessible to them, and, selecting the one which seems to promise the best chance of success, they throw themselves into the pursuit of the things that conduce to that success. If the career is law, they strive to win cases and gain wealth and prestige, accepting the moral code and other standards that they find in actual use; and it is the same, *mutatis mutandis*, in commerce, politics, the ministry, the various handicrafts, and so on.

There is thus nothing morally distinctive about rivalry; it is harmful or beneficent according to the objects and standards with reference to which it acts. All depends upon the particular game in which one takes a hand. It may be said in a broad way, however, that rivalry supplies a stimulus wholesome and needful to the great majority of men, and that it is, on the whole, a chief progressive force, utilizing the tremendous power of ambition, and controlling it to the furtherance of ends that are socially approved. The great mass of what we judge to be evil is of a

* Psychology, vol. ii, p. 409.

negative rather than a positive character, arising not from misdirected ambition but from apathy or sensuality, from a falling short of that active, social humanity which ambition implies.

In order to work effectively in the service of society rivalry must be disciplined and organized. This means, chiefly, that men must associate in specialized groups, each group pursuing ideals of technical efficiency and social service, success in this pursuit being the object of rivalry. Consider, for example, how achievement in athletics is attained in our colleges. In the first place, there is a general interest in sports and an admiration for success in them which makes it an object of general ambition. Many candidates are "tried out" and assigned, according to their promise, to special squads for training, in football, baseball, running, jumping, and so on. In each of these little groups rivalry is made intense, definite, and systematic by traditions, by standards of accomplishment, by regular training, and by expert appreciation and criticism. Occasional public contests serve to arouse the imagination and to exhibit achievement. The whole social self is thus called in to animate a course of endeavor scientifically directed to a specific end. A similar method is used in armies and navies to develop excellence in marksmanship and the like. And is it not much the same in professional groups; among lawyers, for example, dentists, bacteriologists, astronomers, historians, painters, novelists, and even poets? In each of these fields there is a selected group of candidates for distinction, watching one another's work, eager to excel, imagining the judgment of their fellows, testing achievement by expert criticism and by comparison with high examples. There is also a more or less systematic course of training which all must go through, and a tradition to which all refer.

The general fact is that the most effective way of utilizing human energy is through an organized rivalry, which by specialization and social control is, at the same time, organized co-operation.

An ideal social system, from this point of view, would be one in which the work of individuals in each occupation, the work of occupations in relation to one another, that of class in relation to class and of nation in relation to nation, should be motived by a desire to excel, this desire being controlled and subordinated by allegiance to common social ideals.

I have little faith in any system of motives which does not leave room for personal and group ambitions. Self-feeling and social feeling must be harmonized and made to go abreast.

But is it practicable to make emulation in service, as distinct from selfish emulation, the ruling motive of mankind? If it is, and if we can establish ideals of service that make for general welfare and progress, the problem of getting the best out of human nature would seem to be in a way to work itself out.

There appears to be nothing to prevent the higher emulation from becoming general if we can provide the right conditions for it. If college boys, soldiers, and many sorts of professional men will put their utmost energies into the attainment of excellence, without pecuniary reward, impelled only by loyalty to a group ideal and the hope of appreciation, it is clear that the lack of this spirit in other situations is due not to human nature but to the kind of appeal that is made to it.

What, then, are the right conditions? Apparently they are, in general, a group spirit and tradition, ruled by service ideals, in which the individual may merge himself. This will take up the self into its own larger life: the individual will conform to it and his ambition will be to further its ideals. This is what animates the college athlete, the loyal soldier, the man of science, the socialist, and the trade-unionist.

Without doubt it would animate the workman in a factory, if the organization had the same unity of spirit and ideal that are found in the other cases mentioned. In fact, however, this is rarely present in the industrial and commercial world. For this there are various reasons, among which are the following:

1. The fact that the traditional motive and ideal in commerce and capitalistic industry is not service but private gain. This is a condition that idealizes selfishness and is directly opposed to emulation in service. Unless the idea of service can be so enhanced that it subordinates the idea of gain, these occupations will continue to lack social spirit and higher efficiency. Apparently we must look for this enhancement to the development of service groups, embracing handworkers as well as managers, with such power, responsibility,

and sense of honor as we now see in some of the professions.

2. The unstable character of many commercial and industrial activities, making it difficult to form continuing groups and traditions. This is a serious and possibly, in some cases, a fatal obstacle to higher organization.

3. The fact that our present economic organization is autocratic, or oligarchic, and that, consequently, the mass of workers do not and cannot feel that it is their own to such a degree that their selves are identified with it and that they owe it honor and service.

Some critics of the present condition speak of it as "wage-slavery," and if the essence of slavery is being compelled to do work that is in no sense *yours*, it is true that our industrial work is largely of this kind. It is done under a sense of compulsion, without real participation, and hence is servile in spirit, whatever its form. "But," we are told, "if the workman doesn't like it, he can quit." Precisely; in other words, the situation is such that the only way to assert one's self, to prove one's freedom and manhood, is to slight his job, or to strike. The self is not only outside the task but hostile to it. A strike is a time of glorious self-assertion against a hated domination. The misuse of human nature could hardly go further.

4. The prevalence of a narrow economics, which disregards human nature, and particularly the social self. The dogma that nothing but pecuniary interest need be considered in the economic system fortifies and perpetuates a bad situation.

Evidently we need to revise our system of motives, especially those relating to material production, with a view to giving more encouragement to our higher human nature. And this will involve the building up of somewhat democratic occupation groups with traditions, standards, and ideals of service.

By hero-worship is here meant an emulation that strives to imitate some admired character, in a spirit not of rivalry or opposition, but of loyal enthusiasm. It is higher than rivalry, in the sense that it involves a superior grade of mental activity—though, of course, there is no sharp line of separation between them. While the other is a rather gross and simple impulse, common to all men and to the higher animals, the hero-worshipper is an idealist, imaginative; the object that arouses his enthusiasm and his endeavor does so because it bears a certain relation to his aspirations, to his constructive thought. Hero-worship is thus more selective, more significant of the special character and tendencies of the individual, in every way more highly organized than rivalry.

It has a great place in all active, aspiring lives, especially in the plastic period of youth. We feed our characters, while they are forming, upon the vision of admired models; an ardent sympathy dwells upon the traits through which their personality is communicated to us—facial expression, voice, significant movements, and so on. In this way those tendencies in us that are toward them are literally fed; are stimulated, organized, made habitual and

312

familiar. As already pointed out, sympathy appears
to be an act of growth; and this is especially true of
the sort of sympathy we call hero-worship. All autobiographies which deal with youth show that the
early development of character is through a series of
admirations and enthusiasms, which pass away, to be
sure, but leave character the richer for their existence.
They begin in the nursery, flourish with great vigor
in the school-yard, attain a passionate intensity during adolescence, and though they abate rapidly in
adult life, do not altogether cease until the power of
growth is lost. All will find, I imagine, if they recall
their own experience, that times of mental progress
were times when the mind found or created heroes to
worship, often owning allegiance to several at the
same time, each representing a particular need of
development. The active tendencies of the school-
boy lead to admiration of the strongest and boldest
of his companions; or perhaps, more imaginative, he
fixes his thoughts on some famous fighter or explorer;
later it is possibly a hero of statesmanship or literature who attracts him. Whatever the tendency, it
is sure to have its complementary hero. Even science
often begins in hero-worship. "This work," says
Darwin of Humboldt's Personal Narrative, "stirred
up in me a burning zeal to add even the most humble
contribution to the noble structure of Natural Science." * We easily forget this varied and impassioned idealism of early life; but "the thoughts of
youth are long, long thoughts," and it is precisely

* See Darwin's Life and Letters, by his son, vol. i, p. 47.

then and in this way that the most rapid development of character takes place. J. A. Symonds, speaking of Professor Jowett's early influence upon him says, "Obscurely but vividly I felt my soul grow by his contact, as it had never grown before"; and Goethe remarks that "vicinity to the master, like an element, lifts one and bears him on."

If youth is the period of hero-worship, so also is it true that hero-worship, more than anything else, perhaps, gives one the sense of youth. To admire, to expand one's self, to forget the rut, to have a sense of newness and life and hope, is to feel young at any time of life. "Whilst we converse with what is above us we do not grow old but grow young"; and that is what hero-worship means. To have no heroes is to have no aspiration, to live on the momentum of the past, to be thrown back upon routine, sensuality, and the narrow self.

As hero-worship becomes more imaginative, it merges insensibly into that devotion to ideal persons that is called religious. It has often been pointed out that the feeling men have toward a visible leader and master like Lincoln, Lee, Napoleon, or Garibaldi, is psychologically much the same thing as the worship of the ideal persons of religion. Hero-worship is a kind of religion, and religion, in so far as it conceives persons, is a kind of hero-worship. Both are expressions of that intrinsically social or communicative nature of human thought and sentiment which was insisted upon in a previous chapter. That the personality toward which the feeling is directed is

ideal evidently affords no fundamental distinction.
All persons are ideal, in a true sense, and those whom
we admire and reverence are peculiarly so. That is
to say, the idea of a person, whether his body be present to our senses or not, is imaginative, a synthesis,
an interpretation of many elements, resting upon our
whole experience of human life, not merely upon our
acquaintance with this particular person; and the
more our admiration and reverence are awakened the
more actively ideal and imaginative does our conception of the person become. Of course we never *see*
a person; we see a few visible traits which stimulate
our imaginations to the construction of a personal
idea in the mind. The ideal persons of religion are
not fundamentally different, psychologically or so-
ciologically, from other persons; they are personal
ideas built up in the mind out of the material at its
disposal, and serving to appease its need for a sort of
intercourse that will give scope to reverence, submission, trust, and self-expanding enthusiasm. So far
as they are present to thought and emotion, and so
work upon life, they are real, with that immediate
social reality discussed in the third chapter. The
fact that they have attached to them no visible or
tangible material body, similar to that of other persons,
is indeed an important fact, but rather of physiological
than of psychological or social interest. Perhaps it
is not going too far to say that the idea of God is
specially mysterious only from a physiological point
of view; mentally and socially regarded it is of one sort
with other personal ideas, no less a verifiable fact,

and no more or less inscrutable. It must be obvious to any one who reflects upon the matter, I should think, that our conceptions of personality, from the simple and sensuous notions a little child has of those about him, up to the noblest and fullest idea of deity that man can achieve, are one in kind, as being imaginative interpretations of experience, and form a series in which there are no breaks, no gap between human and divine. All is human, and all, if you please, divine.

If there are any who hold that nothing is real except what can be seen and touched, they will necessarily forego the study of persons and of society; because these things are essentially intangible and invisible. The bodily presence furnishes important assistance in the forming of personal ideas, but is not essential. I never saw Shakespeare, and have no lively notion of how he looked. His reality, his presence to my mind, consists in a characteristic impression made upon me by his recorded words, an imaginative interpretation or inference from a book. In a manner equally natural and simple the religious mind comes to the idea of personal deity by a spontaneous interpretation of life as a whole. The two ideas are equally real, equally incapable of verification *to the senses.*

CHAPTER IX

LEADERSHIP OR PERSONAL ASCENDANCY

LEADERSHIP DEFINES AND ORGANIZES VAGUE TENDENCY—POWER AS BASED UPON THE MENTAL STATE OF THE ONE SUBJECT TO IT—THE MENTAL TRAITS OF A LEADER: SIGNIFICANCE AND BREADTH—WHY THE FAME AND POWER OF A MAN OFTEN TRANSCEND HIS REAL CHARACTER—ASCENDANCY OF BELIEF AND HOPE—MYSTERY—GOOD FAITH AND IMPOSTURE—DOES THE LEADER REALLY LEAD?

BUT how do we choose our heroes? What is it that gives leadership to some and denies it to others? Can we make out anything like a *rationale* of personal ascendancy? We can hardly hope for a complete answer to these questions, which probe the very heart of life and tendency, but at least the attempt to answer them, so far as possible, will bring us into an interesting line of thought.

It is plain that the theory of ascendancy involves the question of the mind's relative valuation of the suggestions coming to it from other minds; leadership depending upon the efficacy of a personal impression to awaken feeling, thought, action, and so to become a cause of life. While there are some men who seem but to add one to the population, there are others whom we cannot help thinking about; they lend arguments to their neighbors' creeds, so that the life of their contemporaries, and perhaps of following generations, is notably different because they have

317

lived. The immediate reason for this difference is evidently that in the one case there is something seminal or generative in the relation between the personal impression a man makes and the mind that receives it, which is lacking in the other case. If we could go farther than this and discover what it is that makes certain suggestions seminal or generative, we should throw much light on leadership, and through that on all questions of social tendency.

We are born with a vaguely differentiated mass of mental tendency, vast and potent, but unformed and needing direction—*informe, ingens, cui lumen ademptum.* This instinctive material is believed to be the outcome of age-long social development in the race, and hence to be, in a general way, expressive of that development and functional in its continuance. The process of evolution has established a probability that a man will find himself at home in the world into which he comes, and prepared to share in its activities. Besides the tendency to various sorts of emotion, we have the thinking instinct, the intelligence, which seems to be fairly distinct from emotion and whose function includes the co-ordination and organization of other instinctive material with reference to the situations which life offers.

At any particular stage of individual existence, these elements, together with the suggestions from the world without, are found more or less perfectly organized into a living, growing whole, a person, a man. Obscurely locked within him, inscrutable to himself as to others, is the soul of the whole past, his portion of the energy, the passion, the tendency, of human life. Its existence creates a vague need to live, to feel, to act; but he cannot fulfil this need, at least not in a normal way, without incitement from outside to loosen and direct his instinctive aptitude. There is explosive material stored up in him, but it cannot go off unless the right spark reaches it, and that spark is usually some sort of a personal suggestion, some living trait that sets life free and turns restlessness into power.

It must be evident that we can look for no cut-and-dried theory of this life-imparting force, no algebraic formula for leadership. We know but little of the depths of human tendency; and those who know most are possibly the poets, whose knowledge is little available for precise uses. Moreover, the problem varies incalculably with sex, age, race, inherited idiosyncrasy, and previous personal development. The general notions of evolution, however, lead us to expect that what awakens life and so gives ascendancy will be something important or functional in the past life of the race, something appealing to instincts which have survived because they had a part to perform; and this, generally speaking, appears to be the case.

The prime condition of ascendancy is the presence of undirected energy in the person over whom it is to be exercised; it is not so much forced upon us from without as demanded from within. The mind, having energy, must work, and requires a guide, a form of thought, to facilitate its working. All views of life are fallacious which do not recognize the fact that the primary need is the need to do. Every healthy organism evolves energy, and this must have an outlet. In the human mind, during its expanding period, the excess of life takes the form of a reaching out beyond all present and familiar things after an unknown good; no matter what the present and familiar may be, the fact that it is such is enough to make it inadequate. So we have a vague onward impulse, which is the unorganized material, the undifferentiated protoplasm, so to speak, of all progress; and this, as we have seen, makes the eagerness of hero-worship in the young, imaginative, and aspiring. So long as our minds and hearts are open and capable of progress, there are persons that have a glamour for us, of whom we think with reverence and aspiration; and although the glamour may pass from them and leave them commonplace, it will have fixed itself somewhere else. In youth the mind, eager, searching, forward-looking, stands at what Professor Baldwin calls the alter pole of the socius, peering forth in search of new life. And the idealist at any age needs superiority in others and is always in quest of it. "Dear to us are those who love us, . . . but dearer are those who reject us as unworthy, for they add another life; they build a heaven before us whereof we had not dreamed, and thereby supply to us new powers out of the recesses of the spirit, and urge us to new and unattempted performances." * To cease to admire is a proof of deterioration.

* Emerson, New England Reformers.

LEADERSHIP OR PERSONAL ASCENDANCY

Most people will be able to recall vague yet intensely vivid personal impressions that they have received from faces—perhaps from a single glance of a countenance that they have never seen before or since—or perhaps from a voice; and these impressions often remain and grow and become an important factor in life. The explanation is perhaps something like this: When we receive these mysterious influences we are usually in a peculiarly impressionable state, with nervous energy itching to be worked off. There is pressure in the obscure reservoirs of hereditary passion. In some way, which we can hardly expect to define, this energy is tapped, an instinct is disengaged, the personal suggestion conveyed in the glance is felt as the symbol, the master-key that can unlock hidden tendency. It is much the same as when electricity stored and inert in a jar is loosed by a chance contact of wires that completes the circuit; the mind holds fast the life-imparting suggestion; cannot, in fact, let go of it.

> "——all night long his face before her lived,
> Dark-splendid, speaking in the silence, full
> Of noble things, and held her from her sleep."

It is true of races, as of individuals, that the more vitality and onwardness they have, the more they need ideals and a leadership that gives form to them. A strenuous people like the Anglo-Saxon must have something to look forward and up to, since without faith of some sort they must fall into dissipation or despair; they can never be content with that calm and symmetrical enjoyment of the present which is thought to have been characteristic of the ancient Greeks. To be sure it is said, and no doubt with truth, that the people of Northern Europe are less hero-worshippers than those of the South, in the sense that they are less given to blind enthusiasm for popular idols; but this, I take it, only means that the former, having more constructive power in building up ideals from various personal sources, and more persistence in adhering to them when thus built up, are more sober and independent in their judgment of particular persons, and less liable to extravagant admiration of the hero of the moment. But their idealism is all the more potent for this, and at bottom is just as dependent upon personal suggestion for its definition. Thus it is likely that all leadership will be found to be such by virtue of defining the possibilities of the mind. "If we survey the field of history," says Professor William James, "and ask what feature all great periods of revival, of expansion of the human mind, display in common, we shall find, I think, simply this; that each and all of them have said to the human being, 'the inmost nature of the reality is congenial to *powers* which you possess'";* and the same principle evidently applies to personal leadership.

We are born to action; and whatever is capable of suggesting and guiding action has power over us from the first. The attention of the new-born child is fixed by whatever exercises the senses, through mo-

* Psychology, vol. ii, p. 314.

tion, noise, touch, or color. Persons and animals interest him primarily because they offer a greater amount and variety of sensible stimulus than other objects. They move, talk, laugh, coax, fondle, bring food, and so on. The prestige they thus acquire over the child's mind is shared with such other stimulating phenomena as cars, engines, windmills, patches of sunlight, and bright-colored garments. A little later, when he begins to acquire some control over his activities, he welcomes eagerly whatever can participate in and so stimulate and guide them. The playthings he cares for are those that go, or that he can do something with—carts, fire-engines, blocks, and the like. Persons, especially those that share his interests, maintain and increase their ascendancy, and other children, preferably a little older and of more varied resources than himself, are particularly welcome. Among grown-ups he admires most those who do something that he can understand, whom he can appreciate as actors and producers—such as the carpenter, the gardener, the maid in the kitchen. R. invented the happy word "thinger" to describe this sort of people, and while performing similar feats would proudly proclaim himself a thinger.

It will be observed that at this stage a child has learned to reflect upon action and to discriminate that which is purposeful and effective from mere motion; he has gained the notion of power. Himself constantly trying to do things, he learns to admire those who can do things better than himself, or who can suggest new things to do. His father sitting at his desk probably seems an inert and unattractive phenomenon, but the man who can make shavings or dig a deep hole is a hero; and the seemingly perverse admiration which children at a later age show for circus men and for the pirates and desperadoes they read about, is to be explained in a similar manner. What they want is *evident* power. The scholar may possibly be as worthy of admiration as the acrobat or the policeman; but the boy of ten will seldom see the matter in that light.

Thus the idea of power and the types of personality which, as standing for that idea, have ascendancy over us, are a function of our own changing character. At one stage of their growth nearly all imaginative boys look upon some famous soldier as the ideal man. He holds this place as symbol and focus for the aggressive, contending, dominating impulses of vigorous boyhood; to admire and sympathize with him is to gratify, imaginatively, these impulses. In this country some notable speaker and party leader often succeeds the soldier as a boyish ideal; his career is almost equally dominating and splendid, and, in time of peace, not quite so remote from reasonable aspiration. In later life these simple ideals are likely to yield somewhat to others of a more special character, depending upon the particular pursuit into which one's energies are directed. Every occupation which is followed with enthusiasm has its heroes, men who stand for the idea of power or efficient action as understood by persons of a particular training and habit. The world of commerce and industry is full of hero-worship, and men who have made great fortunes are admired, not unjustly, for the personal prowess such success implies; while people of a finer intellectual development have their notion of power correspondingly refined, and to them the artist, the poet, the man of science, the philanthropist, may stand for the highest sort of successful action.

It should be observed, however, that the simpler and more dramatic or visually imaginable kinds of power have a permanent advantage as regards general ascendancy. Only a few can appreciate the power of Darwin, and those few only when the higher faculties of their minds are fully awake; there is nothing dramatic, nothing appealing to the visual imagination, in his secluded career. But we can all *see* Grant or Nelson or Moltke at the headquarters of their armies, or on the decks of their ships, and hear the roar of their cannons. They hold one by the eye and by the swelling of an emotion felt to be common to a vast multitude of people. There is always something of the intoxication of the crowd in the submission to this sort of ascendancy. However alone our bodies may be, our imaginations are in the throng; and for my part whenever I think of any occasion when a man played a great part before the eyes of mankind, I feel a thrill of irrational enthusiasm. I should imagine, for instance, that scarcely any one could read such a thing as "Sheridan's Ride" without strong feeling. He witnesses the disorder, uncertainty, and dismay of the losing battle, the anxious officers trying to stay the retreat, and longing for the commander who has

325

always led to victory. Then he follows the ride from "Winchester twenty miles away," and shares the enthusiasm of the army when the valiant and beloved leader rides forth upon the field at last, renewing every heart by his presence and making victory out of defeat. In comparison with this other kinds of power seem obscure and separate. It is the drama of visible courage, danger, and success, and the sense of being one of a throng to behold it, that makes the difference.

This need of a dramatic or visually imaginable presentation of power is no doubt more imperative in the childlike peoples of Southern Europe than it is in the sedater and more abstractly imaginative Teutons; but it is strong in every people, and is shared by the most intellectual classes in their emotional moods. Consequently these heroes of the popular imagination, especially those of war, are enabled to serve as the instigators of a common emotion in great masses of people, and thus to produce in large groups a sense of comradeship and solidarity. The admiration and worship of such heroes is possibly the chief feeling that people have in common in all early stages of civilization, and the main bond of social groups. Even in our own time this is more the case than is understood. It was easy to see, during the Spanish-American War, that the eager interest of the whole American people in the military operations, and the general and enthusiastic admiration of every trait of heroism, was bringing about a fresh sense of community throughout the country and so renewing and consolidating the collective life of the nation.

If we ask what are the mental traits that distinguish a leader, the only answer seems to be that he must, in one way or another, be a great deal of a man, or at least appear to be. He must stand for something to which men incline, and so take his place by right as a focus of their thought.

Evidently he must be the best of his kind available. It is impossible that he should stand forth as an archetype, unless he is conceived as superior, in some respect, to all others within range of the imagination. Nothing that is seen to be second-rate can be an ideal; if a character does not bound the horizon at some point we will look over it to what we can see beyond. The object of admiration may be Cæsar Borgia, or Napoleon, or Jesse James the train-robber, but he must be typical, must stand for something. No matter how bad the leader may be, he will always be found to owe his leadership to something strong, affirmative, and superior, something that appeals to onward instinct.

To be a great deal of a man, and hence a leader, involves, on the one hand, a significant individuality, and, on the other, breadth of sympathy, the two being different phases of personal caliber, rather than separate traits.

It is because a man cannot stand for anything except as he has a significant individuality, that self-reliance is so essential a trait in leadership: except as a person trusts and cherishes his own special tendency, different from that of other people and usually opposed by them in its inception, he can never develop anything of peculiar value. He has to free himself from the domination of purposes already defined and urged upon him by others, and bring up something fresh out of the vague underworld of subconsciousness; and this means an intense self, a militant, gloating "I." Emerson's essay on self-reliance only formulates what has always been the creed of significant persons.

On the other hand, success in unfolding a special tendency and giving vogue to it, depends upon being in touch, through sympathy, with the current of human life. All leadership takes place through the communication of ideas to the minds of others, and unless the ideas are so presented as to be congenial to those other minds, they will evidently be rejected. It is because the novelty is not alien to us, but is seen to be ourself in a fresh guise, that we welcome it.

It has frequently been noticed that personal ascendancy is not necessarily dependent upon any palpable deed in which power is manifested, but that there is often a conviction of power and an expectation of success that go before the deed and control the minds of men without apparent reason. There is something fascinating about this immediate and seemingly causeless personal efficacy, and many writers of insight lay great stress upon it. Emerson, for example, is fond of pointing out that the highest sort of greatness is self-evident, without particular works. Most men of executive force possess something of this direct ascendancy, and some, like Napoleon, Cromwell, Bismarck, and Andrew Jackson, have had it in pre-eminent measure. It is not confined to any class, however, but exists in an infinite variety of kinds and degrees; and men of thought may have it as well as men of action. Dante, Milton, Goethe, and their like, bear the authority to dominate the minds of others like a visible mantle upon their shoulders, inspiring a sense of reverence and a tendency to believe and follow in all the impressionable people they meet. Such men are only striking examples of what we are all familiar with in daily life, most persons of decided character having something imposing about them at times. Indeed, there is hardly any one so insignificant that he does not seem imposing to some one at some time.

Notwithstanding the mystery that is often made of this, it appears to be simply a matter of impulsive personal judgment, an impression of power, and a sense of yielding due to interpretation of the visible or audible symbols of personality, discussed in a previous chapter. Another may impress us with his power, and so exercise ascendancy over us, either by grossly performing the act, or by exhibiting traits of personality which convince our imaginations that he can and will do the act if he wishes to. It is in this latter way, through imaginative inference, that people mostly work upon us in ordinary social intercourse. It would puzzle us, in many cases, to tell just how we know that a man is determined, dauntless, magnanimous, intrinsically powerful, or the reverse. Of course reputation and past record count for much; but we judge readily enough without them, and if, like Orlando in "As You Like It," he "looks successfully," we believe in him. The imagination is a sort of clearing-house through which great forces operate by convenient symbols and with a minimum of trouble.

The man of action who, like Napoleon, can dominate the minds of others in a crisis, must have the general traits of leadership developed with special reference to the promptness of their action. His individual significance must take the form of a palpable decision and self-confidence; and breadth of sympathy becomes a quick tact to grasp the mental state of those with whom he deals, so that he may know how to plant the dominating suggestion. Into the vagueness and confusion that most of us feel in the face of a strange situation, such a man injects a clear-cut idea. There is a definiteness about him which makes us feel that he will not leave us drifting, but will set a course, will substitute action for doubt, and give our energies an outlet. Again, his aggressive confidence is transmitted by suggestion, and acts directly upon our minds as a sanction of his leadership. And if he adds to this the tact to awaken no opposition, to make us feel that he is of our sort, that his suggestions are quite in our line, in a word that we are safe in his hands; he can hardly be resisted.

In face-to-face relations, then, the natural leader is one who always has the appearance of being master of the situation. He includes other people and extends beyond them, and so is in a position to point out what they must do next. Intellectually his suggestion seems to embrace what is best in the views of others, and to embody the inevitable conclusion; it is the timely, the fit, and so the prevalent. Emotionally his belief is the strongest force present, and so draws other beliefs into it. Yet, while he imposes himself upon others, he feels the other selves as part of the situation, and so adapts himself to them that no opposition is awakened; or possibly he may take the violent method, and browbeat and humiliate a weak mind: there are various ways of establishing superiority, but in one way or another the consummate leader always accomplishes it.

Take Bismarck as an example of almost irresistible personal ascendancy in face-to-face relations. He had the advantage, which, however, many men of equal power have done without, of an imposing bulk and stature; but much more than this were the mental and moral traits which made him appear the natural master in an assembly of the chief diplomats of Europe. "No idea can be formed," says M. de Blowitz,* "of the ascendancy exercised by the German Chancellor over the eminent diplomatists attending the Congress. Prince Gortchakoff alone, eclipsed by his rival's greatness, tried to struggle against him." His "great and scornful pride," the absolute, contemptuous assurance of superiority which was evident in every pose, tone, and gesture, accompanied, as is pos-

* In Harper's Magazine, vol. 78, p. 870.

sible only to one perfectly sure of himself, by a frankness, good-humor, and cordial insight into others which seemed to make them one with himself, participators in his domination; together with a penetrating intelligence, a unique and striking way of expressing himself, and a perfect clearness of purpose at all times, were among the elements of the effect he produced. He conciliated those whom he thought it worth while to conciliate, and browbeat, ignored, or ridiculed the rest. There was nothing a rival could say or do but Bismarck, if he chose, would say or do something which made it appear a failure.

General Grant was a man whose personal presence had none of the splendor of Prince Bismarck, and who even appeared insignificant to the undiscerning. It is related that when he went to take command of his first regiment soon after the outbreak of the Civil War, the officer whom he was to succeed paid no attention to him at first, and would not believe that he was Grant until he showed his papers. An early acquaintance said of him, "He hadn't the push of a business man." "He was always a gentleman, and everybody loved him, for he was so gentle and considerate; but we didn't see what he could do in the world." * Yet over the finer sort of men he exercised a great ascendancy, and no commander was more willingly obeyed by his subordinates, or inspired more general confidence. In his way he manifested the essential traits of decision, self-confidence, and tact

* Reminiscences quoted by Garland in McClure's Magazine, April, 1897.

332

in great measure. He never appeared dubious, nervous, or unsettled; and, though he often talked over his plans with trusted officers, he only once, I believe, summoned a council of war, and then rejected its decision. He was nearly or quite alone in his faith in the plan by which Vicksburg was taken, and it is well known that General Sherman, convinced that it would fail, addressed him a formal remonstrance, which Grant quietly put in his pocket and later returned to its author. "His pride in his own mature opinion," says General Schofield, "was very great; in that he was as far as possible from being a modest man. This absolute confidence in his own judgment upon any subject he had mastered, and the moral courage to take upon himself alone the highest responsibility, and to demand full authority and freedom to act according to his own judgment, without interference from anybody, added to his accurate estimate of his own ability, and his clear perception of the necessity for undivided authority and responsibility in the conduct of military operations, and in all that concerns the efficiency of armies in time of war, constituted the foundation of that very great character." * He was also a man of great tact and insight. He always felt the personal situation; divining the character and aims of his antagonists, and making his own officers feel that he understood them and appreciated whatever in them was worthy.

In spite of the fact that a boastful spirit is attrib-

* From a letter published in the newspapers at the time of the dedication of the Grant Monument, in April, 1897.

uted to Americans, the complete renunciation of external display so noticeable in General Grant is congenial to the American mind, and characteristic of a large proportion of our most successful and admired men. Undoubtedly our typical hero is the man who is capable of anything, but thinks it unbecoming to obtrude the fact. Possibly it is our self-reliant, democratic mode of life, which, since it offers a constant and varied test of the realities, as distinct from the appearances, gives rise to a contempt of the latter, and of those arts of pretense which impose upon a less sophisticated people. The truth about us is so accessible that cant becomes comparatively transparent and ridiculous.*

There is no better phenomenon in which to observe personal ascendancy than public speaking. When a man takes the floor in an assembly, all eyes are fixed upon him, all imaginations set to work to divine his personality and significance. If he looks like a true and steadfast man, of a spirit kindred with our own, we incline to him before he speaks, and believe that what he says will be congenial and right. We have all, probably, seen one arise in the midst of an audience strange to him, and by his mere attitude and expression of countenance create a subtle sense of community and expectation of consent. Another, on the contrary, will at once impress us as

* Mr. Howells remarks that "in Europe life is histrionic and dramatized, and that in America, except when it is trying to be European, it is direct and sincere."—"Their Silver Wedding Journey," Harper's Magazine, September, 1899.

334

self-conceited, insincere, overexcited, cold, narrow, or in some other way out of touch with us, and not likely to say anything that will suit us. As our first speaker proceeds, he continues to create a sense that he feels the situation; we are at home and comfortable with him, because he seems to be of our sort, having similar views and not likely to lead us wrong; it is like the ease and relaxation that one feels among old friends. There can be no perfect eloquence that does not create this sense of personal congeniality. But this deference to our character and mood is only the basis for exerting power over us; he is what we are, but is much more; is decided where we were vacillating, clear where we were vague, warm where we were cold. He offers something affirmative and onward, and gives it the momentum of his own belief. A man may lack everything but tact and conviction and still be a forcible speaker; but without these nothing will avail. "Speak only what you do know and believe, and are personally in it, and are answerable for every word." In comparison with these traits of mind and character, fluency, grace, logical order, and the like, are merely the decorative surface of oratory, which is well enough in its subordinate place, but can easily be dispensed with. Bismarck was not the less a great orator because he spoke "with difficulty and an appearance of struggle," and Cromwell's rude eloquence would hardly have been improved by lessons in elocution.

Burke is an example of a man who appears to have had all the attributes of a great speaker except tact,

335

and was conspicuously contrasted in this respect with Fox, whose genial nature never failed to keep touch with the situation. A man whose rising makes people think of going to dinner is not distinctively a great orator, even though his speeches are an immortal contribution to literature. The well-known anecdote of the dagger illustrates the unhappy results of losing touch with the situation. In the midst of one of his great discourses on the French Revolution, intending to impress upon his hearers the bloody character of that movement, Burke drew from his bosom a dagger and cast it on the floor. It so happened, however, that the Members of Parliament present were not just then in the mood to be duly impressed by this exhibition, which produced only astonishment and ridicule. Fox could never have done a thing of this sort. With all Burke's greatness, it would seem that there must have been something narrow, strenuous, and at times even repellent, in his personality and manner, some lack of ready fellow feeling, allowing him to lose that sense of the situation without which there can hardly be any face-to-face ascendancy.

The ascendancy which an author exercises over us by means of the written page is the same in essence as that of the man of action or the orator. The medium of communication is different; visible or audible traits give place to subtler indications. There is also more time for reflection, and reader or writer can choose the mood most fit to exert power or to feel it; so that there is no need for that constant preparedness and aggressiveness of voice and manner which the man of action requires. But these are, after all, incidental differences; and the underlying traits of personality, the essential relationship between leader and follower, are much the same as in the other cases. The reader should feel that the author's mind and purpose are congenial with his own, though in the present direction they go farther, that the thought communicated is not at all alien, but so truly his that it offers an opportunity to expand to a wider circle, and become a completer edition of himself. In short, if an author is to establish and maintain the power to interest us and, in his province, to lead our thought, he must exhibit personal significance and tact, in a form appropriate to this mode of expression. He must have a humanity so broad that, in certain of our moods at least, it gives a sense of congeniality and at-homeness. He must also make a novel and characteristic impression of some sort, a fresh and authentic contribution to our life; and must, moreover, be wholly himself, "stand united with his thought," have that "truth to its type of the given force" of which Walter Pater speaks. He must possess belief in something, and simplicity and boldness in expressing it.

Take Darwin again for example, all the better because it is sometimes imagined that personality is unimportant in scientific writing. Probably few thoughtful and open-minded persons can read the Origin of Species without becoming Darwinists, yielding willingly, for the time at least, to his ascendancy,

337

and feeling him as a master. If we consider the traits that give him this authority, it will be found that they are of the same general nature as those already pointed out. As we read his chapters, and begin to build him up in our imaginations out of the subtle suggestions of style, we find ourselves thinking of him as, first of all, a true and simple man, a patient, sagacious seeker after the real. This makes us, so far as we are also simple seekers after the real, feel at home with him, forget suspicion, and incline to believe as he believes, even if we fail to understand his reasons—though no man leaves us less excuse for such failure. His aim is our aim—the truth, and as he is far more competent to achieve it in this field than we are, both because of natural aptitude and a lifetime of special research, we readily yield him the reins, the more so because he never for an instant demands it, but seems to appeal solely to facts.

How many writers are there, even of much ability, who fail, primarily and irretrievably, because they do not make this favorable personal impression; because we divine something insincere, something impatient, some private aim that is not truth, which keeps us uncomfortably on our guard and makes us reluctant to follow them even when they appear most incontrovertible! Mr. Huxley suggested that Darwin harmed his case by excessive and unnecessary deference to the suggestions of his opponents; but it may well be that in the long run, and with the highest tribunal, this trait has added to his power. Many men have been convinced by the character of Darwin, by

338

his obvious disinterestedness and lack of all controversial bias, who would never have followed Huxley. I have had occasion to notice that there is no way of making converts to the idea of evolution so effectual as to set people reading the Origin of Species. Spencerism comes and goes, but Darwinism is an abiding condition.

Darwin's intellectual significance no one will question; and his self-confidence or faith was equally remarkable, and not at all inconsistent with his modesty. In his case it seems a faith in truth itself, so wholly is the self we find in his books identified with the striving after truth. As an act of faith his twenty years of collecting and brooding over the facts bearing upon the principle he had divined, was an exploit of the same nature as that of Columbus, sailing westward for months into an unknown ocean, to a goal which no one else could see. And with what simple confidence does he take his stand upon the truth thus won, and apply it to the geological history of the globe, or the rise of the human body and mind. A good illustration of his faith is his assertion, in the face of ridicule, that the existence of an orchid with a narrow neck eleven inches long proved the existence of a moth with a tongue of equal length. The moth, at that time unknown, was subsequently discovered.*

To illustrate the same principles in a wholly different phase of thought, we might take Charles Lamb. Lamb, too, attracts us first of all by a human and

* Related by W. H. Gibson, in Harper's Magazine for May, 1897.

congenial personality. We feel that in the kinds of
sentiment with which he deals he is at home and adequate, is ourselves and more than we, with a deeper
pathos, a richer, more audacious humor, a truer sensibility. He, too, enlarges life by access to novel and
acceptable modes of being; and he is always boldly
and simply himself. It is a poor notion of Lamb that
does not recognize that he was, in his way, a man of
character, conviction, and faith.

A similar analysis might be applied to great writers
of other sorts—poets, historians, and moralists; also
to painters, sculptors, actors, singers, to every potent
personality after its kind. While there is infinite
variety in leadership—according to the characters of
the persons concerned, the points at which they come
in contact, the means of communication between
them, and so on—there is, nevertheless, a likeness of
principle everywhere present. There is no such radical and complete divergence of the conditions of power
in the various fields of activity as is sometimes imagined. While there are great differences, they may be
looked upon as specific rather than generic. We may
always expect to find a human nature sufficiently
broad and sound—at least in those phases most apparent in the special means of expression chosen—to
be felt as representative; also some timely contribution added to the range of thought or feeling, and faith
in or loyalty to this peculiar contribution.

It is a very natural result of the principles already
noted that the fame and power of a man often tran-

scend the man himself; that is to say, the personal idea associated by the world with a particular name and presence has often little basis in the mind behind that name and presence, as it appears to cool and impartial study. The reason is that the function of the great and famous man is to be a symbol, and the real question in other minds is not so much, What are you? as, What can I believe that you are? What can you help me to feel and be? How far can I use you as a symbol in the development of my instinctive tendency? The scientific historian may insist on asking, What are you? because the instinct he is trying to gratify is the need to make things consistent to the intelligence. But few persons have this need strongly developed, in comparison with those of a more emotional character; and so most will care more for the other questions. The scientific point of view can never be that of the most of mankind, and science, it seems to me, can hardly be more than the critic and chastener of popular faith, not its leader.

Thus we may say of all famous and admired characters that, as personal ideas, they partake of the nature of gods, in that the thought entertained of them is a constructive effort of the idealizing imagination seeking to create a personal symbol of its own tendency.

Perhaps there is no more striking illustration of this than that offered by the mediæval history of the papacy. It is notorious that the idea of the pope, as it was entertained by the religious world, and the pope himself, as he appeared to his intimates, were things having for the most part no close relation to each other. The visible pope was often and for long periods at a time a depraved or insignificant man; but during these very periods the ideal pope, the pope of Europe's thought, might and often did flourish and grow in temporal and spiritual power. The former was only a symbol for the better definition of what the world needed to believe, a lay figure for garments woven by the co-operative imagination of religious men   The world needed to believe in a spiritual authority as a young girl needs to be in love, and it took up with the papacy as the most available framework for that belief, just as the young girl is likely to give her love to the least repugnant of those who solicit it. The same is true in a large measure of the other great mediæval authority, the emperor, as Mr. Bryce so clearly shows in his history of the Holy Roman Empire; and it holds true in some degree of all those clothed with royalty or other great offices. Fame may or may not represent what men were; but it always represents what humanity needs them to have been.

It is also true that when there is a real personal superiority, ascendancy is seldom confined to the traits in which this is manifested, but, once established in regard to these traits, it tends to envelop the leader as a whole, and to produce allegiance to *him* as a concrete person. This comes, of course, from the difficulty of breaking up and sifting that which presents itself to the senses, and through them to the mind, as a single living whole. And as the faults and weaknesses of a great man are commonly much easier to imitate than his excellences, it often

342

happens, as in the case of Michelangelo, that the former are much more conspicuous in his followers than the latter.

Another phase of the same truth is the ascendancy that persons of belief and hope always exercise as against those who may be superior in every other respect, but who lack these traits. The onward and aggressive portion of the world, the people who do things, the young and all having surplus energy, need to hope and strive for an imaginative object, and they will follow no one who does not encourage this tendency. The first requisite of a leader is, not to be right, but to lead, to show a way. The idealist's programme of political or economic reform may be impracticable, absurd, demonstrably ridiculous; but it can never be successfully opposed merely by pointing out that this is the case. A negative opposition cannot be wholly effectual: there must be a competing idealism; something must be offered that is not only less objectionable but more desirable, that affords occupation to progressive instinct. This holds true, for instance, in the case of teachers. One may sometimes observe two men of whom one has a sounder judgment, a clearer head, a more steadfast character, and is more a master of his subject, than the other; yet is hopelessly inferior in influence, because the other has a streak of contagious idealism which he lacks. One has all the virtues except hope; the other has that and all the power. It has been well said that when a man ceases to learn—to be open and forward-looking —he should also cease to teach.

It would be easy to multiply illustrations of this simple but important truth. All vigorous minds, I think, love books and persons that are mentally enfranchising and onward-looking, that seem to overthrow the high board fences of conventional thought and show a distance with purple hills; while it would be possible to mention powerful minds that have quickly lost influence by giving too much the impression of finality, as if they thought their system was the last. They only build another board fence a little beyond the old one. Perhaps the most admirable and original thing about Emerson is the invincible openness and renewal that seem to be in him, and some of us find his best expression in that address on the "Method of Nature" in which, even more than elsewhere, he makes us feel that what is achieved is ever transitory, and that there is everything to expect from the future. In like manner, to take perhaps the most remarkable example of all, the early Christians found in their belief organized hope, in contrast to the organized *ennui* of the Roman system of thought, and this, it would seem, must have been its most direct and potent appeal to most minds.*

It is also because of this ideal and imaginative character in personal ascendancy that mystery enters so

* The fact that the Roman system meant organized *ennui* in thought, the impossibility of entertaining large and hopeful views of life, is strikingly brought out, by the aid of contemporary documents, in Dill's Roman Society. Prisoners of a shrinking system, the later Romans had no outlook except toward the past. Anything onward and open in thought was inconceivable by them.

largely into it. Our allegiance is accompanied by a mental enlargement and renewal through generative suggestions; we are passing from the familiar to the strange, are being drawn we know not whither by forces never before experienced; the very essence of the matter is novelty, insecurity, and that excitement in the presence of dim possibilities that constitutes mystery.

It has often been remarked that to one in love the beloved person appears as a mystery, enveloped, as it were, in a sort of purple cloud. This is doubtless because the lover is undergoing strange alteration in his own mind; fresh vague passions are rising into consciousness out of the dark storehouse of hereditary instinct; he is cast loose from his old anchorage and does not know whither he is driven. The consequent feeling of a power and a strangeness upon him he associates, of course, with the person—commonplace enough, perhaps, to others—who is the symbol and occasion of the experience. Goethe seems to mean something of this sort when he uses the expression *das ewig Weibliche* to suggest the general mystery and allurement of new life.

And it is much the same no matter what sort of ascendancy is exercised over us: there is always excitement and a feeling of newness and uncertainty; imagination is awakened and busies itself with the fascinating personality; his slightest word or action is eagerly interpreted and works upon us. In short, mystery and idealism are so inseparable that a sense of power in others seems to involve a sense of their

345

inscrutability; and, on the other hand, so soon as a person becomes plain, he ceases to stimulate the imagination; we have seen all around him, so that he no longer appears an open door to new life, but has begun to be commonplace and stale.

It is even true that inscrutability in itself, having perhaps nothing important back of it, plays a considerable part in personal ascendancy. The hero is always a product of constructive imagination; and just as some imaginative painters find that the too detailed observation of sensible objects cumbers the inner vision and impedes production, so the hero-worshipper is likely at times to reject altogether the persons he knows in favor of some sort of mask or lay figure, whose very blankness or inertness insures the great advantage that it cannot actively repudiate the qualities attributed to it: it offers *carte blanche* to the imagination. As already suggested, the vital question in ascendancy is not, primarily, What are you? but, What do you enable me to be? What self-developing ideas do you enable me to form? and the power of mere inscrutability arises from the fact that it gives a vague stimulus to thought and then leaves it to work out the details to suit itself. To recur to the matter of falling in love: the young girl who, like Gwendolen in Daniel Deronda, or Isabel in the Portrait of a Lady, fixes her passion upon some self-contained and to her inscrutable person, in preference to others who are worthier but less mysterious, is a common character in life as well as in fiction.

Many other illustrations of the same principle might

346

be given. Thus the fact, instances of which are collected by Mr. Tylor in his work on Primitive Culture, that the insane, the idiotic, and the epileptic are reverenced by primitive peoples, may be interpreted in a similar manner.* Those who are mentally abnormal present in a striking form the inscrutable in personality; they seem to be men, but are not such men as we; our imaginations are alarmed and baffled, so that it is not unnatural that before science has shown us definite relations between these persons and ourselves, they should serve as one of the points about which crystallize our imaginations of unknown power. In the same way a strange and somewhat impassive physiognomy is often, perhaps, an advantage to an orator, or leader of any sort, because it helps to fix the eye and fascinate the mind. Such a countenance as that of Savonarola may have counted for much toward the effect he produced. Another instance of the prestige of the inscrutable is the fascination of silence, when power is imagined to lie behind it. The very name of William the Silent gives one a sort of thrill, whether he knows anything of that distinguished character or not. One seems to see a man darkly potent, mysteriously dispensing with the ordinary channel of self-assertion, and attaining his ends without evident means. It is the same with Von Moltke, "silent in seven languages," whose genius humbled France and Austria in two brief campaigns. And General Grant's taciturnity undoubtedly fascinated the imagination of the people—after his earlier successes had shown that

* See Primitive Culture, by E. B. Tylor, chap. xiv.

there was really something in him—and helped to secure to him a trust and authority much beyond that of any other of the Federal generals. It is the same with personal reserve in every form: one who always appears to be his own master and does not too readily reveal his deeper feelings, is so much the more likely to create an impression of power. He is formidable because incalculable. And accordingly we see that many people deliberately assume, or try to assume, an appearance of inscrutability,

> "And do a wilful stillness entertain,
> With purpose to be dressed in an opinion
> Of wisdom, gravity, profound conceit";

Disraeli, it is said, "was a mystery man by instinct and policy," and we all know others in our own circle of acquaintances.

So with the expression of personality in literature. A book which is perfectly clear at the first cursory reading is by that fact condemned as commonplace. If there were anything vital in it, it would appear at least a little strange, and would not be fully understood until it had been for some time inwardly digested. At the end of that time it would have done its best service for us and its ascendancy would have waned. It is always thus, I imagine, with writers who strongly move us; there is first mystery and a sense of unexplored life, then a period of assimilative excitement, and after that chastened affection, or perhaps revulsion or distrust. A person of mature years and ripe development, who is expecting nothing from literature but the corroboration and renewal of past ideas, may find satisfaction in a lucidity so complete as to occasion no imaginative excitement, but young and ambitious students are not content with it. They seek the excitement because they are capable of the growth that it accompanies. It was a maxim of Goethe that where there is no mystery there is no power; and something of the perennial vitality of his writings may be attributed to the fact that he did not trouble himself too much with the question whether people would understand him, but set down his inmost experiences as adequately as he could, and left the rest to time. The same may be said of Browning, and of many other great writers.

Something similar holds true of power in plastic art. The sort of mystery most proper and legitimate in art, however, is not an intellectual mystery—though some artists have had a great deal of that, like Leonardo, who "conquered by the magnetism of an incalculable personality" *—but rather a sensuous mystery, that is to say a vague and subtle appeal to recondite sources of sensuous impression, an awakening of hitherto unconscious capacity for harmonious sensuous life, like the feeling we get from the first mild weather in the spring. In this way, it seems to me, there is an effect of mystery, of congenial strangeness, in all powerful art. Probably every one would recog-

---

* J. A. Symonds, History of the Renaissance in Italy, The Fine Arts, p. 329. Hamerton has some interesting observations on mystery in art in his life of Turner, p. 352; also Ruskin in Modern Painters, part V, chaps. 4 and 5.

nize this as true of music, even if all do not feel its applicability to painting, sculpture, and architecture.

The well-known fact that mystery is inseparable from higher religious idealism may be regarded as a larger expression of this same necessity of associating inscrutability with personal power. If the imagination cannot be content with the definite in lesser instances, it evidently cannot when it comes to form the completest image of personality that it can embrace.

Although ascendancy depends upon what we think about a man rather than what he is, it is nevertheless true that an impression of his reality and good faith is of the first importance, and this impression can hardly outlast close scrutiny unless it corresponds to the fact. Hence, as a rule, the man who is to exercise enduring power over others must believe in that for which he stands. Such belief operates as a potent suggestion upon the minds of others.

> "While thus he spake, his eye, dwelling on mine,
> Drew me, with power upon me, till I grew
> One with him, to believe as he believed." *

If we divine a discrepancy between a man's words and his character, the whole impression of him becomes broken and painful; he revolts the imagination by his lack of unity, and even the good in him is hardly accepted. Nothing, therefore, is more fatal to ascendancy than perceived insincerity or doubt, and in immediate intercourse it is hard to conceal them.

* Tennyson, The Holy Grail.

350

When Luther came to Rome and saw what kind of a man the Pope was, the papacy was shake...

How far it is possible for a man to work upon others through a false idea of himself depends upon a variety of circumstances. As already pointed out, the man himself may be a mere incident with no definite relation to the idea of him, the latter being a separate product of the imagination. This can hardly be except where there is no immediate contact between leader and follower, and partly explains why authority, especially if it covers intrinsic personal weakness, has always a tendency to surround itself with forms and artificial mystery, whose object is to prevent familiar contact and so give the imagination a chance to idealize. Among a self-reliant, practical people like ours, with much shrewdness and little traditional reverence, the power of forms is diminished; but it is always great. The discipline of armies and navies, for instance, very distinctly recognizes the necessity of those forms which separate superior from inferior, and so help to establish an unscrutinized ascendancy in the former. In the same way manners, as Professor Ross remarks in his work on Social Control,* are largely used by men of the world as a means of self-concealment, and this self-concealment serves, among other purposes, that of preserving a sort of ascendancy over the unsophisticated.

As regards intentional imposture, it may be said in general that all men are subject to be duped in matters of which they have no working knowledge and

* See p. 248.

which appeal strongly to the emotions. The application of this principle to quack medicine, to commercial swindles, and to the ever-reappearing impostures relating to supposed communication with spirits, is too plain to be enlarged upon. While it is an advantage, even to a charlatan, to believe in himself, the susceptibility of a large part of us to be duped by quacks of one sort or another is obvious enough, and shows that the work of free institutions in developing shrewdness is by no means complete.

Probably a close and candid consideration of the matter would lead to the conclusion that every one is something of an impostor, that we all pose more or less, under the impulse to produce a desired impression upon others. As social and imaginative beings we must set store by our appearance; and it is hardly possible to do so without in some degree adapting that appearance to the impression we wish to make. It is only when this adaptation takes the form of deliberate and injurious deceit that much fault can be found with it. "We all," says Stevenson in his essay on Pepys, "whether we write or speak, must somewhat drape ourselves when we address our fellows; at a given moment we apprehend our character and acts by some particular side; we are merry with one, grave with another, as befits the nature and demands of the relation." If we never tried to seem a little better than we are, how could we improve or "train ourselves from the outside inward"? And the same impulse to show the world a better or idealized aspect of ourselves finds an organized expression in the various professions and classes, each of which has to some extent a cant or pose, which its members assume unconsciously, for the most part, but which has the effect of a conspiracy to work upon the credulity of the rest of the world. There is a cant not only of theology and of philanthropy, but also of law, medicine, teaching, even of science—perhaps especially of science, just now, since the more a particular kind of merit is recognized and admired, the more it is likely to be assumed by the unworthy. As theology goes down and science comes up, the affectation of disinterestedness and of exactness in method tends to supplant the affectation of piety.

In general it may be said that imposture is of considerable but always secondary importance; it is a sort of parasite upon human idealism and thrives only by the impulse to believe. A correct intuition on the part of mankind in the choice of their leaders is the only guaranty of the effectual organization of life in any or every sphere; and in the long run and on a large scale this correctness seems to exist. On the whole, the great men of history were real men, not shams, their characters were genuinely representative of the deeper needs and tendencies of human nature, so that in following them men were truly expressing themselves.

We have seen that all leadership has an aspect of sympathy and conformity, as well as one of individuality and self-will, so that every leader must also be a follower, in the sense that he shares the general current of life. He leads by appealing to our own tendency, not by imposing something external upon us. Great men are therefore the symbols or expressions, in a sense, of the social conditions under which they work, and if these conditions were not favorable the career of the great man would be impossible.

Does the leader, then, really lead, in the sense that the course of history would have been essentially different if he had not lived? Is the individual a true cause, or would things have gone on about the same if the famous men had been cut off in infancy? Is not general tendency the great thing, and is it not bound to find expression independently of particular persons? Certainly many people have the impression that in an evolutionary view of life single individuals become insignificant, and that all great movements must be regarded as the outcome of vast, impersonal tendencies.

If one accepts the view of the relation between particular individuals and society as a whole already stated in various connections, the answer to these questions must be that the individual *is* a cause, as independent as a cause can be which is part of a living whole, that the leader does lead, and that the course of history must have been notably different if a few great men had been withdrawn from it.

As to general tendency, it is false to set it over against individuals, as if it were a separate thing; it is only through individuals that general tendency begins or persists. "Impersonal tendency" in society is a mere abstraction; there is no such thing. Whether

354

idiosyncrasy is such as we all have in some measure, or whether it takes the form of conspicuous originality or genius, it is a variant element in life having always some tendency to innovation. Of course, if we believe in the prevalence of continuity and law, we cannot regard it as a new creation out of nothing; it must be a reorganization of hereditary and social forces. But however this may be, the person as a whole is always more or less novel or innovating. Not one of us floats quite inert upon the general stream of tendency; we leave the world somewhat different from what it would have been if we had been carried off by the croup.

Now in the case of a man of genius, this variant tendency may be so potent as to reorganize a large part of the general life in its image, and give it a form and direction which it could not have had otherwise. How any one can look at the facts and doubt the truth of this it is hard to see. Would the life we receive from the last century have been the same if, say, Darwin, Lincoln, and Bismarck had not lived? Take the case of Darwin. No doubt his greatness depended upon his representing and fulfilling an existing tendency, and this tendency entered into him from his environment, that is from other individuals. But it came out of him no longer the vague drift toward evolutionary theory and experiment that it was before, but concrete, common sense, matter-of-fact knowledge, thoroughly Darwinized, and so accredited by his character and labors that the world accepts it as it could not have done if he had not lived. We may apply the same idea to the author of Christianity. Whatever we may or may not believe regarding the nature of Christ's spiritual leadership, there is, I take it, nothing necessarily at variance with a sound social science in the Christian theory that the course of history has been transformed by his life.

The vague instincts which it is the function of the leader to define, stimulate, and organize, might have remained latent and ineffectual, or might have developed in a totally different manner, if he had not lived. No one can guess what the period following the French Revolution, or any period of French history since then, might have been without Napoleon; but it is apparent that all would have been very different. It is true that the leader is always a symbol, and can work only by using existing elements of life; but in the peculiar way in which he uses those elements is causation, is creation, in the only sense, perhaps, in which creation is definitely conceivable. To deny its importance is as absurd as to say that the marble as it comes from the quarry and the marble after Michelangelo is through with it are one and the same thing.

Most, if not all, of our confusion regarding such points as these arises from the almost invincible habit of thinking of "society," or "historical tendency," as a distinct entity from "individuals," instead of remembering that these general and particular terms merely express different aspects of the same concrete fact—human life. In studying leadership we may examine the human army one by one, and inquire why certain persons stand out from the rest as captains colonels, or generals, and what, in particular, it is that they have to do; or, in studying social tendency, we may disregard individuality and look at the movements of the army, or of its divisions and regiments, as if they were impersonal wholes. But there is no separation in fact: the leader is always the nucleus of a tendency, and, on the other hand, all social movement, closely examined, will be found to consist of tendencies having such nuclei. It is never the case that mankind move in any direction with an even front, but there are always those who go before and show the way.

I need hardly add that leadership is not a *final* explanation of anything; but is simply one of many aspects in which human life, always inscrutable, may be studied. In these days we no longer look for final explanations, but are well content if we can get a glimpse of things in process, not expecting to know how they began or where they are to end. The leader is a cause, but, like all causes we know of, he is also an effect. His being, however original, is rooted in the past of the race, and doubtless as susceptible of explanation as anything else, if we could only get at the facts.

CHAPTER X

THE SOCIAL ASPECT OF CONSCIENCE

THE RIGHT AS THE RATIONAL—SIGNIFICANCE OF THIS VIEW—THE
RIGHT AS THE ONWARD—THE RIGHT AS HABIT—RIGHT IS NOT
THE SOCIAL AS AGAINST THE INDIVIDUAL—IT IS, IN A SENSE,
THE SOCIAL AS AGAINST THE SENSUAL—THE RIGHT AS A SYN-
THESIS OF PERSONAL INFLUENCES—PERSONAL AUTHORITY—
CONFESSION, PRAYER, PUBLICITY—TRUTH—DEPENDENCE OF
RIGHT UPON IMAGINATION—CONSCIENCE REFLECTS A SOCIAL
GROUP—IDEAL PERSONS AS FACTORS IN CONSCIENCE—SOME
IDEAS OF RIGHT ARE UNIVERSAL

I AGREE with those moralists who hold that what
we judge to be the right is simply the rational, in a
large sense of that word. The mind is the theatre of
conflict for an infinite number of impulses, variously
originating, among which it is ever striving to produce some sort of unification or harmony. This endeavor to harmonize or assimilate includes deliberate
reasoning, but is something much more general and
continuous than that. It is mostly an unconscious or
subconscious manipulation of the materials presented,
an unremitting comparison and rearrangement of
them, which ever tends to organize them into some
sort of a whole. The right, then, is that which stands
this test; the sanction of conscience attaches to those
thoughts which, in the long run, maintain their places
as part of that orderly whole which the mental instinct
calls for, and which it is ever working with more or

less success to build up. That is right which presents itself, after the mind has done its full work upon the matter, as the mentally necessary, which we cannot gainsay without breaking up our mental integrity.

According to this view of the matter, judgments of right and wrong are in no way isolated or radically different in kind from other judgments. Such peculiarity as they have seems to come chiefly from the unusual intensity of the mental conflict that precedes them. The slightest scrutiny of experience shows, it seems to me, that the sharp and absolute distinction often assumed to exist between conscience and other mental activities does not hold good in life. There are gradual transitions from judgments which no one thinks of as peculiarly moral, through others which some would regard as moral and others would not, to those which are universally so regarded; and likewise moral feeling or sentiment varies a good deal in different individuals, and in the same individual under different conditions.

The class of judgments which every one considers as moral is perhaps limited to such as follow an exciting and somewhat protracted mental struggle, involving an imaginative weighing of conflicting personal ideas. A line of conduct has to be chosen; alternatives present themselves, each of which is backed by strong impulses, among which are some, at least, of sympathetic origin; the mind is intensely, even painfully, aroused, and when a decision is reached, it is accompanied by a somewhat peculiar sort of feeling called the sense of obligation, duty, or right. There would be little agreement, however, as to what sort of situations evoke this feeling. We are apt to feel that any question in regard to which we are much in earnest is a question of right and wrong. To the artist a consciously false stroke of brush or chisel is a moral wrong, a sin; and a good carpenter will suffer remorse if he lets a bad joint go uncorrected.

The fact that the judgment of right is likely to present itself to people of emotional temperament as an imagined voice, admonishing them what they ought to do, is an illustration of that essentially social or interlocutory character of thought, spoken of in an earlier chapter. Our thoughts are always, in some sort, imaginary conversations; and when vividly felt they are likely to become distinctly so. On the other hand, people whose moral life is calm perceive little or no distinction, in this regard, between the conclusions of conscience and other judgments.

Of course, the view that the right is the rational would be untrue, if by rational were meant merely the result of formal reasoning. The judgment of right and the conclusion of formal thought are frequently opposed to each other, because, I take it, the latter is a comparatively narrow, partial, and conventional product of the mind. The former is rational and mentally authoritative in a larger sense; its premises are immeasurably richer; it deals with the whole content of life, with instincts freighted with the inarticulate conclusions of a remote past, and with the unformulated inductions of individual experience. To set the product of a superficial ratiocination over the final output, in conscience, of our whole mental being, is a kind of pedantry. I do not mean to imply that there is usually an opposition between the two—they should work harmoniously together—but only to assert that when there is, conscience must be regarded as of a profounder rationality.

On the other hand, the wrong, the immoral, is, in a similar sense, the irrational. It is that which, after the mind has done its full work upon the matter, presents itself as the mentally isolated, the inharmonious, that which we cannot follow without having, in our more collected moods, a sense of having been untrue to ourselves, of having done ourselves a harm. The mind in its fullest activity is denied and desecrated; we are split in two. To violate conscience is to act under the control of an incomplete and fragmentary state of mind; and so to become less a person, to begin to disintegrate and go to pieces. An unjust or incontinent deed produces remorse, apparently because the thought of it will not lie still in the mind, but is of such a nature that there is no comfortable place for it in the system of thought already established there.

The question of right and wrong, as it presents itself to any particular mind, is, then, a question of the completest practicable organization of the impulses with which that mind finds itself compelled to deal. The working out of the right conclusion may be compared to the process by which a deliberative body comes to a conclusion upon some momentous public measure. Time must be given for all the more important passions, prejudices, traditions, interests, and the like, to be urged upon the members with such cogency as their advocates can give them, and for attempts to harmonize these conflicting forces so that a measure can be framed which the body can be induced to pass. And when a decision is finally reached there is a sense of relief, the greater in proportion as the struggle has been severe, and a tendency, even on the part of the opposition, to regard the matter as settled. Those people who cannot achieve moral unity, but have always a sense of two personalities warring within them, may be compared to certain countries in whose assemblies political parties are so embittered that they never come to an understanding with one another.

The mental process is, of course, only the proximate source of the idea of right, the conflict by which the competitive strength of the various impulses is measured, and some combination of them achieved; behind it is the whole history of the race and of the individual, in which impulses are rooted. Instinctive passions, like love, ambition, and revenge; the momentum of habit, the need of change, personal ascendencies, and the like, all have their bearing upon the final synthesis, and must either be conciliated or suppressed. Thus in case of a strong passion, like revenge let us say, one of two things is pretty sure to happen: either it will succeed in getting its revengeful impulse, more or less disguised perhaps, judged as right; or, if opposing ideas prove stronger, revenge will be kept under by the rise of an intense feeling of wrong that associates itself with it. If one observes that a person has a very vivid sense of the wrong of some particular impulse, one may usually infer that he has had in some way to contend with it; either as a temptation in his own mind, or as injuriously manifested in the conduct of others.

The natural way to solve a moral question, when immediate action is not required, is to let it lie in the mind, turning it over from time to time as attention is directed to it. In this manner the new situation gradually relates itself to all the mental forces having pertinency to it. The less violent but more persistent tendencies connect themselves quietly but firmly to recalcitrant impulse, enwrapping it like the filaments of a spider's web, and bringing it under discipline. Something of this sort is implied in the rule of conduct suggested by Mr. H. R. Marshall, in his excellent work, Instinct and Reason: "Act to restrain the impulses which demand immediate reaction, in order that the impulse order determined by the existence of impulses of less strength, but of wider significance, may have full weight in the guidance of your life." *

It occurs to me, however, that there is no absolute rule that the right is the deliberate. It is usually so, because the danger of irrationality and disintegration comes, in most cases, from the temporary sway of some active impulse, like that to strike or use injurious words in anger. But rationality involves decision as well as deliberation; and there are persons in whom the impulse to meditate and ponder so much outweighs the impulse to decide and act, as itself to endanger the

* See his " Instinct and Reason," p. 569.

unity of life. Such a person may well come to feel that the right is the decisive. It seems likely that in most minds the larger rationality, which gives the sense of right, is the sequel of much pondering, but is definitely achieved in moments of vivid insight.

The main significance of the view that the right is the rational is to deny that there is any sharp distinction in kind between the question of right and wrong and other mental questions; the conclusion of conscience being held to be simply a more comprehensive judgment, reached by the same process as other judgments. It still leaves untouched the remoter problems, mental and social, underlying all judgments; as, for instance, of the nature of impulses, of what determines their relative intensity and persistence, of the character of that process of competition and assimilation among them of which judgments are the outcome; and of the social order as determining impulses both indirectly, through its action upon heredity, and directly through suggestion.

And behind these is that problem of problems, to which all the roads of thought lead, that question of organization or vital process, of which all special questions of society or of the mind are phases. From whatever point of view we look at life, we can see something going on which it is convenient to call organization, development, or the like; but I suppose that all who have thought much about the matter feel that we have only a vague notion of what the fact is that lies behind these words.

I mention these things merely to disclaim any present attempt to fathom them, and to point out that the aim of this chapter is limited to some observations on the working of social or personal factors in the particular sort of organization which we call conscience or moral judgment.

It is useless to look for any other or higher criterion of right than conscience. What is felt to be right *is* right; that is what the word means. Any theory of right that should turn out to be irreconcilable with the sense of right must evidently be judged as false. And when it is urged that conscience is variable, we can only answer that, for this very reason, the right cannot be reduced to a universal and conclusive formula. Like life in all its phases, it is a progressive revelation out of depths we do not penetrate.

For the individual considering his own conduct, his conscience is the only possible moral guide, and though it differ from that of every one else, it is the only right there is for him; to violate it is to commit moral suicide. Speculating more largely on conduct in general he may find the right in some collective aspect of conscience, in which his own conscience appears as member of a larger whole; and with reference to which certain particular consciences, at variance with his own, like those of certain sorts of criminals, may appear as degenerate or wrong—and this will not surprise him, because science teaches us to expect degenerate variations in all forms of life. But, however broad a view he takes, he cannot do otherwise than refer the matter to his conscience; so that what *I* think, or—to generalize it—what *we* think, must, in one form or another, be the arbiter of right and wrong, so far as there can be any. Other tests become valid only in so far as conscience adopts them.

It would seem that any scientific study of the matter must consist essentially in investigating the conditions and relations of concrete right—the when, where, and why of what people *do* think is right. Social or moral science can never be a final source or test of morality; though it can reveal facts and relations which may help conscience in making its authoritative judgment.

The view that the right is the rational is quite consistent with the fact that, for those who have surplus energy, the right is the *onward*. The impulse to act, to become, to let out the life that rises within from obscure springs of power, is the need of needs, underlying all more special impulses; and this onward *Trieb* must always count in our judgments of right: it is one of the things conscience has to make room for. There can be no harmony in a mental life which denies expression to this most persistent and fundamental of all instinctive tendencies: and consequently the equilibrium which the active mind seeks, and a sense of which is one with the sense of right, is never a state of rest, but an *equilibrium mobile*. Our situation may be said to resemble that of an acrobat balancing himself upon a rolling sphere, and enabled to stand upright only on condition of moving continually forward. The right never remains precisely the same two days in succession; but as soon as any particular state of right is achieved, the mental centre of gravity begins to move onward and away from it, so that we can hold our ground only by effecting a new adjustment. Hence the merely negative can never be the right to a vigorous person, or to a vigorous society, because the mind will not be content with anything so inadequate to its own nature. The good self must be what Emerson calls a "crescive self," and the right must mark a track across the "waste abyss of possibility" and lead out the energies to congenial exertion.

This idea is nowhere, perhaps, more cogently stated and illustrated than in M. Guyau's penetrating work, A Sketch of Morality. He holds that the sense of duty is, in one aspect, a sense of a power to do things, and that this power tends in itself to create a sense of obligation. We can, therefore we must. "Obligation is an internal expansion—a need to complete our ideas by converting them into action." * Even pain may be sought as part of that larger life which the growing mind requires. "Leopardi, Heine, or Lenau would probably not have exchanged those hours of anguish in which they composed their finest songs for the greatest possible enjoyment. Dante suffered. . . . Which of us would not undergo a similar suffering? Some heart-aches are infinitely sweet." † And so with benevolence and what is called self-sacrifice. ". . . charity is but one with overflowing fecundity; it is like a

* M. J. Guyau, Esquisse d'une Morale sans Obligation ni Sanction, English Translation, p. 93.
† Idem, p. 149.

maternity too large to be confined within the family. The mother's breast needs life eager to empty it; the heart of the truly humane creature needs to be gentle and helpful to all." * "The young man is full of enthusiasm; he is ready for every sacrifice because, in point of fact, it is necessary that he should sacrifice something of himself—that he should diminish himself to a certain extent; he is too full of life to live only for himself." †

The right, then, is not merely the repressive discipline with which we sometimes identify it, but is also something warm, fresh, and outward-looking. That which we somewhat vaguely and coldly call mental development is, when at its best, the revelation of an expanding, variegating, and beautiful whole, of which the right act is a harmonious member.

When, on the other hand, we say that right is largely determined by habit, we only emphasize the other aspect of that progressive mingling of continuity with change, which we see in mental life in all its phases. Habit, we know, makes lines of less resistance in thought, feeling, and action; and the existence of these tracks must always count in the formation of a judgment of right, as of any other judgment. It ought not, apparently, to be set over against novel impulses as a contrary principle, but rather thought of as a phase of all impulses, since novelty always consists, from one point of view, in a fresh combination of habits. It is much the same question as that of suggestion and

* Idem, p. 87.   † Idem, p. 82.

choice, or of invention and imitation. The concrete fact, the real thing, in each case, is not one of these as against the other, or one modified by the other, but a single, vital act of which these are aspects, having no separate existence.

Whether a person's life, in its moral or any other aspect, is obviously changeful, or, on the contrary, appears to be merely repetitive or habitual, depends upon whether the state of his mind, and of the conditions about it, are favorable to rapid changes in the system of his thought. Thus if he is young and vigorous, and if he has a natural open-mindedness and keenness of sensibility, he will be so much the more likely, other things equal, to incorporate fresh elements of thought and make a new synthesis, instead of running on habit. Variety of life in the past, preventing excessive deepening of the mental ruts, and contact with strong and novel influences in the present, have the same tendency.

The rigidly habitual or traditionary morality of savages is apparently a reflection of the restriction and sameness of their social life; and a similar type of morals is found even in a complex society, as in China, when the social system has become rigid by the equilibration of competing ideas. On the other hand, the stir and change of the more active parts of our society make control by mere habit impossible. There are no simple dominant habits; tendencies are mixed and conflicting, so that the person must either be intelligently moral or else degenerate. He must either make a fresh synthesis or have no synthesis at all.

369

What is called principle appears to be simply a habit of conscience, a rule formed originally by a synthesis of various impulses, but become somewhat mechanical and independent of its origin—as it is the nature of habit to do. As the mind hardens and matures there is a growing inaptitude to take in novel and powerful personal impressions, and a corresponding ascendancy of habit and system; social sentiment, the flesh and blood of conduct, partly falls away, exposing a skeleton of moral principles. The sense of duty presents itself less and less as a vivid sympathetic impulse, and more and more as a sense of the economy and restfulness of a definite standard of conduct. When one has come to accept a certain course as duty he has a pleasant sense of relief and of lifted responsibility, even if the course involves pain and renunciation. It is like obedience to some external authority; any clear way, though it lead to death, is mentally preferable to the tangle of uncertainty.

Actions that appear memorable or heroic are seldom achieved at the moment of decisive choice, but are more likely to come after the habit of thought which produces the action has become somewhat mechanical and involuntary. It is probably a mistake to imagine that the soldier who braves death in battle, the fireman who enters the burning building, the brakeman who pursues his duty along the icy top of a moving train, or the fisherman who rows away from his vessel into the storm and mist, is usually in an acute state of heroism. It is all in the day's work; the act is part of a system of thought and conduct which has become

370

habitual and would be painful to break. Death is not imagined in all its terrors and compared with social obligation; the case is far simpler. As a rule there is no time in a crisis for complicated mental operations, and whether the choice is heroic or cowardly it is sure to be simple. If there is any conflict of suggestions it is brief, and the one that gains ascendancy is likely to be followed mechanically, without calculation of the future.

One who studies the "sense of oughtness" in children will have no difficulty in seeing that it springs largely from a reluctance to break habits, an indisposition, that is, to get out of mental ruts. It is in the nature of the mind to seek a principle or unifying thought—the mind is a rule-demanding instinct—and in great part this need is met by a habit of thought, inculcated perhaps by some older person who proclaims and enforces the rule, or perhaps by the unintended pressure of conditions which emphasize one suggestion and shut out others. However the rule originates, it meets a mental want, and, if not too strongly opposed by other impulses, is likely to be adopted and felt as obligatory just because it is a consistent way of thinking. As Mr. Sully says, "The truth is that children have a tremendous belief in law." *

The books on child-study give many instances of the surprising allegiance which children often give to rule, merely as rule, and even an intermittent observer will be sure to corroborate them. Thus a child five

* Studies of Childhood, p. 284.

371

years old, when on a visit, was invited to "open his mouth and shut his eyes," and upon his doing so a piece of candy was put into the former. When he tasted it he pulled it out and exclaimed, "Mama don't want me to have candy." Now this did not seem to be affectation, nor was the child other than fond of sweets, nor afraid of punishment or blame; he was simply under the control of a need for mental consistency. The no-candy rule had been promulgated and enforced at home; he had adopted it as part of his system of thought, and, when it was broken, his moral sense, otherwise the harmony of his mind, was shocked to a degree that the sweet taste of the candy could not overcome. Again, R. was subjected nearly every evening for several years to a somewhat painful operation called "bending his foot," intended to correct a slight deformity. After becoming accustomed to this he would sometimes protest and even cry if it were proposed to omit it. I thought I could see that moral allegiance to a rule, merely as such, weakened as he grew older; and the explanation of this I took to be that the increasing competition of suggestions and conflict of precepts made this simple, mechanical unity impossible, and so forced the mind, still striving for harmony, to exert its higher organizing activity and attempt a larger sort of unification. It is the same principle as that which prevents the civilized man from retaining the simple allegiance to rule and habit that the savage has; his complex life cannot be unified in this way, any more than his accounts can be notched on a stick; and he is forced, if he is to achieve any unity of life, to seek it in some more elaborate standard of behavior. Under uniform conditions the habitual is the rational, and therefore the moral; but under complex conditions this ceases to be the case.

Of course this way of looking at the matter does not do away with all the difficulties involved in it, but does, it seems to me, put habitual and other morality on the common ground of rationality, and show the apparently sharp division between them to be an illusion.

Those who think as I do will reject the opinion that the right is, in any general sense, the social as opposed to the individual. As already stated, I look upon this antithesis as false when used to imply a radical opposition. All our human thought and activity is either individual or social, according to how you look at it, the two being no more than phases of the same thing, which common thought, always inclined to confuse words with things, attempts to separate. This is as true in the ethical field as in any other. The consideration of other persons usually enters largely into questions of right and wrong; but the ethical decision is distinctly an assertion of a private, individualized view of the matter. Surely there is no sound general principle in accordance with which the right is represented by the suggestions of the social environment, and the wrong by our more private impulses.

The right is always a private impulse, always a self-assertion, with no prejudice, however, to its social character. The "ethical self" is not less a self for being ethical, but if anything more of a self, because it is a fuller, more highly organized expression of personality. All will recognize, I imagine, that a strong sense of duty involves self-feeling, so that we say to ourselves emphatically *I* ought. It would be no sense of duty at all if we did not feel that there was something about it peculiar to us and antithetical to some of the influences acting upon us. It is important for many purposes to emphasize the fact that the ethical self is always a public self; but it is equally true and important that it is always a private self.

In short, ethical thinking and feeling, like all our higher life, has its individual and social aspects, with no peculiar emphasis on either. If the social aspect is here at its highest, so also is the individual aspect.

The same objection applies to any form of the antithesis self *versus* other, considered as a general statement of moral situations. It is a fallacious one, involving vague and material notions of what personality is—vague because material, for we cannot, I think, reflect closely upon the facts of personality without seeing that they are primarily mental or spiritual, and by no means even analogous to the more obvious aspects of the physical. As a matter of fact, ego and alter, self and sympathy, are correlative, and always mingled in ethical judgments, which are not distinguished by having less self and more other in them, but by being a completer synthesis of all pertinent impulses. The characteristic of a sense of right is not

374

ego or alter, individual or social, but mental unification, and the peculiar feeling that accompanies it.

Egoism can be identified with wrong only when we mean by it some narrow or unstable phase of the self; and altruism, if we take it to mean susceptibility to be impressed by other people, is equally wrong when it, in turn, becomes narrow or unstable, as we see it in hysterical persons. As I have already said, I hold altruism, when used, as it seems to be ordinarily, to denote a supposed peculiar class of impulses, separate from another supposed class called egoistic, to be a mere fiction, engendered by the vaguely material idea of personality just mentioned. Most higher kinds of thought are altruistic, in the sense that they involve a more or less distinct reference to other persons; but when intensely conceived, these same kinds of thought are usually, if not always, self-thoughts, or egoistic, as well.

The question whether a man shall keep his dollar or give it to a beggar, for example, looks at first sight like a question of ego *versus* alter, because there are two physical bodies present and visibly associated with the conflicting impulses. In this merely physical sense, of referring to one material body rather than another, it is in fact such a question, but not necessarily in any properly mental, social, or moral sense.

Let us look at the matter a moment with reference to various possible meanings of the words altruism and altruistic. Taking the latter word as the most convenient for our purpose, I can think of three meanings, any one of which would answer well enough to the vague current usage of it: first, that which is suggested by another person, that is by his appearance, words, or other symbols; second, that which is for the benefit of another; third, good or moral.

In the first sense, which carries no moral implication at all, it is altruistic to give to the beggar, but the word is also applicable to the greater part of our actions, since most of them are suggested by others in some way. And, of course, many of the actions included are what are generally called selfish ones. To strike a man with whom we are angry, to steal from one of whom we are envious, to take liberties with an attractive woman, and all sorts of reprehensible proceedings suggested by the sight of another person, would be altruistic in this sense, which I suppose, therefore, cannot be the one intended by those who use the word as the antithesis to egoistic.

If we use the word in the second sense, that of being for the benefit of another, to give to the beggar may or may not be altruistic; thoughtful philanthropy is inclined to say that it is usually for his harm. It may, perhaps, be said that we at least intend to benefit or please him, that this is the main thing, and that it is a question whether the action has an I-reference or a you-reference in the mind of the actor. As to this I would again call attention to what was said of the nature of I and you as personal ideas in Chapter III, and of the nature of egotism in Chapter VI. Our impulses regarding persons cannot, in my opinion, be classified in this way. What could be more selfish than the action of a mother who cannot refuse her child indigestible sweetmeats? She gives them both to please the child and to gratify a shallow self which is identified with him. To refuse the money to the beggar may be as altruistic, in the sense of springing from the desire to benefit others, as to give it. The self for which one wishes to keep the dollar is doubtless a social self of some sort, and very possibly has better social claims upon him than the beggar: he may wish to buy flowers for a sick child.

I need hardly add that to give the money is not necessarily the moral course. The attempt to identify the good with what refers to others as against what refers to one's self is hopelessly confusing and false, both theoretically and in practical application.

In short, it is hard to discover, in the word altruism, any definite moral significance.

The individual and the group are related in respect to moral thought quite as they are everywhere else; individual consciences and the social conscience are not separate things, but aspects of one thing, namely, the moral Life, which may be regarded as individual by fixing our attention upon a particular conscience in artificial isolation, or as general, by attending to some collective phase, like public opinion upon a moral question. Suppose, for instance, one were a member of the Congress that voted the measure which brought on the war with Spain. The question how he should vote on this measure would be, in its individual aspect, a matter of private conscience; and so with all other members. But taking the vote as a whole, as a synthesis, showing the moral drift of the group, it appears

377

as an expression of a social conscience. The separation is purely artificial, every judgment of an individual conscience being social in that it involves a synthesis of social influences, and every social conscience being a collective view of individual consciences. The concrete thing, the moral Life, is a whole made up of differentiated members. If this is at all hard to grasp, it is only because the fact is a large one. We certainly cannot get far unless we can learn to *see* organization, since all our facts present it.

The idea that the right is the social as opposed to the sensual is, it seems to me, a sound one, if we mean by it that the mentally higher, more personal, or imaginative impulses have on the whole far more weight in conscience than the more sensual. The immediate reason for this seems to be that the mind of one who shares the higher life is so thronged with vivid personal or social sentiments, that the merely sensual cannot be the rational except where it is allied with these, or at any rate not opposed to them. It is for the psychologist to explain the mental processes involved, but apparently the social interests prevail in conscience over the sensual because they are the major force; that is, they are, on the whole, so much more numerous, vivid, and persistent, that they determine the general system of thought, of which conscience is the fullest expression. We may, perhaps, represent the matter nearly enough for our purpose by comparing the higher and lower kinds of thought to the human race and the inferior animals. The former is so much more powerful,

378

on the whole, though not always so individually, that it determines, in all settled countries, the general organization of life, erecting cities and railroads, clearing forests, and the like, to suit itself, and with only incidental regard to other animals. The latter are preserved within the system only in so far as they are useful, or at any rate not very troublesome, to mankind. So all sensual impulses are judged by their relation to a system of thought dominated by social sentiment. The pleasures of eating, harmless in themselves, begin to be judged wrong so soon as they are indulged in such a way as to blunt the higher faculties, or to violate justice, decency, or the like. A shipwrecked man, it is felt, should rather perish of hunger than kill and eat another man, because the latter action violates the whole system of social thought. And in like manner it is held that a soldier, or indeed any man, should prefer honor and duty to life itself.

The working of personal influence upon our judgments of right is not different in kind from its working upon other judgments: it simply introduces vivid impulses, which affect the moral synthesis something in the way that picking up a weight will change one's centre of gravity and force him to alter his footing.

As was suggested above, the morality of mere rule and habit becomes the less conspicuous in the life of children the more they are subjected to fresh personal influences. If their sympathies are somewhat dull, or if they are secluded, their minds naturally become grooved; and all children, perhaps, become much bound

379

to habit in matters where personal influence is not likely to interfere. But in most children, and in most matters, it will be found that the moral judgment and feeling are, from the very earliest, intensely sympathetic and personal, charged with shame, affection, anger, jealousy, and desire to please. The mind has already to struggle for harmony among vivid emotions, aroused by the appeals of life to hereditary instinct, each giving intensity to certain ideas of conduct, and tending to sway the judgment of right in their sense.

If the boy who refused the candy, as mentioned above, had possessed a vivid imagination of personal attitudes, which he did not, his situation might have been much more intricate. He might have been drawn to accept it not only by the sweet taste but by a desire to please the friends who offered it; and on the other hand he might have been deterred by a vision of the reproving face and voice of his mother. Thus M., nearly sixteen months old, had been frowned at and called naughty in a severe tone of voice when she tried to claw her brother's face. Shortly after, while sitting with him on the bed, her mother being at a distance, she was observed to repeat the offense and then, without further cause or suggestion, to bow her head and look abashed and guilty. Apparently she had a sense of wrong, a conviction of sin, perhaps consisting only in a reminiscence of the shame she had previously felt when similar behavior was followed by rebuke.

Here, then, we have a simple manifestation of a moral force that acts upon every one of us in countless ways, and every day of his life—the imagined approval

380

or disapproval of others, appealing to instinctive emotion, and giving the force of that emotion to certain views of conduct. The behavior that connects itself with such social sentiment as we like and feel the impulse to continue, is so much the more likely to be judged as right; but if the sentiment is one from which we are averse, the behavior is the more likely to be judged as wrong. The child's moral sense, says Perez, "begins as soon as he understands the signification of certain intonations of the voice, of certain attitudes, of a certain expression of countenance, intended to reprimand him for what he has done or to warn him against something he was on the point of doing. This penal and remunerative sanction gives rise by degrees to a clear distinction of concrete good and evil." *

A child who is not sensitive to praise or blame, but whose interests are chiefly impersonal, or at any rate only indirectly personal, sometimes appears to have no moral sense at all, to be without the conviction of sin or any notion of *personal* wrong. He has little experience of those peculiarly acute and trying mental crises which result from the conflict of impulses of sympathetic origin with one another or with animal appetites. This was much the case with R. in his earliest years. Living in quiet surroundings, somewhat isolated from other children, with no violent or particularly mischievous impulses, occupied all day long with blocks, sand-pile, and other impersonal interests, not sensitive to blame nor inclined to take it seriously, he gave the impression of being non-moral, an unfallen

* See his First Three Years of Childhood, p. 287.

spirit. M. was the very opposite of all this. From the first week she was visibly impulsive, contentious, sensitive, sympathetic; laying traps for approval, rebelling against criticism, sudden and quick to anger, sinning, repenting, rejoicing; living almost altogether in a vivid personal world.

A character of the latter sort has an intenser moral life, because the variety of strong impulses introduced by a sensitive and personally imaginative temperament are sure to make crises for the mind to wrestle with. The ethics of personal feeling which it has to work out seems widely apart from the ethics of rule and habit, as in fact it is, so far as regards the materials that enter into the moral synthesis. The color and content, all the concrete elements of the moral life, are as different as are the different characters of people: the idea of right is not a fraction of thought alike in all minds, but a comprehensive, integrating state of mind, characteristic of the personality of which it is an expression.

The idea of justice is, of course, a phase of the idea of right, and arises out of the mental attempt to reconcile conflicting impulses. As Professor Baldwin points out, the child is puzzled by contradictions between his simpler impulses, such as those to appropriate food and playthings, and other impulses of more imaginative or sympathetic origin. Needing to allay this conflict he readily grasps the notion of a *tertium quid*, a reconciling rule or law which helps him to do so.

Our mature life is not radically distinguished from childhood as regards the working of personal influence upon our moral thought. If there is progress it is in the way of fulness of experience and better organization: the mental life may become richer in those sympathetic or imaginative impulses which we derive from healthy intercourse with the world, and without a good store of which our judgments of right must be narrow and distorted; there may at the same time be a completer ordering and discipline of these materials, a greater power to construct the right, the unifying thought, out of diverse elements, a quicker recognition of it when achieved, and a steadier disposition to act upon it. In most cases, perhaps, a person after thirty years of age gains something in the promptness and steadfastness of his moral judgment, and loses something in the imaginative breadth of his premises. But the process remains the same, and our view of right is still a sort of microcosm of our whole character. Whatever characteristic passions we have will in some way be represented in it, and until we stiffen into mental rigidity and decline, it will change more or less with every important change in our social surroundings.

To a very large class of minds, perhaps to the largest class, the notion of right presents itself chiefly as a matter of personal authority. That is, what we feel we ought to do is simply what we imagine our guide or master would do, or would wish us to do. This, for instance, is the idea very largely inculcated and practised by the Christian church. It is not anything opposed to or different from the right as a mental synthesis, but simply means that admiration, reverence, or some other strong sentiment, gives such overwhelming force to the suggestions of a certain example, that they more or less completely dominate the mind. The authority works through conscience and not outside of it. Moreover, the relation is not so one-sided as it would seem, since our guide is always, in one point of view, the creation of our own imaginations, which are sure to interpret him in a manner congenial to our native tendency. Thus the Christ of Fra Angelico is one thing, and the Christ of Michelangelo, directing the ruin of the damned, is quite another.

The ascendancy of personal authority is usually greater in proportion as the mind is of a simple, visually imaginative, rather than reflective turn. People of the sort commonly called "emotional," with ready and vivid personal feeling but little constructive power, are likely to yield to an ascendant influence as a whole, with little selection or reconstruction. Their individuality is expressed chiefly in the choice of a master; having chosen, they are all his. If they change masters they change morals at the same time. The mental unity of which they, like all the rest of us, are in search, is found in allegiance to a concrete personality, which saves them the impossible task of abstract thought. Such people, however, usually feel an attraction toward stability in others, and secure it for themselves by selecting a steadfast personality to anchor their imaginations to.

This, of course, is possible or congenial only to those who lack the mental vigor to make in a more intellectual manner that synthesis of which moral judgment

384

is the expression. Those who have this vigor make use of many examples, and if they acknowledge the pre-eminence of any one, he is likely to be vaguely conceived and to be in reality no more than the symbol of their own moral conclusions.

The immediate power of personal images or influences over our sense of right is probably greater in all of us than we realize. "It is wonderful," says George Eliot in Middlemarch, "how much uglier things will look when we only think we are blamed for them . . . and, on the other hand, it is astonishing how pleasantly conscience takes our encroachments on those who never complain, or have nobody to complain for them." That is to say, other persons, by awaking social self-feeling in us, give life and power to certain sentiments of approval or disapproval regarding our own actions. The rule, already suggested, that the self of a sensitive person, in the presence of an ascendant personality, tends to become his interpretation of what the other thinks of him, is a prime factor in determining the moral judgments of all of us. Every one must have felt the moral renewal that comes with the mere presence of one who is vigorously good, whose being enlivens our aspiration and shames our backsliding, who makes us really feel the desirability of the higher life and the baseness and dulness of the lower.

In one of Mr. Theodore Child's papers on French art he relates that Dagnan said after the death of Bastien-Lepage, "With every new picture I paint in future I shall try to think if he would have been satisfied with it." Almost the same has been said by an

385

American author with reference to Robert Louis Stevenson. And these instances are typical of the general fact that our higher selves, our distinctively right views and choices, are dependent upon imaginative realization of the points of view of other persons. There is, I think, no possibility of being good without living, imaginatively of course, in good company; and those who uphold the moral power of personal example as against that of abstract thought are certainly in the right. A mental crisis, by its very difficulty, is likely to call up the thought of some person we have been used to look to as a guide, and the confronting of the two ideas, that of the person and that of the problem, compels us to answer the question, What would he have thought of it? The guide we appeal to may be a person in the room, or a distant friend, or an author whom we have never seen, or an ideal person of religion. The strong, good men we have once imagined live in our minds and fortify there the idea of worthiness. They were free and noble and make us unhappy to be less.

Of course the influence of other persons often goes by contraries. The thought of one who is repugnant to us brings a strong sense of the wrong of that for which he stands, and our conviction of the hatefulness of any ill trait is much enlivened by intimate contact with one who exhibits it.

The moral potency of confession, and of all sorts of publicity, rests upon the same basis. In opening ourselves to another we are impelled to imagine how our conduct appears to him; we take an outside view of ourselves. It makes a great difference to whom we confess: the higher the character of the person whose mind we imagine, the more enlightening and elevating is the view of ourselves that we get. Even to write our thoughts in a diary, and so to confess, not to a particular person, but to that vague image of an interlocutor that connects itself with all articulate expression, makes things look different.

It is, perhaps, much the same with prayer. To pray, in a higher sense, is to confront our moral perplexities with the highest personal ideal we can form, and so to be unconsciously integrating the two, straightening out the one in accordance with the other. It would seem that social psychology strongly corroborates the idea that prayer is an essential aspect of the higher life; by showing, I mean, that thought, and especially vivid thought, is interlocutory in its very nature, and that aspiration almost necessarily takes, more or less distinctly, the form of intercourse with an ideal being.

Whatever publishes our conduct introduces new and strong factors into conscience; but whether this publicity is wholesome or otherwise depends upon the character of the public; or, more definitely, upon whether the idea of ourselves that we impute to this public is edifying or degrading. In many cases, for instance, it is ruinous to a person's character to be publicly disgraced, because he, or she, presently accepts the degrading self that seems to exist in the minds of others. There are some people to whom we should be ashamed to confess our sins, and others, perhaps, to whom we should not like to own our virtues. Certainly it should not be assumed that it is good for us to have our acts displayed before the generality of persons: while this may be a good thing as regards matters, like the tax-roll, that relate to our obvious duty to the immediate community, it has in most things a somewhat vulgarizing effect, tending to promote conformity rather than a distinctive life. If the scholar's study were on the market-place, so that the industrious townspeople could see how many hours of the day he spends in apparent idleness, he might lack courage to pursue his vocation. In short, we need privacy as against influences that are not edifying, and communion with those that are.

Even telling the truth does not result so much from a need of mental accuracy, though this is strong in some minds, as from a sense of the unfairness of deceiving people of our own sort, and of the shame of being detected in so doing. Consequently the maxim, "Truth for friends and lies for enemies," is very generally followed, not only by savages and children, but, more or less openly, by civilized people. Most persons feel reluctant to tell a lie in so many words, but few have any compunctions in deceiving by manner, and the like, persons toward whom they feel no obligation. We all know business men who will boast of their success in deceiving rivals; and probably few of us hold ourselves to quite the same standard of honor in dealing with one we believe to be tricky and ill disposed toward us, that we would if we thought him honest and well meaning. "Conscience is born of

388

love" in this as in many matters. A thoughtful observer will easily see that injustice and not untruth is the essence of lying, as popularly conceived.

It is because of our need to recall vanished persons, that all goodness and justice, all right of any large sort, depend upon an active imagination. Without it we are the prisoners of the immediate environment and of the suggestions of the lower organism. It is only this that enables us to live with the best our lives have afforded, and maintain higher suggestions to compete with the baser ones that assail us. Let us hear Professor James again: "When for motives of honor and conscience I brave the condemnation of my own family, club, and 'set'; when as a Protestant I turn Catholic; as a Catholic, freethinker; as a 'regular practitioner,' homeopath, or what not, I am always inwardly strengthened in my course, and steeled against the loss of my actual social self by the thought of other and better *possible* social judges than those whose verdict goes against me now. The ideal social self which I thus seek in appealing to their decision may be very remote; it may be represented as barely possible. I may not hope for its realization during my lifetime; I may even expect the future generations, which would approve me if they knew me, to know nothing about me when I am dead and gone." * As regards the nearness or remoteness of the companion it would perhaps be sufficient to say that if imagined he is actually present, so far as

* Psychology, vol. i, p. 315.

our mental and moral life are concerned, and except as affecting the vividness of our idea of him, it makes no immediate difference whether we ever saw him or whether he ever had any corporeal existence at all.

The alteration of conscience due to the advent in thought of a new person is often so marked that one view of duty is quite evidently supplanted by a fresh one, due to the fresh suggestion. Thus, to take an example probably familiar to all who are used to mental application, it sometimes happens that a student is fagged and yet feels that he must think out his problem; there is a strong sense of oughtness backing this view, which, so long as it is unopposed, holds its ground as the call of duty. But now a friend may come in and suggest to him that he ought to stop, that if he goes on he will harm himself and do poor work. Here is another view of right, and the mind must now make a fresh synthesis and come, perhaps, to feel that its duty is to leave off.

Because of its dependence upon personal suggestion, the right always reflects a social group; there is always a circle of persons, more or less extended, whom we really imagine, and who thus work upon our impulses and our conscience; while people outside of this have not a truly personal existence for us. The extent of this circle depends upon many circumstances, as for instance upon the vigor of our imaginations, and the reach of the means of communication through which personal symbols are impressed upon them.

THE SOCIAL ASPECT OF CONSCIENCE

In these days of general literacy, many get their most potent impressions from books, and some, finding this sort of society more select and stimulating than any other, cultivate it to the neglect of palpable persons. This kind of people often have a very tender conscience regarding the moral problems presented in novels, but a rather dull one for those of the flesh-and-blood life about them. In fact, a large part of the sentiments of imaginative persons are purely literary, created and nourished by intercourse with books, and only indirectly connected with what is commonly called experience. Nor should it be assumed that these literary sentiments are necessarily a mere dissipation. Our highest ideals of life come to us largely in this way, since they depend upon imaginative converse with people we do not have a chance to know in the flesh. Indeed, the expansion of conscience that is so conspicuous a fact of recent years, the rise of moral sentiment regarding international relations, alien races, and social and industrial classes other than our own, could not have taken place without the aid of cheap printing and rapid communication. Such understanding and sense of obligation as we have regarding the populace of great cities, for instance, is due chiefly to writers who, like the author of How the Other Half Lives, describe the life of such people in a vivid, personal way, and so cause us to imagine it.

Not to pursue this line of thought too far, it is enough for our purpose to note that conscience is always a group conscience, however the group may be formed, so that our moral sentiment always reflects our time, our country, and our special field of personal imagination. On the other hand, our sense of right ignores those whom we do not, through sympathy, feel as part of ourselves, no matter how close their physical contiguity. To the Norman conqueror the Saxon was an inferior animal, whose sentiments he no more admitted to his imagination, I suppose, than a farmer does those of his cattle, and toward whom, accordingly, he did not feel human obligation. It was the same with the slaveholder and the slave, and so it sometimes is with employer and wage-earner. The behavior of the Europeans toward the Chinese during the recent invasion of China showed in a striking manner how completely moral obligation breaks down in dealing with people who are not felt to be of kindred humanity with ourselves.

In minds capable of constructive imagination the social factor in conscience may take the form of ideal persons, whose traits are used as a standard of behavior.

Idealization, of this or any other sort, is not to be thought of as sharply marked off from experience and memory. It seems probable that the mind is never indifferent to the elements presented to it, but that its very nature is to select, arrange, harmonize, idealize. That is, the whole is always acting upon the parts, tending to make them one with itself. What we call distinctively an ideal is only a relatively complex and finished product of this activity. The past, as it lives in our minds, is never a mere repetition of old experience, but is always colored by our present feeling, is always idealized in some sense; and it is the same with our anticipation of the future, so that to wholesome thought expectation is hope. Thus the mind is ever an artist, re-creating things in a manner congenial to itself, and special arts are only a more deliberate expression of a general tendency.

An ideal, then, is a somewhat definite and felicitous product of imagination, a harmonious and congenial reconstruction of the elements of experience. And a personal ideal is such a harmonious and congenial reconstruction of our experience of persons. Its active function is to symbolize and define the desirable, and by so doing to make it the object of definite endeavor. The ideal of goodness is only the next step beyond the good man of experience, and performs the same energizing office. Indeed, as I have already pointed out, there is no separation between actual and ideal persons, only a more or less definite connection of personal ideas with material bodies.

There are all degrees of vagueness or definition in our personal ideals. They may be no more than scattered imaginings of traits which we have met in experience and felt to be worthy; or they may assume such fulness and cohesion as to be distinct ideal persons. There may even be several personal ideals; one may cherish one ideal of himself and a different one for each of his intimate friends; or his imagination may project several ideals of himself, to correspond to various phases of his development.

393

Probably the phrase "ideal person" suggests something more unified and consistent than is actually present in the minds of most people when they conceive the desirable or good in personal character. Is it not rather ideal traits or sentiments, fragments of personal experience, phases of past intercourse returning in the imagination with a new emphasis in the presence of new situations? We have at times divined in other people courage, generosity, patience, and justice, and judged them to be good. Now, when we find ourselves in a situation where these traits are called for, we are likely to be reminded by that very fact of our previous experience of them; and the memory of it brings these sentiments more vividly to life and gives them more authority in conscience. Thus a person hesitating whether to smuggle in dutiable goods is likely to think in his perplexity of some one whom he has come to regard as honorable in such matters, and of how that one would feel and act under like conditions.

This building up of higher personal conceptions does not lend itself to precise description. It is mostly subconscious; the mind is continually at work ordering and bettering its past and present experiences, working them up in accordance with its own instinctive need for consistency and pleasantness; ever idealizing, but rarely producing clean-cut ideals. It finds its materials both in immediate personal intercourse and through books and other durable media of expression. "Books, monuments, pictures, conversation, are portraits in which he finds the lineaments he is forming." "All that is said of the wise man . . . describes to each reader his own idea, describes his unattained but attainable self." * "A few anecdotes, a few traits of character, manners, face, a few incidents, have an emphasis in your memory out of all proportion to their apparent significance, if you measure them by the ordinary standards. They relate to your gift. Let them have their weight, and do not reject them and cast about for illustrations more usual in literature. What your heart thinks great is great. The soul's emphasis is always right." †

Idealism in this vague form has neither first, second, nor third person. It is simply an impression of the desirable in personality, and is impulsively applied to your conduct, my conduct, or his conduct, as the case may be. The sentiment occurs to us, and the connection in which it occurs determines its moral application. We sometimes speak as if it required an unusual effort of virtue to apply the same standards to ourselves as to others; and so it does, in one sense; but in another it is easier and more common to do this than not to do it. The simplest thing, as regards the mental process concerned, is to take ideas of conduct as they come, without thinking specially where they come from, and judge them by the standard that conscience presents to us. Injustice and personal wrong of all sorts, as between one's self and others, commonly consist, not in imagining the other man's point of view and refusing to give it weight; but in not imagining it, not admitting him to the tribunal

* Emerson, History.   † Idem, Spiritual Laws.

at all. It is in exerting the imagination that the effort of virtue comes in. One who entertains the thought and feeling of others can hardly refuse them justice; he has made them a part of himself. There is, as we have seen, no first or second person about a sentiment; if it is alive in the mind that is all there is to the matter.

It is perhaps the case, however, that almost every person of imagination has at times a special and somewhat definite ideal self, concerning which he has the "my" feeling, and which he would not use in judging others. It is, like all ideals, a product of constructive imagination working upon experience. It represents what we should like to see ourselves, and has an especially vigorous and varied life in early youth, when the imagination projects models to match each new aspiration that gains power over it. In a study of the Continued Stories of children, by Mabel W. Learoyd, many interesting facts are given illustrating sustained self-idealization. These continued stories are somewhat consecutive series of imaginations on the part of the young, recalled and described at a later period. Two-thirds are said to embody an ideal, and the author, in an idealized form, is the hero of many of them.* An instance of this same process continued into old age is the fact mentioned by Mr. E. W. Emerson in his Emerson in Concord,† that the poet's diary contains frequent allusion to one Osman, who stands for an ideal self, a more perfect Emerson of his aspiration.

* Amer. Jour. of Psychology, vol. 7, p. 86.
† See pp. 101, 210, 226.

THE SOCIAL ASPECT OF CONSCIENCE

It would always be found, I think, that our ideal self is constructed chiefly out of ideas about us attributed to other people. We can hardly get any distinct view of ourselves except in this way, that is by placing ourselves at the standpoint of some one else. The impressions thus gained are worked over and over, like other mental material, and, according to the imaginative vigor of the mind, more or less reorganized, and projected as an ideal.

With some this ideal is quite definite and visible before the eye of the mind. I have heard the expression "seeing yourself" applied to it. Thus one woman says of another, "She always sees herself in evening dress," meaning that her ideal of herself is one of social propriety or distinction, and that it takes the form of an image of her visible person as it appears to others in a shape expressing these traits. This is, of course, a phase of the reflected self, discussed in the fifth chapter. Some people "see themselves" so constantly, and strive so obviously to live up to the image, that they give a curious impression of always acting a part, as if one should compose a drama with himself as chief personage, and then spend his life playing it. Perhaps something of this sort is inevitable with persons of vivid imagination.

Once formed and familiarized the ideal self serves, like any ideal only more directly, as an incitement to growth in its direction, and a punishment to retrogression. A man who has become used to imagining himself as noble, beneficent, and respected has a real picture in his mind, a fair product of aspiring thought,

397

a work of art. If his conduct violates this imagination he has a sense of ugliness and shame; there is a rent in the picture, a rude, shapeless hole, shattering its beauty, and calling for painful and tedious repairs before it can be even tolerable to look upon. Repentance is the pain of this spectacle; and the clearer and more firmly conceived the ideal, the greater the pain.

The ideal person or persons of an ethical religion are the highest expression of this creative outreaching of the mind after the admirable in personality. It can hardly be supposed, by any one who is willing to go into the psychology of the matter at all, that they are radically different from other ideal persons, or in any way sharply divided from the mass of personal thought. Any comparative study of idealism, among nations in various stages of civilization, among persons of different intellectual power, among the various periods of development in one individual, can hardly fail, I should say, to leave a conviction that all hangs together, that there is no chasm anywhere, that the most rudimentary idealizing impulse of the savage or the child is of a piece with the highest religious conceptions. The tendency of such a view, of course, is not to drag down the exalted, but to show all as part of a common life.

All ideals of personality are derived from intercourse, and all that attain any general acceptance have a social organization and history. Each historical epoch or nation has its somewhat distinctive personal ideals, which are instilled into the individual from the general store of thought. It is especially true that the persons of religion have this character. They are communal and cumulative, are gradually built up and become in some degree an institution. In this way they may acquire richness, clearness, sanctity, and authority, and may finally be inculcated as something above and outside of the human mind. The latter is certain to happen if they are made the basis of a discipline to be applied to all sorts of people. The dogma that they are extra-human serves, like the forms and ceremonies of a court, to secure to them the prestige of distance and inaccessibility.

It is a chief function of religious organization to make the moral synthesis more readily attainable, by establishing a spiritual discipline, or system of influences and principles, which shall constantly stimulate one's higher sentiments, and furnish a sort of outline or scaffolding of suggestions to aid him in organizing his thought. In doing this its main agent is the inculcation of personal ideals, although the teaching of creeds is also, perhaps, important to the same purpose. It is apparently part of the legitimate function of organized moral thought to enter the vaguer fields of speculation about conduct and inculcate provisional ideas, relating for instance to the origin and meaning of life—matters which the mind must and will explore, with or without a guide. To have suggested to them definite ways of thinking regarding such matters helps to make mental unity possible, and to save men from the aimless and distracting wanderings that often end in despair. Of course these ideas must be in harmony with the general state of thought, consistent, for example, with the established results of science. Otherwise they only increase the distraction. But a *credible creed* is an excellent thing, and the lack of it is a real moral deficiency.

Now in times of intellectual unsettlement, like the present, the ideal may become disorganized and scattered, the face of God blurred to the view, like the reflection of the sun in troubled waters. And at the same time the creeds become incredible, so that, until new ones can be worked out and diffused, each man must either make one for himself—a task to which few are equal—or undergo distraction, or cease to think about such matters, if he can. This state of things involves some measure of demoralization, although it may be part of a movement generally beneficent. Mankind needs the highest vision of personality, and needs it clear and vivid, and in the lack of it will suffer a lack in the clearness and cogency of moral thought. It is the natural apex to the pyramid of personal imagination, and when it is wanting there will be an unremitting and eventually more or less successful striving to replace it. When it reappears it will, of course, express in all its lineaments a new era of thought; but the opinion that it is gone to stay, which is entertained by some, seems very ill grounded.

Comparative studies of the moral ideas of different societies, such as Wm. G. Sumner's work on Folkways, make it clear that the sense of right does, in fact, vary with the group, and that "the mores can make anything right or anything wrong." Stealing, cannibalism, and many other things that we condemn, may be regarded as permissible, creditable, or even obligatory. Matters of decency, as in dress or manners, are almost wholly conventional, as appears, for instance, when certain Africans spit upon one as a sign of good-will.

It is notable, however, that there are, after all, some ideas of right that are practically universal. Here, for example, are three things that all tribes, so far as I can discover, regard as obligatory:

1. Loyalty to the group. Dante's judgment that traitors belong in the lowest pit of Hell expresses a universal sentiment of mankind.

2. Kindness to members of the group.

3. Adherence to the customs of the tribe.

These are universal because they spring from universal conditions of social life. All men live in co-operating groups, and without loyalty and kindness they cannot co-operate successfully. And conservatism must be cherished, especially among savages, who have no recorded traditions, because it is the means of insuring stability and preserving the results of experience.

Morals are profoundly functional, and beneath many strange divergences there is found a core of likeness corresponding to a similarity in the life-process itself.

CHAPTER XI

PERSONAL DEGENERACY

IS A PHASE OF THE QUESTION OF RIGHT AND WRONG—RELATION
TO THE IDEA OF DEVELOPMENT—JUSTIFICATION AND MEANING
OF THE PHRASE "PERSONAL DEGENERACY"—HEREDITARY AND
SOCIAL FACTORS IN PERSONAL DEGENERACY—DEGENERACY AS
A MENTAL TRAIT—CONSCIENCE IN DEGENERACY—GROUP DE-
GENERACY—CRIME, INSANITY, AND RESPONSIBILITY—PRACTI-
CAL EFFECT OF THE ORGANIC VIEW UPON RESPONSIBILITY—
UPON PUNISHMENT

I WISH to touch upon this subject only in so far as
to suggest a general way of conceiving it in accord
with the views set forth in the preceding chapters.

The question of personal degeneracy is a phase of
the question of right or wrong and is ultimately determined by conscience. A degenerate might be defined as one whose personality falls distinctly short
of a standard set by the dominant moral thought of a
group. It is the nature of the mind to form standards of better or worse in all matters toward which
its selective activity is directed; and this has its collective as well as its individual aspect, so that not
only every man but every group has its preferences
and aversions, its good and bad. The selective, organizing processes which all life, and notably the life
of the mind, presents, involve this distinction; it is
simply a formulation of the universal fact of preference. We cannot view things in which we are inter-

ested without liking some and disliking others; and somewhat in proportion to our interest is our tendency to express these likes and dislikes by good and bad or similar words. And since there is nothing that interests us so much as persons, judgments of right and wrong regarding them have always been felt and expressed with peculiar zest and emphasis. The righteous and the wicked, the virtuous and the vicious, the good and bad under a hundred names, have been sharply and earnestly discriminated in every age and country.

Although this distinction between personal good and bad has always been a fact of human thought, a broader view of it is reached, in these days, through the idea of evolution. The method of nature being everywhere selective, growth is seen to take place not by making a like use of the elements already existing, but by the fostering of some to the comparative neglect or suppression of others. Or, if this statement gives too much the idea of a presiding intelligence outside the process itself, we may simply say that the functions of existing elements in contributing to further growth are extremely different, so much so that some of them usually appear to have no important function at all, or even to impede the growth, while others appear to be the very heart of the onward or crescent life. This idea is applicable to physiological processes, such as go on within our bodies, to the development of species, as illustrated with such convincing detail by Darwin, and to all the processes of thought and of society; so that the forces that are observed in the present, if viewed with reference to function or tendency, never appear to be on the same level of value, but are strung along at different levels, some below a mean, some above it. Thus we not only have the actual discrimination of good and bad in persons, but a philosophy which shows it as an incident of evolution, a reflection in thought of the general movement of nature.

Or, to regard the process of evolution in more detail, we find degeneracy or inferiority implied in that idea of variation which is the starting-point of Darwinism. All forms of life, it seems, exhibit variations; that is, the individuals are not quite alike but differ from one another and from the parents in a somewhat random manner, so that some are better adapted to the actual conditions of life, and some worse. The change or development of a species takes place by the cumulative survival and multiplication, generation after generation, of fit or fortunate variations. The very process that produces the fittest evidently implies the existence of the unfit; and the distinctly unfit individuals of any species may be regarded as the degenerate.

It will not do to transfer these ideas too crudely to the mental and social life of mankind; but it will hardly be disputed that the character of persons exhibits variations which are partly at least incalculable, and which produce on the one hand leadership and genius and on the other weakness and degeneracy. We probably cannot have the one without having

404

something, at least, of the other, though I believe that the variations of personality are capable, to a great degree, of being brought under rational control.

This truth that all forms of deficient humanity have a common philosophical aspect is one reason for giving them some common name, like degeneracy. Another is that the detailed study of fact more and more forces the conclusion that such things as crime, pauperism, idiocy, insanity, and drunkenness have, in great measure, a common causation, and so form, practically, parts of a whole. We see this in the study of heredity, which shows that the transmitted taint commonly manifests itself in several or all of these forms in different generations or individuals of the same stock; and we see it in the study of social conditions, in the fact that where these conditions are bad, as in the slums of great cities, all the forms become more prevalent. A third reason for the use of a special term is that it is desirable that the matter receive more dispassionate study than formerly, and this may possibly be promoted by the use of words free, so far as possible, from irrelevant implications. Many of the words in common use, such as badness, wickedness, crime, and the like, reflect particular views of the facts, such as the religious view of them as righteousness or sin, and the legal view as criminal or innocent, while degeneracy suggests the disinterestedness of science.

I do not much care to justify the particular word degeneracy in this connection, further than to say

405

that I know of none more convenient or less objectionable. It comes, of course, from *de* and *genus* through *degenerare*, and seems to mean primarily the state of having fallen from a type. It is not uncommon in English literature, usually meaning inferiority to the standard set by ancestors, as when we say a degenerate age, a degenerate son, etc.; and recently it has come into use to describe any kind of marked and enduring mental defect or inferiority. I see no objection to this usage unless it be that it is doubtfu! whether the mentally or morally inferior person can in all cases be said *to have fallen* from a higher state. This might be plausibly argued on both sides, but it does not seem worth while.

I use the phrase personal degeneracy, then, to describe the state of persons whose character and conduct fall distinctly below the type or standard regarded as normal by the dominant sentiment of the group. Although it must be admitted that this definition is a vague one, it is not more so, perhaps, than most definitions of mental or social phenomena. There is no sharp criterion of what is mentally and socially up to par and what is not, but there are large and important classes whose inferiority is evident, such as idiots, imbeciles, the insane, drunkards, and criminals; and no one will question the importance of studying the whole of which these are parts.

It is altogether a social matter at bottom; that is to say, degeneracy exists only in a certain relation between a person and the rest of a group. In so far as any mental or physical traits constitute it they do so because they involve unfitness for a normal social career, in which alone the essence of the matter is found. The only palpable test of it—and this an uncertain one—is found in the actual career of the person, and especially in the attitude toward him of the organized thought of the group. We agree fairly well upon the degeneracy of the criminal, largely because his abnormality is of so obvious and troublesome a kind that something in particular has to be done about it, and so he becomes definitely and formally stigmatized by the organs of social judgment. Yet even from this decisive verdict an appeal is successfully made in some cases to the wider and maturer thought of mankind, so that many have been executed as felons who, like John Brown, are now revered as heroes.

In short, the idea of wrong, of which the idea of degeneracy is a phase, partakes of the same uncertainty that belongs to its antithesis, the idea of right. Both are expressions of an ever-developing, always selective life, and share in the indeterminateness that necessarily goes with growth. They assume forms definite enough for the performance of their momentous practical functions, but always remain essentially plastic and variable.

Concerning the causation of degeneracy, we may say, as of every aspect of personality, that its roots are to be looked for somewhere in the mingling of hereditary and social factors from which the individual life springs. Both of these factors exhibit marked

407

variation; men differ in their natural traits very much as other animals do, and they also find themselves subject to the varying influences of a diversified social order. The actual divergences of character and conduct which they exhibit are due to the composition of these two variables into a third variable, the man himself.

In some cases the hereditary factor is so clearly deficient as to make it natural and justifiable to regard heredity as the cause; in a much larger number of cases there is good reason to think that social conditions are more particularly to blame, and that the original hereditary outfit was fairly good. In a third class, the largest, perhaps, of all, it is practically impossible to discriminate between them. Indeed, it is always a loose way of speaking to set heredity and environment over against each other as separable forces, or to say that either one is the cause of character or of any personal trait. They have no separate existence after personal development is under way; each reacts upon the other, and every trait is due to their intimate union and co-operation. All we are justified in saying is that one or the other may be so aberrant as to demand our special attention.

Congenital idiocy is regarded as hereditary degeneracy, because it is obvious that no social environment can make the individual other than deficient, and we must work upon heredity if we wish to prevent it. On the other hand, when we find that certain conditions, like residence in crowded parts of a city, are accompanied by the appearance of a large per cent of criminality, among a population whom there is no reason to suppose naturally deficient, we are justified in saying that the causes of this degeneracy are social rather than hereditary. Probably much of the criminality, in the latter case, is due to the conjunction of degrading surroundings with a degree of hereditary deficiency that a better training would have rendered harmless, or at least inconspicuous; but, practically, if we wish to diminish this sort of degeneracy, we must work upon social conditions.

A sound mental heredity consists essentially in teachability, a capacity to learn the things required by the social order; and the congenital idiot is degenerate by the hereditary factor alone, because he is incapable of learning these things. But a sound heredity is no safeguard against personal degeneracy; if we have teachability all turns upon what is taught, and this depends upon the social environment. The very faculties that lead a child to become good or moral in a good environment may cause him to become criminal in a criminal environment; it is all a question of what he finds to learn. It may be said, then, that of the four possible combinations between good and bad heredity and good and bad environment, three—bad heredity with bad or good environment, and good heredity with bad environment—lead to degeneracy. Only when both elements are favorable can we have a good result. Of course, by bad environment in this connection must be understood bad in its action upon this particular individual, not as judged by some other standard.

409

As the social surroundings of a person can be changed, and his hereditary bias cannot, it is expedient, in that vast majority of cases in which causation is obscure, to assume as a working hypothesis that the social factor is at fault, and to try by altering it to alter the person. This is more and more coming to be done in all intelligent treatment of degeneracy.

As a mental trait, marking a person off as, in some sense, worse than others in the same social group, degeneracy appears to consist in some lack in the higher organization of thought. It is not that one has the normal mental outfit plus something additional, called wrong, crime, sin, madness, or the like, but that he is in some way deficient in the mental activity by which sympathy is created and by which all impulses are unified with reference to a general life. The criminal impulses, rage, fear, lust, pride, vanity, covetousness, and so on, are the same in general type as those of the normal person; the main difference is that the criminal lacks, in one way or another, the higher mental organization—a phase of the social organization—to which these impulses should be subordinate. It would not be very difficult to take the seven deadly sins—Pride, Envy, Anger, Sloth, Covetousness, Gluttony, and Lust—and show that each may be regarded as the undisciplined manifestation of a normal or functional tendency. Indeed, as regards anger this was attempted in a previous chapter.

"To describe in detail the different varieties of

degeneracy that are met with," says Doctor Maudsley, "would be an endless and barren labor. It would be as tedious as to attempt to describe particularly the exact character of the ruins of each house in a city that had been destroyed by an earthquake: in one place a great part of the house may be left standing, in another place a wall or two, and in another the ruin is so great that scarcely one stone is left upon another." *

In the lowest phases mental organization can hardly be said to exist at all: an idiot has no character, no consistent or effective individuality. There is no unification, and so no self-control or stable will; action simply reflects the particular animal impulse that is ascendant. Hunger, sexual lust, rage, dread, and, in somewhat higher grades, a crude, naïve kindliness, are each felt and expressed in the simplest manner possible. There can, of course, be little or no true sympathy, and the unconsciousness of what is going on in the minds of other persons prevents any sense of decency or attempt to conform to social standards.

In the higher grades we may make the distinction, already suggested in speaking of egotism, between the unstable and the rigid varieties. Indeed, as was intimated, selfishness and degeneracy are of the same general character; both being defined socially by a falling short of accepted standards of conduct, and mentally by some lack in the scope and organization of the mind.

There is, then, one sort of persons in whom the

* The Pathology of Mind, p. 425.

most conspicuous and troublesome trait is mere mental inconsistency and lack of character, and another who possess a fair degree, at least, of consistency and unity of purpose, but whose mental scope or reach of sympathy is so small that they have no adequate relation to the life about them.

An outgrowing, impressionable sort of mind, if deficient in the power to work up its material, is necessarily unstable and lacking in momentum and definite direction: and in the more marked cases we have people of the hysterical type, unstable forms of dementia and insanity, and impulsive crime. "The fundamental defect in the hysterical brain," says Doctor Dana, "is that it is circumscribed in its associative functions; the field of consciousness is limited just as is the field of vision. The mental activity is confined to personal feelings, which are not regulated by connotation of past experiences, hence they flow over too easily into emotional outbursts or motor paroxysms. The hysterical person cannot think." * It is evident that something similar might be said of all manifestations of instability.

On the other hand, an ingrowing sort of mind, whose tendency is rather to work over and over its cherished thoughts than to open out to new ones, may have a marked deficiency of sensibility and breadth of perception. If so, the person is likely to exhibit some form of gross and persistent egotism, such as sensuality, avarice, narrow and ruthless ambition, fanaticism, of a hard, cold sort, delusion of

* C. L. Dana, Nervous Diseases, p. 425.

greatness, or those kinds of crime that result from habitual insensibility to social standards rather than from transient impulse.

As conscience is simply the completest product of mental organization, it will of course share in whatever defect there may be in the mental life as a whole. In the lower grades of idiocy we may assume that there is no system in the mind from which a conscience could spring. In a higher degenerate of the unstable type, there is a conscience, but it is vacillating in its judgments, transient in duration, and ineffectual in control, proportionally to the mental disintegration which it reflects. We all, probably, can think of people conspicuously lacking in self-control, and it will perhaps be evident, when we reflect upon them, that their consciences are of this sort. The voice of conscience, with them, is certain to be chiefly an echo of temporary emotions, because a synthesis embracing long periods of time is beyond their range; it is frequently inaudible, on account of their being engrossed by passing impulses, and their conduct is largely without any rational control at all. They are likely to suffer sharp and frequent attacks of remorse, on account of failure to live up to their standards, but it would seem that the wounds do not go very deep as a rule, but share in the general superficiality of their lives. People of this sort, if not too far gone in weakness, are probably the ones who profit most by punishment, because they are helped by the sharp and definite pain which it associates with acts that they recog-

413

nize as wrong, but cannot keep from doing without a vivid emotional deterrent. They are also the ones who, in their eagerness to escape from the pains of fluctuation and inconsistency, are most prone to submit blindly to some external and dogmatic authority. Unable to rule themselves, they crave a master, and if he only *is* a master, that is, one capable of grasping and dominating the emotions by which they are swayed, they will often cleave to him and kiss the rod.

With those whose defect is rigidity rather than instability, conscience may exist and may control the life; the trouble with it is, that it is not in key with the consciences of other people. There is an original poverty of the impulses that extends to any result that can be worked out of them. It may appear startling to some to assert that conscience may dictate the wrong, but such is quite clearly the fact, if we identify the right with some standard of conduct accepted among people of broad sympathies. Conscience is the only possible moral guide—any external authority can work morally upon us only through conscience—but it always partakes of the limitations of one's character, and so far as that is degenerate the idea of right is degenerate also. As a matter of fact, the very worst men of the hard, narrow, fanatical, or brutal sorts, often live at peace with their consciences. I feel sure that any one who reflects imaginatively upon the characters of people he has known of this sort will agree that such is the case. A bad conscience implies mental division, inconsistency between thought and deed, and men of this sort are often quite at one with themselves. The usurer who grinds the faces of the poor, the unscrupulous speculator who causes the ruin of innocent investors to aggrandize himself, the fanatical anarchist who stabs a king or shoots a president, the Kentucky mountaineer who regards murderous revenge as a duty, the assaulter who causes pictures commemorative of his crimes to be tattooed on his skin, are diverse examples of wrongdoers whose consciences not only do not punish, but often instigate their ill deeds.

The idea, cherished by some, that crime or wrong of any sort is invariably pursued by remorse, arises from the natural but mistaken assumption that all other people have consciences similar to our own. The man of sensitive temperament and refined habit of thought feels that he would suffer remorse if he had done the deed, and supposes that the same must be the case with the perpetrator. On the contrary, it seems likely that only a very small proportion of those whom the higher moral sentiment regards as wrong-doers suffer much from the pricks of conscience. If the general tenor of a man's life is high, and the act is the fearful outcome of a moment of passion, as is often the case with unpremeditated murder, he will suffer, but if his life is all of a piece, he will not. All authorities agree that the mass of criminals, and the same is clearly true of ill-doers within the law, have a habit of mind of which the ill deed is the logical outcome, so that there is nothing sudden or catastrophic about it. Of course, if we apply the word conscience only to the mental synthesis of a mind rich in higher

415

sentiments, then such people have no consciences, but it seems a broader view of the matter to say that they have a conscience, in so far as they have mental unity, but that it reflects the general narrowness and perversion of their lives. In fact, people of this description usually, if not always, have standards of their own, some sort of honor among thieves, which they will not transgress, or which, if transgressed, cause remorse. It is impossible that mental organization should not produce a moral synthesis of some sort.

In many cases degenerate conduct is due to the fact that the individual lives in a group having degenerate standards: it does not indicate intrinsic inferiority on his part at all. I mean, for example, that a boy who runs away from school, plunders freight-cars, breaks windows, and the like, may do these things merely from suggestion and emulation—just as other boys under other influences turn their energies into athletics and the activities of Boy Scouts—without being exceptional in any way unless as to the sort of "bunch" he runs with. And the same may be true of any kind of misconduct. These things exist in groups, and the degenerate individual, so far as he is human, is a *socius* like the rest of us. The group forms his conscience, and what it countenances or admires will not seem wrong to him, no matter how the rest of society may regard it. If it becomes traditional for the members of a certain college fraternity to drink, gamble, and cheat their way through examinations, the freshman will fall into these practices as a matter of course.

In fact the great wrongs are done mainly by people of normal capacity who believe they are doing right. Their consciences are supported by the mores, or collective moral feeling of a group. It was thus that the Germans went into the Great War.

There is nothing in this way of conceiving degeneracy which tends to break down the practical distinctions among the various forms of it, as, for instance, that between crime and insanity. Though the line between these two is arbitrary and uncertain, as must always be the case in the classification of mental facts, and as is confessed by the existence of a class called the criminal insane, yet the distinction itself and the difference in treatment associated with it are sound enough in a general way.

The contrast between our attitudes toward crime and toward insanity is primarily a matter of personal idea and impulse. We understand the criminal act, or think we do, and we feel toward it resentment, or hostile sympathy; while we do not understand the insane act, and so do not resent it, but regard it with pity, curiosity, or disgust. If one man strikes down another to rob him, or in revenge, we can imagine the offender's state of mind, his motive lives in our thought and is condemned by conscience precisely as if we thought of doing the act ourselves. Indeed, to understand an act *is* to think of doing it ourselves. But, if it is done for no reason that we can comprehend, we do not imagine, do not get a personal impression of the case at all, but have to think of it as merely

417

mechanical. It is the same sort of difference as that between a person who injures us accidentally and one who does it "on purpose."

Secondarily, it is a matter of expediency. We feel that the act which we can imagine ourselves doing ought to be punished, because we perceive by our own sympathy with it that more of this sort of thing is likely to take place if it is not put down. We want the house-breaker to be stigmatized, disgraced, and imprisoned, because we feel that, if this is not done, he and others will be encouraged to more house-breaking; but we feel only pity for the man who thinks he is Julius Cæsar, because we suppose there is nothing to be feared either from him or his example. This practical basis of the distinction expresses itself in the general, and I think justifiable, reluctance to ap-ply the name and treatment of insanity to behavior which seems likely to be imitated. It is felt that whatever may be the mental state of the man who commits an act of violence or fraud, it is wholesome that people in general, who draw no fine distinctions, but judge others by themselves, should be taught by example that such conduct is followed by moral and legal penalties. On the other hand, when the behavior is so evidently remote from ordinary habits of thought that it can be a matter only of pity or curiosity, there is no occasion to do anything more than the good of the person affected seems to require.

The same analysis applies to the whole question of responsibility or irresponsibility. It is a matter of imaginative contact and personal idea. To hold a man responsible, is to imagine him as a man like ourselves, having similar impulses but failing to control them as we do, or at least as we feel we ought to do. We think of doing as he does, find it wrong, and impute the wrong to him. The irresponsible person is one who is looked upon as a different sort of being, not human with reference to the conduct in question, not imaginable, not near enough to us to be the object of hostile sentiment. We *blame* the former; that is, we visit him with a sympathetic resentment; we condemn that part of ourselves that we find in him. But in the latter we do not find ourselves at all.

It is worth noting in this connection, that we could not altogether cease to blame others without ceasing to blame ourselves, which would mean moral apathy. It is sometimes thought that the cool analysis of such questions as this tends toward indifferentism; but I do not see that this is the case. The social psychologist finds in moral sentiment a central and momentous fact of human life, and if perchance he does not himself feel it very vividly, he should have the candor to confess himself so much the less a man. Indeed, if there is such a thing as an indifferentist, in the sense of one who does not feel any cogency in moral sentiment, he must be quite unsuited to the pursuit of social or moral science, because he lacks power to sympathize with, and so observe, the facts upon which this sort of science must be based.

What is the practical effect upon responsibility of the view that wrong does not originate merely in the

419

individual will, but has always a history in heredity and social transmission? It tends, I think, not to diminish responsibility but to change its character, to make it an organic whole, including every individual whose will contributes to the wrong in question. It makes more people responsible, and mitigates, without removing, the blame that falls upon the immediate wrong-doer. When a boy is caught stealing brass fixtures from an unfinished house the judge of the Juvenile Court will first of all blame the boy, but, far from stopping there, he will bring into court also the leader of the gang who set him the example, and his parents, who failed to give him suitable care and discipline. The judge may well censure, also, the school authorities for not interesting him in healthy work and recreation, and the city government and influential classes for failing to provide a better environment for him to grow up in. The tendency of any study of indirect causes is to fix more and more responsibility upon those who have wealth, knowledge, and influence, and therefore the power to bring a better state of things to pass. It is impossible not to see, as one looks into these questions, that there is little use in blaming or punishing those who have been brought up in demoralizing surroundings, and that the chief hope of improvement is in arousing the consciences of those who are able to do away with such surroundings and so check the evil at its source.

Under the organic view punishment is not done away with: it has its uses as an influence upon the will, upon the will of actual wrong-doers and of those who might become such. This view does, however, tend to depreciate the importance of punishment as compared with educational and constructive methods. If we can make the whole process healthy, vice, crime, and the like will be kept off as disease is from a healthy body.

In so far as we use punishment its efficacy depends mainly upon two things:

1. It must be evidently just; so that both the offender and the onlooker can see that it is what society must do for the protection of its members. If arbitrary, or gratuitously painful or humiliating, it arouses such resentment as one would feel at being mauled by a bully; brutalizing and alienating the offender. Much of our punishment is of this kind.

2. It must be reasonably certain. Otherwise those who contemplate it will take the chance. Under our present methods most offenders escape, and the criminal class regard punishment as merely one of the risks of a somewhat hazardous occupation.

CHAPTER XII

FREEDOM

THE MEANING OF FREEDOM—FREEDOM AND DISCIPLINE—FREEDOM
AS A PHASE OF THE SOCIAL ORDER—FREEDOM INVOLVES INCI-
DENTAL STRAIN AND DEGENERACY

GOETHE remarks in his Autobiography * that the
word freedom has so fair a sound that we cannot
do without it even though it designate an error. Certainly it is a word inseparable from our higher sentiments, and if, in its popular use at the present day, it
has no precise meaning, there is so much the more
reason why we should try to give it one, and to continue its use as a symbol of something that mankind
cherishes and strives for.

The common notion of freedom is negative, that is,
it is a notion of the absence of constraint. Starting
with the popular individualistic view of things, the
social order is thought of as something apart from,
and more or less a hindrance to, a man's natural development. There is an assumption that an ordinary
person is self-sufficient in most respects, and will do
very well if he is only left alone. But there is, of
course, no such thing as the absence of restraint, in
the sense of social limitations; man has no existence
apart from a social order, and can develop his personality only through the social order, and in the same
degree that it is developed. A freedom consisting in

* Aus Meinem Leben, book XI.

the removal of limiting conditions is inconceivable. If the word is to have any definite meaning in sociology, it must therefore be separated from the idea of a fundamental opposition between society and the individual, and made to signify something that is both individual and social. To do this it is not necessary to do any great violence to accepted ideas of a practical sort; since it is rather in theory than in application that the popular view is objectionable. A sociological interpretation of freedom should take away nothing worth keeping from our traditional conception of it, and may add something in the way of breadth, clearness, and productiveness.

The definition of freedom naturally arising from the chapters that have gone before is perhaps this: that it is *opportunity for right development,* for development in accordance with the progressive ideal of life that we have in conscience. A child comes into the world with an outfit of vague tendencies, for all definite unfolding of which he is dependent upon social conditions. If cast away alone on a desert island he would, supposing that he succeeded in living at all, never attain a real humanity, would never know speech, or social sentiment, or any complex thought. On the other hand, if all his surroundings are from the first such as to favor the enlargement and enrichment of his life, he may attain the fullest development possible to him in the actual state of the world. In so far as the social conditions have this favoring action upon him he may be said to be free. And so every person, at every stage of his growth, is free or unfree in proportion as he does or does not find himself in the midst of conditions conducive to full and harmonious personal development. Thinking in this way we do not regard the individual as separable from the social order as a whole, but we do regard him as capable of occupying any one of an indefinite number of positions within that order, some of them more suitable to him than others.

No doubt there are elements of vagueness in this conception. What is full and harmonious personal development? What is the right, the opportunity to achieve which is freedom? The possibilities of development are infinitely various, and unimaginable until they begin to be realized, so that it would appear that our notion gives us nothing definite to go by after all. This is largely true: development cannot be defined, either for the race or for individuals, but is and must remain an ideal, of which we can get only partial and shifting glimpses. In fact, we should cease to think of freedom as something definite and final, that can be grasped and held fast once for all, and learn to regard it as a line of advance, something progressively appearing out of the invisible and defining itself, like the forms of a mountain up which one is climbing in a mist. This vagueness and incompleteness are only what we meet in every direction when we attempt to define our ideals. What is progress? What is right? What is beauty? What is truth? The endeavor to produce unmistakable and final definitions of these things is now, I suppose, given up, and we have come to recognize that the good, in all its forms, is evolved rather than achieved, is a process rather than a state.

The best definition of freedom is perhaps nothing other than the most helpful way of thinking about it; and it seems to me that the most helpful way of thinking about it is to regard it in the light of the contrast between what a man is and what he might be, as our experience of life enables us to imagine the two states. Ideas of this sort are suggested by defining freedom as opportunity, and their tendency is to stimulate and direct practical endeavor. If the word helps us to realize, for instance, that it is possible to make healthy, intelligent, and hopeful children out of those that are now sickly, dull, and unhappy, so much the better. On the other hand, the definition of it as letting people alone, well enough suited, perhaps, to an overgoverned state of society, does not seem especially pertinent to our time and country.

We have always been taught by philosophy that the various forms of the good were merely different views of the same thing, and this idea is certainly applicable to such notions as those of freedom, progress, and right. Thus freedom may be regarded as merely the individual aspect of progress, the two being related as the individual and the social order were asserted to be in the first chapter, and no more distinct or separable. If instead of contrasting what a particular man is with what he might be, we do the same for mankind as a whole, we have the notion of progress. Progress which does not involve liberation is evidently no progress at all; and, on the other hand, a freedom that is not part of the general onward movement of society is not free in the largest sense. Again, any practicable idea of freedom must connect it with some standard of right, in which, like opposing claims in a clearing-house, the divergent tendencies of each person, and of different persons, are disciplined and reconciled. The wrong is the unfree; it is that which tends, on the whole, to restrict personal development. It is no contribution to freedom to turn loose the insane or the criminal, or to allow children to run on the streets instead of going to school. The only test of all these things—of right, freedom, progress, and the like—is the instructed conscience; just as the only test of beauty is a trained æsthetic sense, which is a mental conclusion of much the same sort as conscience.

So far as discipline is concerned, freedom means not its absence but the use of higher and more rational forms as contrasted with those that are lower or less rational. A free discipline controls the individual by appealing to his reason and conscience, and therefore to his self-respect; while an unfree control works upon some lower phase of the mind, and so tends to degrade him. It is freedom to be disciplined in as rational a manner as you are fit for.

Thus freedom is relative to the particular persons and states who are to enjoy it, some individuals within any society, and some societies as wholes, being capable of a higher sort of response than others.

FREEDOM

I can perceive, during my own lifetime, an actual growth of freedom in most of our institutions. Family discipline has become more a matter of persuasion and example, less one of mere authority and the rod. In the school, mechanical modes of teaching, enlivened by punishment, have given way to sympathy, interest, and emulation. In the church we are no longer coerced by dogma, forms, and the fear of Hell, but are persuaded through our intelligence, sympathy, and desire for service. Governments, on the whole, rely more upon education, investigation, and public opinion, less upon the military and police functions. In armies and navies harsh discipline and awe of rank are in part supplanted by appeals to patriotism, fellowship, and emulation, and by cultivating that spiritual condition known as morale. In prisons there is an increase of methods that, by appealing to intelligence, responsibility, and honor, tend to elevate rather than degrade the offender.

The growth of freedom is most questionable in the industrial system; but even here we have ideals, agitation, and experiments in the free participation of the individual in the process. These give us hope that the present organization—for the most part unfree— may gradually be liberalized.

The social order is antithetical to freedom only in so far as it is a bad one. Freedom can exist only in and through a social order, and must be increased by all the healthy growth of the latter. It is only in a large and complex social system that any advanced degree of it is possible, because nothing else can supply the multifarious opportunities by means of which all sorts of persons can work out a congenial development through the choice of influences.

In so far as we have freedom in the United States at the present time, in what does it consist? Evidently, it seems to me, in the access to a great number and variety of influences by whose progressive selection and assimilation a child may become, within vague limits set by the general state of our society, the best that he is naturally fitted to become. It consists, to begin with infancy, in a good family life, in intelligent nurture and training, adapted to the special traits of character which every child manifests from the first week of life. Then it involves good schooling, admitting the child through books and teachers to a rich selection from the accumulated influences of the best minds of the past. Free technical and professional education, so far as it exists, contributes to it, also the facility of travel, bringing him in contact with significant persons from all over the world; public libraries, magazines, good newspapers, and so on. Whatever enlarges his field of selection without permanently confusing him adds to his liberty. In fact, institutions—government, churches, industries, and the like—have properly no other function than to contribute to human freedom; and in so far as they fail, on the whole, to perform this function, they are wrong and need reconstruction.

Although a high degree of freedom can exist only through a complex social order, it by no means follows that every complex social order is free. On the contrary, it has more often been true in the past that very large and intricately organized states, like the Roman Empire, were constructed on a comparatively mechanical or unfree principle. And in our own time a vast and complex empire, like Russia or China, may be less free than the simplest English-speaking colony. There are serious objections to identifying progress, as Herbert Spencer sometimes appears to do, with the mere differentiation and co-ordination of social functions. But the example of the United States, which is perhaps on the whole the most intricately differentiated and co-ordinated state that ever existed, shows that complexity is not inconsistent with freedom. To enter fully into this matter would require a more careful examination of the institutional aspect of life than I wish to undertake at present; but I hold that the possibility of organizing large and complex societies on a free principle depends upon the quickness and facility of communication, and so has come to exist only in recent times. The great states of earlier history were necessarily somewhat mechanical in structure.

It happens from time to time in every complex and active society, that certain persons feel the complexity and insistence as a tangle, and seek freedom in retirement, as Thoreau sought it at Walden Pond. They do not, however, in this manner escape from the social institutions of their time, nor do they really mean to do so; what they gain, if they are successful, is a saner relation to them. Thoreau in his hut remained as truly a member of society, as dependent for suggestion upon his books, his friends, and his personal memories, and upon verbal expression for his sense of self, as did Emerson in Concord or Lowell in Cambridge; and I imagine that if he had cared to discuss the matter he would have admitted that this was the case. Indeed, the idea of Thoreau as a recluse was not, I think, his own idea, but has been attached to him by superficial observers of his life. Although he was a dissenter from the state and the church of his time, his career would have been impossible without those institutions, without Harvard College, for instance, which was a joint product of the two. He worked out his personal development through congenial influences selected from the life of his time, very much as others do. He simply had peculiar tendencies which he developed in a peculiar way, especially by avoiding a gregarious mode of life unsuited to his temperament. He was free through the social order, not outside of it, and the same may be said of Edward Fitzgerald and other seclusive spirits. No doubt the commonplace life of the day is a sort of slavery for many sensitive minds that have not, like these, the resolution to escape from it into a calmer and broader atmosphere.

Since freedom is not a fixed thing that can be grasped and held once for all, but a growth, any particular society, such as our own, always appears partly free and partly unfree. In so far as it favors, in every child, the development of his highest possibilities, it is free, but where it falls short of this it is not. So far as children are ill-nurtured or ill-taught, as family training is bad, the schools inefficient, the local government ill-administered, public libraries lacking, or private associations for various sorts of culture deficient, in so far the people are unfree. A child born in a slum, brought up in a demoralized family, and put at some confining and mentally deadening work when ten or twelve years old, is no more free to be healthy, wise, and moral than a Chinese child is free to read Shakespeare. Every social ill involves the enslavement of individuals.

This idea of freedom is quite in accord with a general, though vague, sentiment among us; it is an idea of fair play, of giving every one a chance; and nothing arouses more general and active indignation among our people than the belief that some one or some class is not getting a fair chance. There seems, however, to be too great complacency in the way in which the present state of things is interpreted, a tendency to assume that freedom has been achieved once for all by the Declaration of Independence and popular suffrage, and that little remains but to let each person realize the general blessing to the best of his ability. It is well to recognize that the freedom which we nominally worship is never more than partly achieved, and is every day threatened by new encroachments, that the right to vote is only one phase of it, and possibly, under present conditions, not the most important phase, and that we can maintain and increase it only by a sober and determined application of our best thought and endeavor. Those lines of Lowell's "Commemoration Ode" are always applicable:

> "—the soft Ideal that we wooed
> Confronts us fiercely, foe-beset, pursued,
> And cries reproachful: Was it then my praise,
> And not myself was loved? Prove now thy truth.
> I claim of thee the promise of thy youth."

In our view of freedom we have a right to survey all times and countries and from them form for our own social order an ideal condition, which shall offer to each individual all the encouragements to growth and culture that the world has ever or anywhere enjoyed. Any narrowness or lack of symmetry in life in general is reflected in the contraction or warping of personal development, and so constitutes a lack of freedom. The social order should not exaggerate one or a few aspects of human nature at the expense of others, but extend its invitations to all our higher tendencies. Thus the excessive preoccupation of the nineteenth century with material production and physical science may be regarded as a partial enslavement of the spiritual and æsthetic sides of humanity, from which we are now struggling to escape. The freedom of the future must, it would seem, call more and more for a various, rich, and tolerant environment, in which all sorts of persons may build themselves up by selective development. The day for any sort of dogmatism and coercive uniformity appears to be past, and it will be practicable to leave people

432

more and more to control by a conscience reflecting the moral opinion of the group to which their inclination and capacity attach them.

The substitution of higher forms of control for lower, the offering more alternatives and trusting the mind to make a right selection, involves, of course, an increased moral strain upon individuals. Now this increase of moral strain is not in all cases exactly proportioned to the ability to bear it well; and when it is not well borne the effect upon character is more or less destructive, so that something in the way of degeneracy results.

Consequently every general increase of freedom is accompanied by some degeneracy, attributable to the same causes as the freedom. This is very plainly to be seen at the present time, which is one, on the whole, of rapid increase of freedom. Family life and the condition of women and children have been growing freer and better, but along with this we have the increase of divorce and of spoiled children. Democracy in the state has its own peculiar evils, as we all know; and in the church the decay of dogmatism and unreasoning faith, a moral advance on the whole, has nevertheless caused a good many moral failures. In much the same way the enfranchisement of the negroes is believed to have caused an increase of insanity among them, and the growth of suicide in all countries seems to be due in part to the strain of a more complex society. It is not true, exactly, that freedom itself causes degeneracy, because if one is subjected to more strain than is good for him his real freedom is rather contracted than enlarged, but it should rather be said that any movement which has increase of freedom for its general effect can never be so regulated as to have only this effect, but is sure to act upon some in an opposite manner.

Nor is it reasonable to sit back and say that this incidental demoralization is inevitable, a fixed price of progress. On the contrary, although it can never be altogether dispensed with, it can be indefinitely reduced, and every social institution or influence that tends to adapt the stress of civilization to the strength of the individual does reduce it in some measure.

INDEX

ADOLESCENCE, the self in, 200
Affectation, 202 ff., 352
Altruism, 39, 124; in relation to egoism, 126 ff., 148, 222 ff., 374 ff.
Ambition, 306 f.
Americanism, unconscious, 71
Anger, 25 f.; development of, 264 ff.; animal, 272
Anglo-Saxons, cantankerousness of, 299; idealism of, 321
Antipathy, 267 ff.
Appreciation, necessary to production, 92
Art, creative impulse in, 92; personal symbols in, 107 ff.; mental life a work of, 157 f.; plastic, mystery in, 348 f.; as idealization, 398
Ascendancy, personal, 317–357
Asceticism, 185, 249
Athletics, organized rivalry in, 308
Augustine, St., 248
Aurelius, Marcus, on freedom of thought, 71; self-feeling of, 248
Author, an, as leader, 336 ff.
Authority, personal, in morals, 383 ff., 414. See also Leadership.

BALDWIN, PROF. J. M., 52; on social persons, 125; 207, 302, 320
Bastien-Lepage, 385

Belief, ascendancy of, 343 f., 350 f.
Beowulf, on honor, 240 f.
Bismarck, 285; ascendancy of, 329, 331
Blame, nature of, 417 ff.
Blowitz, M. de, 331
Body, relation of, to the self, 175 f., 194
Booth, Charles, 306
Brotherhood, extension of the sense of, 144 f.
Brown, John, 407
Browning, 349
Bryant, Sophie, on antipathy, 267
Bryce, Prof. James, 75, 342
Burke, Edmund, 233, 335 f.
Burroughs, John, on the physiognomy of works of genius, 109

CÆSAR, as a personal idea, 133
Cant, 353
Capitalism, 310
Casaubon, Mr., 254 f.
Chagrin, 273
Charity, 270, 375. See also Altruism, Right
Chicago, aspect of the crowd in, 74
Child, Theodore, 385
Child, a, unlovable at birth, 82
Children, imitation in, 56 ff.; sociability of, 81 ff.; imaginary conversation of, 88 ff.;

435

study of expression by, 97 ff.; growth of sentiment in, 114 ff.; development of self in, 174, 177; use of "I" by, 189 ff.; reflected self in, 196 ff.; anger of, 264 f.; hero-worship of, 313; ascendancy over, 322 f.; habitual morality in, 371 f.; moral growth of, 379 ff.; causes of degeneracy in, 409, 416; what constitutes freedom for, 425 f., 428, 431; spoiled, 433

China, organization of, 429

Chinese, European lack of moral sense regarding, 392

Choice, in relation to suggestion, 51–80

Christ, self-feeling of, 174; indignation felt by, 278; as leader, 356; as moral authority, 384

"Christian's Secret of a Happy Life," 70

Church, inculcation of personal authority in the, 383; freedom in the, 427, 432

City life, effect upon sympathy, 146 f.

Class atmospheres, 72 ff.

Classes, social, 13 f., 18

Collectivism, 39

Columbus, 299, 339

Communicate, the impulse to, 92 ff.

Communication, of sentiment, 138 f.; effect of modern, 145; influence of means of, 390, 428

Competition, 275, 287 f.

Confession, 90 f., 386 f.

Conformity, 293 ff.

Conscience, 47, 211, 233, 276, 280, 289; social aspect of, 358–401; in degeneracy, 413

ff.; is the test of freedom, etc., 426. See also Right

Conservatism, 304

"Continued Stories," 396 f.

Controversy, 274

Conversation, imaginary, 88 ff., 389, 391

Country life, effect upon sympathy, 146

Creeds, the nature and use of, 399

Crime and heredity, 18; treatment of, 262, 283; as degeneracy, 412, 415 ff.; and insanity, 417 ff.

Criminal impulses, nature of, 410 f.

Cromwell, 329

Crowd-feeling, 325 f.

Crowds, suggestibility of, 77

Culture, relation of, to social organization, 151 f.

DAGNAN, 385

Dante, 67 f., 219

Darwin, Charles, 12, 23, 26, 102, 103, 196, 207, 222, 275, 313; power as a writer, 337, 355, 403

"Das ewig Weibliche," 202, 345

Degeneracy, from too much choice, 76, 147; self-feeling in, 259 ff.; personal, 402–421; incidental to freedom, 433 f.

Delusions of greatness and of persecution, 259 f.

Democracy of sentiment, 147

Descartes, seclusion of, 228

Determinism, 39

Dialogue, composing in, 91 f.

Diaries, as intercourse, 92; moral effect of, 387 f.

Dill's "Roman Society," 344

Discipline, in relation to freedom, 426 f.

Disraeli, B., 249, 348
Divorce, increase of, incidental to freedom, 433
Double causation theory of society, 43 f.
Dreams, as imaginary conversation, 90
Duplicity, 266
Duty, sense of, See Conscience

ECONOMICS, influence of a narrow, 311
Education, culture in, 150 f.; as freedom, 425, 427. See also Children
Ego, the empirical, 168; the metaphysical, 169, 194; and alter in morals, 374 ff.
Egoism, 39; and altruism, 126 ff., 216 ff., 374 ff.
Egotism, 126, 211 ff.; as a mental trait, 217 ff.; varieties of, 218 ff.; as degeneracy, 412 f.
Element of society, 167
Eliot, George, 208, 254, 294, 346, 385
Eloquence, 334 ff.
Emerson, E. W., 396
Emerson, R. W., 41, 93, 154, 160, 205, 241, 275, 297, 299, 320, 328, 367, 395, 396
Emulation, 293–316
Endogenous minds, 231 f., 414
Environment, 301; and heredity, 6 ff., 15, 16 f., 407 f. See also Suggestion
Equilibrium mobile of conscience, 366
Ethics, physiological theories of, 239 f. See also Conscience Right
Eugenics, 12 ff.
Evolution, 45, 47, 50, 54, 177; in relation to leadership, 354; to degeneracy, 404 ff.

Evolutionary point of view, 3 f., 35, 50
Exhaustion, causes suggestibility, 78
Exogenous minds, 231 f., 414
Experience, social, is imaginative, 132 f.
Expression, emotional, 26; facial, 97 ff.; vocal, 101 f.; interpretation of, 102 f. suggestion of, in literature and art, 107 ff.
Eye, expressiveness of, 98 f.; in literature, 108

FACE. See Expression
Fame, often transcends the man, 340 f.
Family, freedom in the, 427
Fear, 25 f., of animals, 101; social, 289 ff.
Feeling. See Sentiment
Findlay, Professor, 28
Fitzgerald, Edward, seclusiveness of, 430
Forms, used to maintain ascendancy, 351
Fox, Charles, 336
Fra Angelico, 279, 384
Francis, St., 83
Freedom, 9; cooperative, 49 f.; lack of in industry, 311; 422–434
Free-will, 39, 49 f., 55, 66
Friendship, 153 f.
Frith's "Autobiography," 111

GALTON, FRANCIS, 18
Games, athletic, 287
Genius, 18, 41, 140, 200, 219; disorders of self incident to, 258 f.; 269, 297, 354 ff. See also Leadership
Gibbon, Edward, 303
Gibson, W. H., 339

Giddings, Prof. F. H., on imitation, 63

Gloating, 174

God, as love, 159 f.; appropriated, 186; as ideal self, 244; idea of, 314 f., 400 f. See also Religion

Gods, famous persons partake of the nature of, 341

Goethe, on individuality in art, 69; on the composition of "Werther," 91; personality in his style, 110; 154, 155, 165, 181, 225, 227, 235, 241, 273, 285, 297, 314, 345, 349, 422

Gothic architecture, rise of, 74

Grant, General, 78,112; ascendancy of, 332 f., 347

Gregarious instinct, 28 f.

Groups, self of, 209 f.; degeneracy of, 416

Gummere, F. B., 240

Guyau, on the onward self, 367 f.

Habit, limits suggestibility, 79; in relation to the self, 187; to the sense of right, 368 ff., 379

Hall, President G. Stanley, 109; on the self, 194, 290

Hamerton, P. G., 228, 349

Hamlet, use of "I" in, 176

Hatred, 284

Hazlitt, W., 284

Hedonizing, instinctive, 96

Herbert, George, 186

Hereditary element in sociability, 86

Hereditary tendency, 318 ff.

Heredity and environment, 4 ff.; human and animal, 19 ff.; as a cause of degeneracy, 407 ff.

Heroism, 370

Hero-worship, 243, 312 ff., 320 f.

History, nature of, 3 ff., 30 f.

Honor, 238 ff.

Hope, ascendancy of, 343 f.

Hostility, 264–292

Howells, W. D., 334

Hugo, Victor, 259

Human nature, general discussion of, 31 ff.

Humility, 243 ff.

Huxley, Thomas, 274 f., 338

Hysterical temperament, 375, 412 f.

"I," in relation to love, 162 ff.; the reflected or looking-glass, 183 f., 196 ff., 206, 209, 240, 246 f., 380 ff.; meaning of, 168–210; exists within the general life, 175 ff.; as related to the rest of thought, 179 f.; inanimate objects as, 183; is rooted in the social order, 185 ff.; how children learn the meaning of, 189 ff.; various phases of, 211–263; use of in literature and conversation, 222 ff.; in self-reverence, 241; in leadership, 328

Ideal persons, as factors in conscience, 392 ff.; of religion, 314 ff., 398 ff.

Idealism, ascendancy of, 343

Idealization, 312, 392 ff.

Ideas, personal. See Personal ideas

Idiocy, congenital, 408; as mental degeneracy, 411

Idiots, kindliness of, 87 f., 158

Imaginary conversation, of children, 88 f.; all thought is, 90 ff.

Imaginary playmate, 88 f.

INDEX

Imagination, in relation to personal ideas, 112 f., 132 ff.; the locus of society, 134; social, a requisite to power, 140; narrowness of, in egotism, 214; essential to goodness, 389

Imitation, 51 ff.; in children, 56 ff.; not mechanical, 61 ff.; by parents, 61 f.; in relation to smiling, 84 f.; 99, 106, 293, 297, 301; the doctrine of objectionable, 302; 342, 369

Imitative instinct, the supposed, 62 ff.

Immortality, self-feeling in the idea of, 186 f.

Imposture, 351 ff.

Indifferentism, 419.

Indignation, 273, 280 ff.

Individual, the, in relation to society, 35–50, 356 f., 422; as a cause, 354 f.; and social, in morals, 373 ff.

Individualism, 39 ff., 44, 45, 48

Individuality, Goethe's view of, in art, 69

Industrial system, effect of upon the individual, 151 f.

Insane, reverence for the, 347

Insanity, in relation to sympathy, 144; the self in, 259 f.; and crime, 417 ff.

Instinctive emotion, 24 ff.

Instincts, in human life, 22 ff.; whether divisible into social and unsocial, 46 f.

Institution, ideal persons may become an, 398 f.

Institutions, in relation to sympathy, 166; growth of freedom in, 426

Intercourse, relation to thought, 92 f.

Interlocutor, imaginary, drawn from the environment, 89 f.

Invention, 302 f., 369. See also Imitation

Involuntary, the, why ignored, 66 f. See also Will

JAMES, HENRY, 214, 268, 346

James, Prof. William, on social persons, 125; on the self, 170; 175, 306, 322, 389

Jerome, St., 49, 186

Jowett, Prof., 314

Justice, the sentiment of, 125; based on sympathy, 142; relation to love, 160; 268, 382, 395

KEMPIS, THOMAS à, 70, 161, 186, 244, 248, 250 f., 256

LABOR QUESTION, 261, 311

Lamb, Charles, 111, 223; literary power of, 339 f.

Language involves an interlocutor, 91 f. See also Expression

Leader, mental traits of a, 327 ff.; does he really lead? 354

Leadership, 140 f., 206, 317–357

Learoyd, Mabel W., 396

Lecky, W. H., 253

Leonardo, mystery of, 349

Likeness and difference in sympathy, 153 f.

Lincoln, 118

Literature, creative impulse in, 92; personal symbols in, 107 ff.; self-feeling in, 224 f.; ascendancy in, 336 ff.; mystery in, 348

Lombroso, Prof. Cesare, 259

Love, of the sexes, 25, 155 f.; and sympathy, 157 ff.; scope of, 159 f.; nature of, 160 ff.; Thomas à Kempis and Emerson on, 161; two kinds of, 162

439

ff.; and self, 162 ff.; 187 ff., 226; as a social ideal, 279 f.; of enemies, 283; 342, 345

Lowell, J. R., 173, 296, 300, 432

Luther, Martin, 212 f., 351

Lying, in relation to sympathy, 143, 388 f.

M., a child of the author, 60, 63, 83, 97 ff., 189 ff., 196 f., 380

Macaulay, physiognomy in his style, 112

McDougall, Professor, 27

Machinery, effect of upon the workman, 151 f.

Maine, Sir Henry, 295

Man of the world, traits of the contemporary, 286

Manners, conformity in, 293 f.; as an aid to ascendancy, 351

Marshall, H. R., 363

Material bent of our civilization, 71, 432

Maudsley, Dr., on degeneracy, 411

Meredith, George, 214

Michelangelo, 111, 343, 384

Middle Ages, suggestibility in the, 73

Milieu, power of the, 70 ff.

Milton, 108

Moltke, silence of, 347

Monasticism, in relation to the self, 249 f., 257 f.

Montaigne, on the need to communicate, 92; 111, 222, 223

Moore, K. C., on the smiling of infants, 82

Morality. See Conscience, Right

Motley, J. L., 109

Murder, 415

Music, sensuous mystery of, 350

Mystery, a factor in ascendancy, 344 ff.

NANSEN, 299

Napoleon, how we know him, 121; ascendancy of, 330; place in history, 356

New Testament, 174, 245, 277

Nietzsche, 29

Nirvana, the ideal of disinterested love, 163

Non-conformity, 293 ff.

Non-resistance, doctrine of, 276 ff.

Norsemen, motive of, 303

Norton, Prof. C. E., 74

"ONE," use of, compared with "I," 224 f.

Onward, right as the, 366 ff.

Opposition, personal, its nature, 130 f.; spirit of, 298 ff.

Oratory, ascendancy in, 334 ff.

Organic view, of the individual, 35 f.; questions relating to, 47 ff.; in relation to responsibility, 419 ff.

Organization, of personal thought, 87; effect of upon the individual, 145 ff.; or vital process, problem of, 364

Originality, 354 ff. See also Genius, Leadership, Invention

Other-worldism, 252

PAINTING, personal symbols in, 107 f. See also Art, Expression

Papacy, symbolic character of, 341 f.

Particularism, 29, 39

Pascal, 248, 252

Passion, why a cause of pain, 285 f.; influence upon idea of right, 362 f.

INDEX

Pater, Walter, 337
Patriotism, 210
Patten, Prof. Simon N., 275
Paul, St., 248
Perez, Dr. B., 82 f.; on the eye, 98 f.; 265, 381
Personal authority, influence upon sense of right, 383 ff.
Personal character, interpretation of, 102, 105; communication of, 106 f.
Personal ideas, 97 ff.; sensuous nucleus of, 104 ff.; sentiment their chief content, 114 ff., 133; compared to a system of lights, 131 f.; affect the physical organism, 133 f.; affect the sense of right, 379 ff.
Personal symbols in art and literature, 107 ff.
Persons, real and imaginary, inseparable, 95 f.; incorporeal, their social reality, 122; social, interpenetrate one another, 124 ff.; ideal, as factors in conscience, 392 ff.; ideal, of religion, 314 ff., 398 ff.
Philanthropy, motive of, 300 f.
Pioneer, self-feeling of the, 299
Pity, is it altruism? 129; relation to sympathy, 137 f.; 270
Power, based on sympathy, 140 f.; idea of, 324; advantage of visible forms of, 325 f. See also Ascendancy
Prayer, as personal intercourse, 387
Pretense, contempt of, in America, 324
Preyer, W., 63, 82
Pride, 230 ff.
Primitive individualism, 45
Principle, moral, 370 f.

Process, social, 4 ff., imitation, etc., as, 302; vital, problem of, 364
Processes, social, reflected in sympathy, 153 ff.
Progress, relation of to heredity, 14 f., 30 f.; to freedom, 425
Psychoanalysis, 25, 29, 262 f.
Publicity, moral effect of, 386 ff.
Punishment, 283, 418, 420 f.

R., a child of the author, 58 ff., 64, 85 f., 87, 89, 190 ff., 372, 381
Race questions, 10, 14, 17, 262
Race-suicide, 13
Rational, right as the, 358 ff.
Reason and instinct, 29 ff.
Recapitulation theory of mental development, 57
Refinement, as affecting hostility, 269
Religion, solitary, 49; suggestibility in, 79, 80; self-feeling of founders of, 213; self-discipline in, 244 f., 248 ff.; as hero-worship, 314 ff.; mediæval, 342; mystery in, 350; ideal persons of, 398 ff.
Remorse, 285, 360, 398, 415 f.
Repentance, 398
Resentment, 230, 242, 266 ff.
Resistance, imaginative, 278 ff.
Responsibility, in crime, etc., 418 ff.
Right, based on sympathy, 142 ff.; relation to egotism, 216; to the self in general, 220; social standards of, as affecting hostility, 287 ff.; as the rational, 358 ff.; conscience the final test of, 365 f.; as the onward, 366 ff.; as habit, 368 ff.,

379; as a phase of the self, 373 f.; the social as opposed to the sensual, 378 f.; action of personal ideas in forming the sense of, 379 ff.; as a microcosm of character, 382; reflects a social group, 390 ff., 401; and wrong, 402 ff.; idea of, 407; universal ideals of, 416; freedom as, 423 ff.

Riis, Jacob A., 391

Rivalry, 305 ff.; in service, 308 ff.; conditions of, 310 f.

Roget's "Thesaurus," 229

Roman Empire, 344, 429

Rousseau, 269, 291

Rule of conduct, Marshall's, 363

Ruskin, 349

Russia, 429

SANITY, based on sympathy, 144

Savonarola, physiognomy of, 347

Schiller, 147, 154

Science, and faith, 339; cant of, 353; moral, limits of, 366; physical, 432

Sculpture, personal symbols in, 107 f.

Seclusion, moral effect of, 388

Secretiveness, 93, 227

"Seeing yourself," 397 f.

Selection, biological, 10 ff.; in sympathy, 155 ff.

Selective method of nature, 402 f.

Self, in relation to other personal ideas, 126 ff., 132; antithesis with "other," 148, 220 ff.; in morals, 395 f.; in relation to love, 162 ff., 187 ff., 226; inanimate objects as, 183; social, 168–263; observa-

tion of in children, 189 ff.; of a group, 209 f.; the narrow or egotistical, 211 ff.; every cherished idea is a, 217; reflected or looking-glass, 183 f., 196 ff., 206, 208, 240, 246 f.; in social problems, 260 ff.; influence of upon conscience, 380 ff.; maladies of the social, 246; transformation of, 253 ff.; effect of uncongenial environment upon, 256 ff.; 275, 352; crescive, 367; ethical, 373 f.; ideal social, 389, 396 ff.

Self-control, 285

Self-feeling, 25, 169 ff.; quotations illustrating, 173 f.; of reformers, etc., 212; intense, essential to production, 224 ff.; control of, 248 ff.; in mental disorder, etc., 259 f.; in non-conformity, 298

Self-image as a work of art, 237

Self-neglecting, 226

Self-reliance, 327 ff.

Self-respect, 236 ff., 270

Self-reverence, 241 ff.

Self-sacrifice, 220, 367. See also Humility, Altruism

Selfishness, nature of, 211 ff.; as a mental trait, 217 ff.

"Sense of other persons," 207

Sensual, as opposed to the social, 378 f.

Sensuality, 214

Sentiment, personal, genesis of, 114 ff.; is differentiated emotion, 115; in personal ideas, 115 ff.; relation to persons, 117; more communicable than sensation, 136 f.; moral, 357 ff.; 417

Sentiments, as related to selfishness, 212; literary, 391

INDEX

Seven deadly sins, 410

Sex, in sympathy, 155 f.; in the self, 202 ff.

Shakespeare, 46, 108, 111; on the genesis of sentiment, 115 f.; 137, 140, 173, 177, 179, 219, 226, 241, 286, 316

Shame, fear of, 291 f.; sense of, 380

"Sheridan's Ride," 325

Sherman, General, 333

Shinn, Miss, 198

Sidis, Dr. B., 73

Sidney, Sir Philip, 118

Silence, fascination of, 347 f.

Simplicity, 205

Sin, 405, 410

Sincerity in leadership, 350 ff.

Smiles, earliest, 82 ff.; interpretation of, 100 f.

Sociability and personal ideas, 81–135

"Social," meanings of the word, 38 f.

Social faculty view, 46 f.

Social groups, sensible basis of the idea of, 113; relation of to the individual, 144

Social order, reflected in sympathy, 144 ff.; freedom in relation to, 427 ff.

Social reality, the immediate is the personal idea, 119

Socialism, 39 ff., 124

Society, and the individual, 35–50, 166 f., 354 f.; in morals, 373 ff., 423: is primarily a mental fact, 119; is a relation among personal ideas, 119; each mind an aspect of, 119 f.; the idea of, 120; must be studied in the imagination, 120 ff.; is the collective aspect of personal thought,

134; a phase, not a separable thing, 135

Sociology, too much based on material notions, 120, 124 f., 132 ff.; must observe personal ideas, 120 ff.; deals with personal intercourse in primary and secondary aspects, 135

Solitude, apparent, 48 f., 92

Sophocles, 173

Spanish-American war, consolidating effect of, 326

Specialization, effect of, 148 ff.

Speech, 16. See also Expression

Spencer, Herbert, on egoism and altruism, 126 f.; nature of his system, 127; on progress, 429

Spencerism, 339

Stability and instability in the self, 230 ff.

Stable and unstable types of mind, 218 ff., 230 ff., 411 f.

Stanley, Prof. H. M., 63, 170, 232, 244

Sterne, L., 225

Stevenson, R. L., physiognomy in his style, 113; 123, 129, 223, 226, 291, 352, 386

Strain of the present age, 146 f.

Struggle for existence, as a view of life, 303

Style, the personal idea in, 107 ff.; what it is, 109; personal ascendancy in, 336 ff.

Stylites, St. Simeon, 49

Suger, the Abbot, 74

Suggestibility, 76 ff.

Suggestion, and choice, 51–80; definition of, 51; in children, 56 ff.; contrary, 59, 298; scope of in life, 65 ff.

Sumner, Wm. G., 400

443

INDEX

Superficiality of the time, 145, 229

Symbols, personal, 103 ff.; in art and literature, 107 ff.

Symonds, J. A., 187, 200 f., 314, 349

Sympathies, reflect the social order, 145 ff.

Sympathy, or understanding as an aspect of society, 136–166; meaning of, 136 ff.; as compassion, 136; a measure of personality, 140 ff.; universal, 147 f.; reflects social processes, 153 ff.; selective, 155 ff.; and love, 157 ff.; a particular expression of society, 165 ff.; hostile, 191, 266 ff.; in leadership, 324 ff.; lack of, in degeneracy, 412; with criminal acts a test of responsibility, 417 ff.

Tact, 215 f.; in ascendancy, 328 f.

Tarde, G., 52, 302

"Tasso," quoted, 155, 181

Teachability of human heredity, 19 ff., 29 ff., 34

Tennyson, 162, 241, 321, 350

Tests, mental, 15 f.

Thackeray, 111, 223

Thoreau, H. D., his relation to society, 93 f., 429 f.; 188, 223, 227, 228, 267, 276, 301

Thorndike, Professor, 32

Toleration, 294 f.

Truth, motive for telling, 388 f.

Tylor, E. B., 78, 347

Vanity, 230, 234 ff.

Variation, degeneracy as, 404 f.

Wagner, Richard, 111

War, and instinct, 27 f.; hostile feeling in, 288; dramatic power of leadership in, 324 f.

War, the Great, 73, 210

Washington, 118

Whitman, Walt, 223

Will, free, 39; individual and social, 53; popular view of, 54; is it externally determined? 55 f., 67 f.; activity of, reflects society, 75 f.

William the Silent, 347

Withdrawal, physical, 249; imaginative, 250 ff.

Wrong, as the irrational, 361; emphasized by example, 386; degeneracy as, 402 ff.; idea of, 407; not always opposed by conscience, 415 f.; the unfree, 426

Wundt, on "Ich," 170

Youth, sense of, 161, 312

444